P9-DFB-343

Front Endsheet: "The Grand Canyon of the Yellowstone," painted by Thomas Moran, 1872; U.S. Department of the Interior

The New America's Wonderlands

Our National Parks

NATIONAL
GEOGRAPHIC
SOCIETY

The New America's Wonderlands

Our National Parks

THE NEW AMERICA'S WONDERLANDS
PUBLISHED BY THE NATIONAL GEOGRAPHIC SOCIETY
MELVIN M. PAYNE, *President*
MELVILLE BELL GROSVENOR, *Editor-in-Chief*
GILBERT M. GROSVENOR, *Editor*

A VOLUME IN THE WORLD IN COLOR LIBRARY
PREPARED BY
NATIONAL GEOGRAPHIC BOOK SERVICE
JULES B. BILLARD, *Chief*

Staff for this Book

ROSS BENNETT, *Editor*

CHARLES O. HYMAN, *Art Director*

ANNE DIRKES KOBOR, *Illustrations Editor*

CONNIE BROWN, *Designer*

THOMAS B. ALLEN, SEYMOUR L. FISHBEIN, MARY SWAIN HOOVER, EDWARD LANOUETTE, DAVID F. ROBINSON, VERLA LEE SMITH
Editor-Writers

SHIRLEY L. SCOTT, *Chief Researcher*

MARY H. DICKINSON, ELEANOR MILUTINOVICH, PAMELA MUCCI, MARGARET SEDEEN
Editorial Research

WILHELM R. SAAKE, *Production Manager*

KAREN F. EDWARDS, *Production*

LINDA BRUMBACH, BARBARA G. STEWART
Picture Research

JAMES R. WHITNEY, *Engraving and Printing*

LIISA HOLLINGSWORTH, SARAH ROBINSON, *Assistants*

JOHN D. GARST, JR., VIRGINIA L. BAZA, MARGARET A. DEANE, NANCY SCHWEICKART, SNEJINKA STEFANOFF, MILDA R. STONE, ALFRED L. ZEBARTH, *Map Design and Production*

WERNER JANNEY, *Style*

VIRGINIA S. THOMPSON, MARTHA K. HIGHTOWER, *Index*

Introduction by Conrad L. Wirth, *Former Director, National Park Service*

Articles by
Thomas B. Allen, Harvey Arden, Ross Bennett, David S. Boyer, William S. Ellis, Rowe Findley, Seymour L. Fishbein, Donald J. Frederick, Edward Lanouette, Bart McDowell, David F. Robinson, Shirley L. Scott, Merle Severy, Charles H. Sloan, Verla Lee Smith, Kenneth F. Weaver, Gordon Young, *and* Paul A. Zahl *of the National Geographic staff; and* William Belknap, Jr., Frank and John Craighead, Walter Meayers Edwards, Ernest Gruening, Paul Jensen, Aubrey Stephen Johnson, John M. Kauffmann, Nathaniel T. Kenney, Carl F. Miller, Edwards Park, *and* Louis Schellbach

383 illustrations, 379 in full color, insert map

Sunrise paints shadows on Point Reyes National Seashore; DeWitt Jones. Overleaf: *El Capitan (left) and Half Dome tower above Yosemite Valley in California's Sierra Nevada; Galen Rowell*

First edition 400,000 copies; second 250,000; third 425,000

Library of Congress CIP data page 463

Foreword

"Look at this monster!" the President said in admiration, holding up a huge National Geographic photograph of the world's tallest living thing, a coast redwood soaring 367.8 feet into the California sky. "What if this tree were cut? It must be saved!"

It *was* saved, along with 1,000-year-old giants in neighboring groves, when in 1968 Lyndon B. Johnson signed into law Redwood National Park. I'll not forget that day, and others like it, witnessing the creation of new and varied parks for the American people.

When the Society first published *America's Wonderlands* in 1959 there were some 180 park units. Since then, as a member of the National Parks Advisory Board and Council, I have seen that number grow to nearly 300. And as I visit the new North Cascades, Voyageurs, and Guadalupe Mountains national parks, cast my lure in the waters of Lake Chelan National Recreation Area, or stroll the dunes of Assateague Island National Seashore, I never cease to marvel at the grandeur, the variety, the spirit-healing resources safeguarded there for us all.

Today we have more parks—also more visitors. So many, in fact, that in favorite parks like Yellowstone and Yosemite peak seasons seem to be "standing room only." Yet despite inconvenience and frustration, increasing numbers of Americans will flock to the parks; experts predict 300 million visits in 1981. How do we preserve the solitude of our parks and at the same time welcome more and more people?

After World War II, an unprecedented surge of visitors threatened to trample some parks flat. One alarmed conservationist suggested closing them. You can't fence people out, of course. When Congress created the Park Service in 1916 the law directed it to "conserve the scenery and ... provide for the enjoyment of the same." True to that charter the Park Service met the postwar challenges—first with the ten-year Mission 66 program, launched in 1956 by Park Director Conrad Wirth, which added new sites, modernized facilities, and set long-range goals, and then with its complementary program called Parkscape—USA, inaugurated by Wirth's successor, George B. Hartzog, Jr., which emphasized recreation parks close to urban centers.

Now, not only are people flocking to parks better equipped to serve them, but parks are coming to the people. The millions who live in cities far from the wonders of a Glacier or Big Bend National Park can find a meaningful park experience almost on their doorstep. Take the twin recreation areas recently authorized a continent apart: Gateway, in the vicinity of New York Harbor, and Golden Gate, around San Francisco Bay. They are just two of some 30 areas that embrace lakeshores, seashores, and scenic riverways where Americans can boat, fish, swim, and hike.

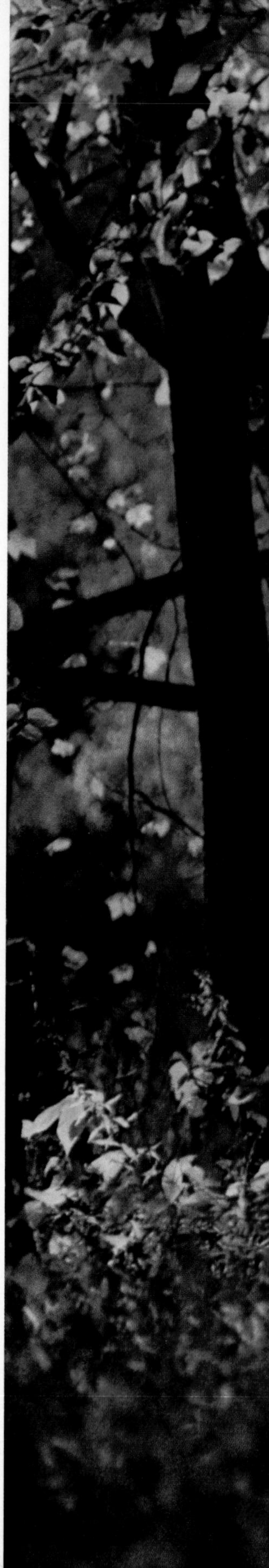

Sylvan stillness bowered in gold enfolds a young leaf-gatherer in Great Smoky Mountains National Park. Despite a growing flood of visitors, popular scenic parks such as this one still offer quiet havens for those who want to get away from it all.

BRUCE DALE, NATIONAL GEOGRAPHIC PHOTOGRAPHER

Nor has the search for parklands ended. In Alaska, our last frontier, the Park Service proposes vast new reserves that will add millions of acres to the system—the trackless Gates of the Arctic, the icy mountain fastness of the Wrangell-St. Elias region, the Kobuk Valley and its incongruous sand dunes half a world away from the torrid zone.

Nearer home, the Park Service seeks not only to broaden its variety of recreationlands but to make better use of older parks. Instead of jamming roads and polluting the air in Yosemite Valley, cars now stay parked and free shuttle buses move the tourist throngs. Thus visitor and vegetation can breathe easier.

New interpretative programs transform the visitor from spectator into participant. Not that ranger talks are anything new. But the scope of programs and exhibits, ranging from animal and plant life to the rocks beneath our feet and the skies over our heads, today makes many of our parks into outdoor universities fascinating for young and old.

Reviewing these pages reminds me how my father, Gilbert Grosvenor, fired my enthusiasm for scenic sanctuaries by taking me as a boy on field trips to the national parks. I recall Stephen Mather, first Director of the Park Service, with whom my father, as President of the National Geographic Society, worked so closely to save our nation's natural wonders. Our Society has contributed to the Park System in significant ways. One was sponsorship of an ecological survey of California's coast redwoods that led to creation of Redwood National Park. Others included the discovery of Alaska's Valley of Ten Thousand Smokes; first expedition to explore Carlsbad Caverns; substantial donation toward the purchase of a tract of big trees for Sequoia's Giant Forest; gift of the archeological trove, Russell Cave; opening up of Wetherill Mesa; unearthing of Pueblo Bonito—even a project to analyze through aerial sensing devices the prehistoric occupation of Chaco Canyon.

Indicative of the strong role the Society has played in the crusade for an unspoiled America is the amazing response to this book. Ever since it appeared, *America's Wonderlands* has been a towering best seller. Earlier editions totaled 650,000 copies. Now completely re-illustrated and extensively revised in text, it measures the giant strides of our Park Service. This volume invites a new generation to come, use, and enjoy America's "crown jewels"—national parks that, in Conrad Wirth's words, "strengthen bodies, refresh minds, uplift the spirits . . . enrich leisure."

Melville Bell Grosvenor

Contents

The Golden West

The Pacific Northwest

The East

Alaska, Hawaii, Virgin Islands

Conrad L. Wirth

Introduction

It was 1925 and Willie Marshman, Effy Buckley, and I had been touring the West Coast in an old secondhand car with a canvas top and running boards. We were heading back east on a zigzag course to see as much of the country as possible, not knowing whether we would ever get west again. We slept on old army cots alongside the car.

The park rangers told us about the bears as we entered Yellowstone and that car lights would drive them away at night. We went into camp the first day at Morris Junction Campground, spent the late afternoon catching up on our laundry, and were in our cots by ten o'clock. Shortly after midnight Willie was awakened by something tickling his face. It was the hair of a bear's belly and the bear was trying to get in the car. He had his front feet on the running board and his back feet on the ground. Eventually the bear backed off to go around to the other side of the car and Willie finally got strength enough to yell in one breath, "Connie turn on the lights!"

I jumped up, climbed in the car, and turned on the lights. As I did, I felt something next to me and turned to look. There I was eye to eye with a fair-size bear. The bear jumped out of the car and ran through the woods. As for me, I fell out of the car right on top of Effy.

Little did I realize then that in a few years I would be in the Park Service working to keep invading campers like myself from hurting or disturbing the bears of Yellowstone, and that the then superintendent of Yellowstone, Horace M. Albright, would become Park Service Director and the man who would hire me.

I spent 33 years in the Park Service, retiring after 12 years as Director, but I've never forgotten that first national park visit.

Your first visit to a national park may be quite different from mine. I hope so; that bear sure spoiled our night's rest. But we spent three very enjoyable days in the park. The important thing is for you to receive a full dividend from your experience, as we did, not only through lungs filled with clean air and eyes soothed by natural beauty, but spirits enriched perhaps beyond immediate understanding.

I myself don't know how to describe this ability of the parks to lift up the soul. One of the best writers on the parks, Freeman Tilden, referred to an ancient undefined Greek concept of a "fifth essence," beyond fire, air, earth, and water. "Any thoughtful person," Tilden wrote, "may find and meditate upon this Fifth Essence in his own backyard. Not a woodland brook, not a mountain, not a field of grass rippling in the breeze does not proclaim the existence of it. But... a consummate expression of this ultimate wealth of the human spirit.... is to be found in the National Park System....Many a man has come to find merely serenity or scenic pictures—and has unexpectedly found a renewal and affirmation of himself."

I'm sure Freeman Tilden would have added "and an eye-to-eye confrontation with a bear" if he had known of our experience.

The parks mean different things to different people. In Glacier National Park years later when I was Director, I saw a middle-aged couple packing their car. "Good morning," I said. "How do you like the park?"

"Best of the ten we've seen this vacation," the man replied. "But mister, please don't keep me from my packing. We have only three more days of vacation and three parks still to see." While he bustled around, I found out from his wife that they had arrived in Glacier the night before. "We drove over Going-to-the-Sun Road," she said, "and we saw Indians on the hotel lawn. This is a wonderful place."

Too rushed to get much out of the parks? Perhaps. But they were having the time of their lives. I defend their right to see Glacier any

Spray roils from the Lower Falls of Yellowstone's Grand Canyon, a scenic glory of the first national park. Overleaf: *Sunrise paints Arizona's Grand Canyon in one of many moods, silhouetting the flat top of Wotans Throne and the dome of Vishnu Temple.*

SAM ABELL. OVERLEAF: JOSEF MUENCH

Official survey party led by Dr. Ferdinand V. Hayden rattles into the Yellowstone area in 1871. A year later President Grant signed the bill preserving this wilderness as a "public park or pleasuring ground."

WILLIAM HENRY JACKSON, NATIONAL ARCHIVES

Twenty men encircle Sequoia National Park's General Sherman tree in this 1915 photograph by Gilbert H. Grosvenor, then editor of the National Geographic. *A picnic among the sequoias for conservation leaders saw Stephen T. Mather, later the first Director of the Park Service, at the head of the table with Dr. Grosvenor on his left.*

GILBERT H. GROSVENOR

way they want, at whatever pace they want.

Later that summer I met two young men at the ranger patrol cabin on the Southeast Arm of Yellowstone Lake. They had the barest amount of worn-out camping gear. Untrimmed hair and bushy beards gave them the look of old-time mountain men, a style that has become fashionable among our younger visitors today.

"How long have you been out?" I asked.

"Two months," said one. "And what a time we've had! A cow moose kept us treed all one night. We can tell you, I bet, where the biggest cutthroat trout in the world live. We've gained fifteen pounds on beans, bacon, sourdough biscuits, and fish." They had a patched-up canoe and planned to paddle back along the shore to their car at Fishing Bridge.

"Maybe you could take these fellows over in the patrol boat," I said to the ranger. "If you do, find out where they caught those trout."

I don't know who talked longest and loudest about their trip, the Glacier pair or the two Yellowstone canoeists. But I have faith in the ability of the parks to spray some of Mr. Tilden's "fifth essence" on every visitor.

Sooner or later each park guest meets a ranger, the backbone of the service. All uniformed personnel, men and women, seasonal and career employees, including the superintendents, constitute the ranger staff. They are well educated and trained to help the visitor. They are the housekeepers, the interpreters, and the law officers. Some seasonal rangers go forth into other occupations; President Ford served as one in Yellowstone as a youth.

Many of our first rangers were born outdoorsmen without much formal education. Some, like Billy Nelson of Yosemite, would be called "characters" today. He had King Albert of the Belgians out on a pack trip. They were camped in a grove of sequoias and Billy was cooking.

"Hey, King," he suddenly shouted over the crackle of the campfire, "shoot me that side of bacon, will you?" Members of the royal party and the Yosemite superintendent blanched. But the King cheerily threw Billy the bacon.

GEN. SHERMAN

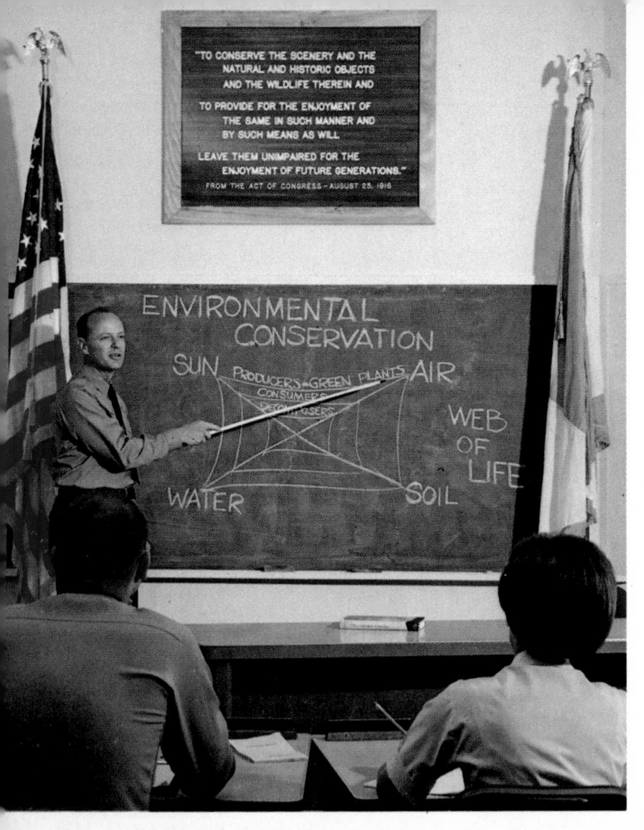

"TO CONSERVE THE SCENERY AND THE
NATURAL AND HISTORIC OBJECTS
AND THE WILDLIFE THEREIN AND
TO PROVIDE FOR THE ENJOYMENT OF
THE SAME IN SUCH MANNER AND
BY SUCH MEANS AS WILL
LEAVE THEM UNIMPAIRED FOR THE
ENJOYMENT OF FUTURE GENERATIONS."
FROM THE ACT OF CONGRESS - AUGUST 25, 1916
ENVIRONMENTAL
CONSERVATION
SUN
PRODUCERS-GREEN PLANTS
AIR
CONSUMERS
DECOMPOSERS
WEB
OF
LIFE
WATER
SOIL

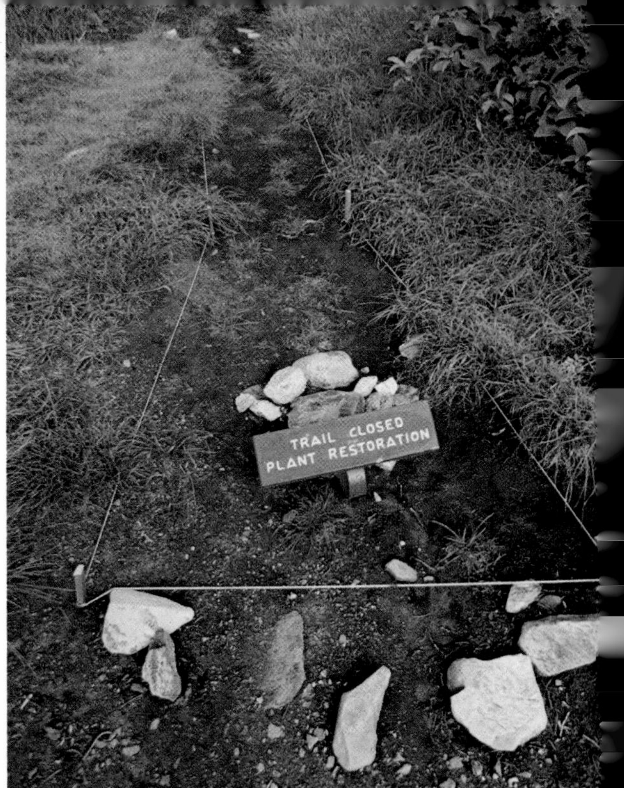

TRAIL CLOSED
PLANT RESTORATION

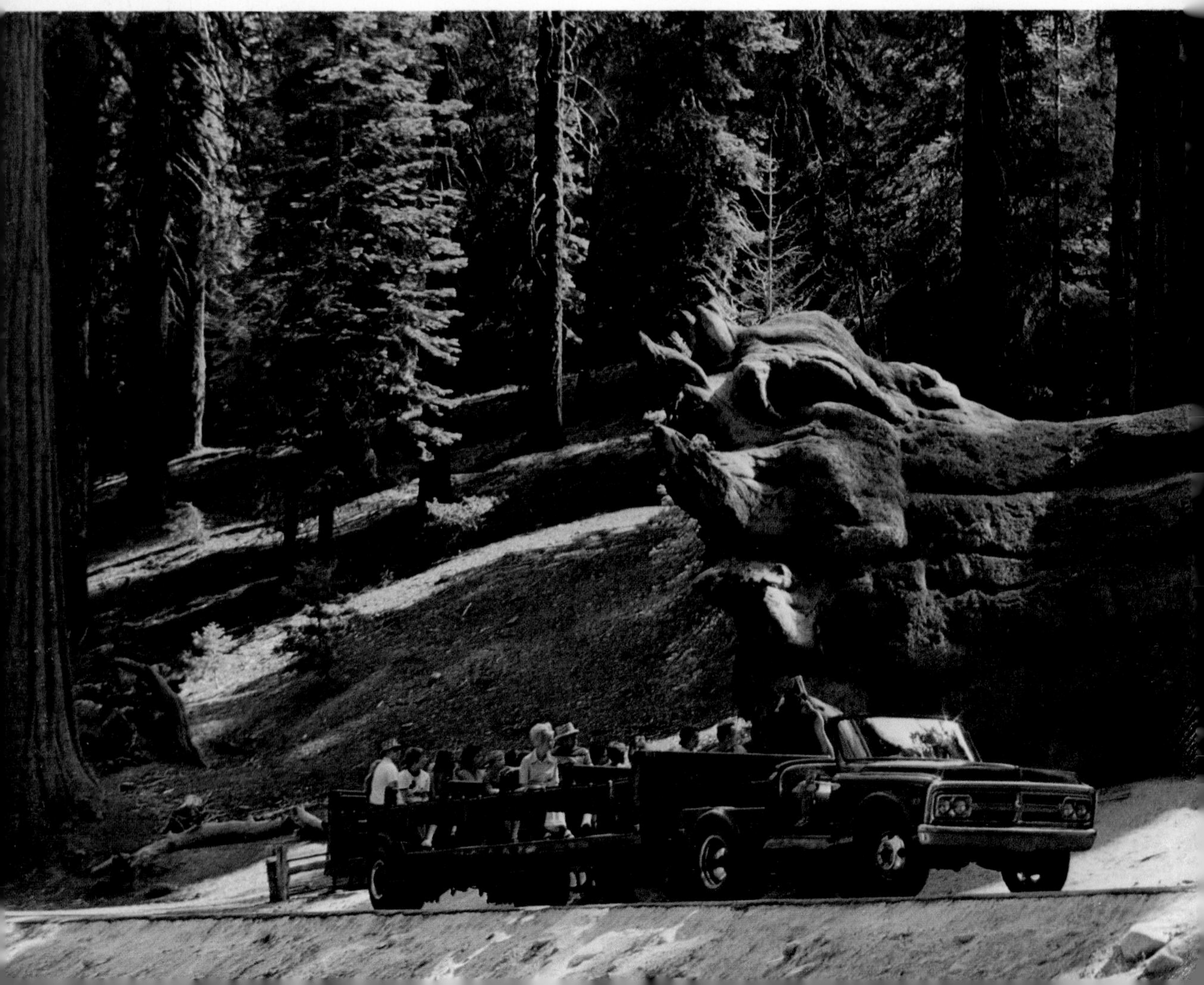

Men and women rangers at Grand Canyon's Albright Training Center (far left) study conservation. Put into practice, the lessons close an overused trail in the North Cascades. Getting motorists out of their cars and into mass "people movers" also helps preserve the parks. This quiet tram in Yosemite's Mariposa Grove of giant sequoias can hold 50 visitors.

From then on it was "King" and "Billy" in conversation between the two men.

Present-day rangers are sent to one of the ranger schools, at Grand Canyon, Arizona, or Harpers Ferry, West Virginia, for graduate or specialized training. Most new rangers, after a trial period in some park, go to Grand Canyon, where they learn basic responsibilities and, of course, the objectives and history of the National Park System and Service.

During the first half of the 19th century, men like Emerson and Thoreau called for setting aside scenic nature preserves. But it wasn't until September 19, 1870, at a campfire in Yellowstone, that the idea of a national park came to fruition. While the flames danced under the starry sky, a group of men discussed what should be done with this outstanding country that they had been exploring for nearly five weeks. They argued about staking personal claims, but Cornelius Hedges, later a judge in Montana Territory, suggested that Yellowstone's unique beauty ought to belong to all the people as a national park.

The others were persuaded, and promised to support the new concept. They kept their word: Two years later Congress passed a bill and President Ulysses S. Grant signed it, establishing Yellowstone as the world's first national park. Yellowstone was a huge success, and before the turn of the century Sequoia, Yosemite, General Grant Grove, and Mount Rainier were added to the new system.

The Antiquities Act of 1906 gave Presidents the power to make national monuments of historically or scientifically interesting places by proclamation. This important law, conceived to protect Indian ruins of the Southwest from souvenir hunters, has done much to preserve the history of man on this continent.

Before 1916 the Department of the Interior administered the parks out of the Secretary's office. Borax tycoon Stephen T. Mather complained about this setup to his friend, Secretary of the Interior Franklin K. Lane. Replied Lane: "If you don't like the way the national parks are being run, come . . . and run them yourself." Mather accepted.

One of the first men he met in Washington was Gilbert Grosvenor, then Editor, later President and Chairman of the Board of Trustees of the National Geographic Society. In 1915 Dr. Grosvenor went on a camping trip that Mather arranged in the Sierra Nevada for some influential people he hoped would help sell his park ideas. Mather and Grosvenor spread blankets beneath giant trees and talked probably half the night about the parks. One result of the trip was a contribution by the Society to help the Government acquire this magnificent grove of ancient sequoias. Dr. Grosvenor also gave enthusiastic support to Mather's plan for a specialized Park Service, helped write the legislation that established it as a bureau of the Department of the Interior, and formed a lasting friendship with the parks.

In 1933, an executive reorganization order by President Franklin D. Roosevelt transferred all military parks, monuments, and memorials to the Park Service along with the park system of Washington, D. C., including the White House. The Park Service doesn't tell the First Lady how to run her household, of course, but it keeps the grounds and historic mansion in good order.

Today the Park Service looks after some 30 million acres of land in nearly 300 units scattered throughout the United States, Puerto Rico, and the Virgin Islands. About a third are primarily scenic. Only 38 bear the official title "national park," but the word "park" generally refers to all areas.

When the Park Service was established in 1916, it had only 37 areas; by 1956, at the start of the Mission 66 project, it administered 182.

Mission 66 was a ten-year program to bring the National Park System up to the standard the American people wanted—and had a right to expect—by 1966, the 50th anniversary of the service. Between 1941 and 1955 the system

CLOCKWISE FROM CLASSROOM: WALTER MEAYERS EDWARDS; DAVID HISER; DEAN CONGER, NATIONAL GEOGRAPHIC PHOTOGRAPHER

Signing a Grand Teton trail log, a cross-country skier joins a growing army of winter park users. Snowmobilers snarl into Yellowstone to catch the wildlife show; for the less adventurous, heated snow buses provide tours. Romping trio footprints a slope beneath the Diamond, a technical climb on Longs Peak in Rocky Mountain National Park.

DAVID HISER

had deteriorated almost to the point of no return, the result of wartime austerity in funding.

The appropriation for 1940 had been $21 million, plus Civilian Conservation Corps help estimated at $20 million—a total of some $40 million. For 1955 it was only $32½ million. In the years between, funds were a good deal less, dropping as low as $5 million in 1945.

Travel in 1941 had been 21 million visitor days; by 1955 it had more than doubled, to 50 million. After 15 years of patching and re-patching roads and buildings, there no longer was any room for makeshift solutions. The parks, in people accommodations, were rural slums.

Conservationist-writer Bernard de Voto's famous column on the parks came out just as Mission 66 was being set up, and it really struck fire. He proposed that half the parks should be closed and the money appropriated by Congress go toward caring for those left open.

Mission 66 provided for $750 million over the ten-year period, and each year it was adjusted for increased costs of material and labor, as well as for the protection and development of additional parks. Seven new natural areas were added, such as *(continued on page 30)*

Mount Angeles slope camouflages mountain goats in Olympic National Park, Washington.

KEITH GUNNAR

Sipapu Bridge opens a sandstone window on Natural Bridges National Monument in Utah

Mountainous surf dwarfs scuba divers on the beach at Redwood National Park, California.

DICK DURRANCE II, NATIONAL GEOGRAPHIC PHOTOGRAPHER

Pele, Hawaiian goddess of volcanoes, vents her wrath in sputtering lava of Kilauea Iki.

DON REESER

Canyonlands in Utah; 39 historic areas, such as Theodore Roosevelt Birthplace in New York; and 15 recreation areas, such as Padre Island in Texas. Since June 30, 1966, some 40 additional areas have been acquired, many as a result of studies started during Mission 66.

Often the bureaus and the departments receive credit for advancements, and they deserve it. But it is equally true that without the backing of Congress little would be accomplished. August 7, 1961, was a landmark day in Park Service history. On that day the President signed into law the bill establishing Cape Cod National Seashore. For the first time, Congress authorized funds ($16 million) to buy land and establish an area in the National Park System.

All of the early parks had come out of tracts of land owned by or given to the Federal Government. Most were in the West because the East never had any substantial amount of public domain. When the time came to create eastern parks, private owners held the land from which parks could be made. When Congress declined to buy any with taxpayers' money, private philanthropy stepped in. Substantial folk from Boston and New York gave their summer-home property on Maine's Mount Desert Island, and Acadia National Park joined the people's estate. John D. Rockefeller, Jr., and others donated the properties necessary to round out Acadia. Mr. Rockefeller also gave $5,000,000 to match state contributions that established Great Smoky Mountains National Park in Tennessee and North Carolina.

We owe Linville Falls on the Blue Ridge Parkway to Mr. Rockefeller, and he contributed thousands of acres in Jackson Hole for Grand Teton National Park. His son Laurance, a National Geographic Society Trustee, gave us one of our most enchanting national parks, Virgin Islands. The Rockefeller family's magnificent gifts have made it the greatest single private benefactor of the National Park System.

Shenandoah came as a gift from Virginia, mainly through the efforts of Governor Harry F. Byrd, who also proposed the Blue Ridge Parkway. It was a chore rounding up the land for Shenandoah. On it lived hundreds of proud mountaineers who had built their own log cabins and could shoot a squirrel in the eye. One owner wouldn't sell. No mountaineer was he, but former President Herbert Hoover.

"Take it as a gift," he said, and deeded over his Camp Rapidan, where he had rested during weekend retreats from the White House.

Foundations established by Mrs. Ailsa Mellon Bruce and by Paul Mellon donated half the price of Cape Hatteras National Seashore in North Carolina, the first seashore in the system. North Carolina gave the other half, which means that each of its citizens played a part in this generous act. These two Mellon Foundations also put up funds to study our ocean, gulf, and Great Lakes shorelines in the interest of preserving outstanding waterfronts. After Cape Hatteras a dozen more national seashores and lakeshores were acquired, including Georgia's Cumberland Island.

We have Texas to thank for Big Bend National Park, and Florida's generosity gave us Everglades National Park, a subtropical place of mystery. Strange hammocks, islands of rank vegetation, stud its flat expanses of waving marsh grass. I can imagine thin smokes rising from campfires of the brightly clad Seminoles, Indians who once roamed this area and who still live in the adjoining regions.

Back in 1956 the proposal for Mission 66 summed up its report in part by stating: "National Parks are an investment in the physical, mental, and spiritual well-being of Americans as individuals. They are a gainful investment contributing to the economy of the nation. They are, moreover, an investment in something as simple, yet as fundamental as good citizenship —love of country, and appreciation of the natural and historic fabric of America." Today those words are more meaningful than ever.

DAVID MUENCH

The Rocky Mountains

Jagged peak, showy beargrass mark Glacier Park's land of contrasts.

William S. Ellis

Yellowstone

NATIONAL PARK, IDAHO-WYOMING-MONTANA

The land itself is raw and timeless, a wilderness realm seemingly set aside at the time of creation. But as a national park, the country's oldest, Yellowstone measures its age in years—more than a hundred.

For millions its name offers a sense of identity with America. No matter that among all national parks visitation is higher at Great Smoky Mountains or that the scenery at Glacier, many claim, is more spectacular. Yellowstone stands as the doyen of national parks in this country and, indeed, in the world.

As I drove through its west entrance on a day stifled by August heat, my thoughts were of a time, years ago, when an aunt returned from a vacation and, as aunts are given to do, distributed souvenirs of places she had visited. For me there was a coin bank in the shape of a moose, with "Yellowstone" burned into its wooden base. It is still among my belongings.

Such mementos of the park are found in homes across the country: pictures of Old Faithful erupting and black bears panhandling for food along the roads; lamps with trick shades that depict the flow of the Lower Falls of the Yellowstone River; samplers with embroidered sketches of trumpeter swans treading through the shallows of a park lake....

"Campgrounds all full," the ranger informed me, though I had not intended to camp. Unfolding a map, he directed me to the nearest accommodations within the park. Ahead lay Yellowstone's famed Grand Loop Road, with many of its 142 miles laced through forests of lodgepole pine. At some points the road skirts geyser basins where the earth steams and belches with infernal indigestion. It straddles mountains, crosses the Continental Divide twice within a few miles, and snaps like a taut string across gentle meadows.

Higher than Niagara, Lower Falls of the Yellowstone River hurtles 308 feet into the golden canyon that named the park. Changing light and iron oxides paint the rhyolite walls ocher and orange and red.

JOSEPH J. SCHERSCHEL, NATIONAL GEOGRAPHIC PHOTOGRAPHER

Visitors catch the cool drift of Old Faithful's lofty plume. A jet of superheated water, the geyser pulses 100 to 200 feet into the air approximately every hour. More than 200 geysers dot Yellowstone, some in backcountry areas accessible only on foot.

SAM ABELL. OPPOSITE: ED COOPER

There are two lanes and a speed limit. Traffic signs and the flashing red eyes of patrol cars, breakdowns and tie-ups, wrecks and wreckers—these too are present.

Thirty-nine miles to Canyon Village.

I drove slowly, savoring the feast of scenery spread all around. The Madison River ran beside the road, whipped to froth in some places and, in others, placid and sequined with reflected sunlight. A fisherman stood waist-deep in the waters, his arm a blur of motion as he snapped a fly on target.

Several miles along, the road passed through the shadows of cinnamon-colored cliffs. Then, by a patch of forest where tall, shallow-rooted pines rose from a floor of rotting snags, I came upon dozens of vehicles, all stopped in a road-blocking tangle. I asked a motorist what the problem was. "Bear," he replied. He pointed, and I saw the animal lumbering along from car to car, accepting handouts—offered in violation of a park law against feeding the animals.

"Crazy, ain't it, all this fuss to see something you can see in a zoo anytime." He paused to watch the bear vacuum up a plug of bologna. "I'll tell you something else you can see without coming to Yellowstone. Traffic jams."

The park is beset by its own popularity. Two million people in half a million cars come each year, in winter as well as summer, to view its splendors—the world's greatest concentration of geysers, hot pools, and other thermal features, some 10,000 in all.

More than a century ago Jim Bridger told of seeing wondrous things in the region that would eventually become the park, things such as a column of water as thick as his body spouting 60 feet into the air. They called him a liar.

Born in Richmond, Virginia, Bridger made his way to Indian country in the West before his twentieth birthday. He could neither read nor write, but he was shrewd and wise, an expert

Wisps of steam waft from Grand Prismatic Pool in the Midway Geyser Basin. The scalding waters, 370 feet in diameter, wear a frayed collar of yellow, brown, and red algae. A boardwalk brings viewers to the rim. Overleaf: *Dissolved limestone welling from deep within the earth creates a frothy fantasy at Minerva Terrace in the Mammoth Hot Springs area.*

JONATHAN S. BLAIR. OVERLEAF: JOSEPH J. SCHERSCHEL, NATIONAL GEOGRAPHIC PHOTOGRAPHER

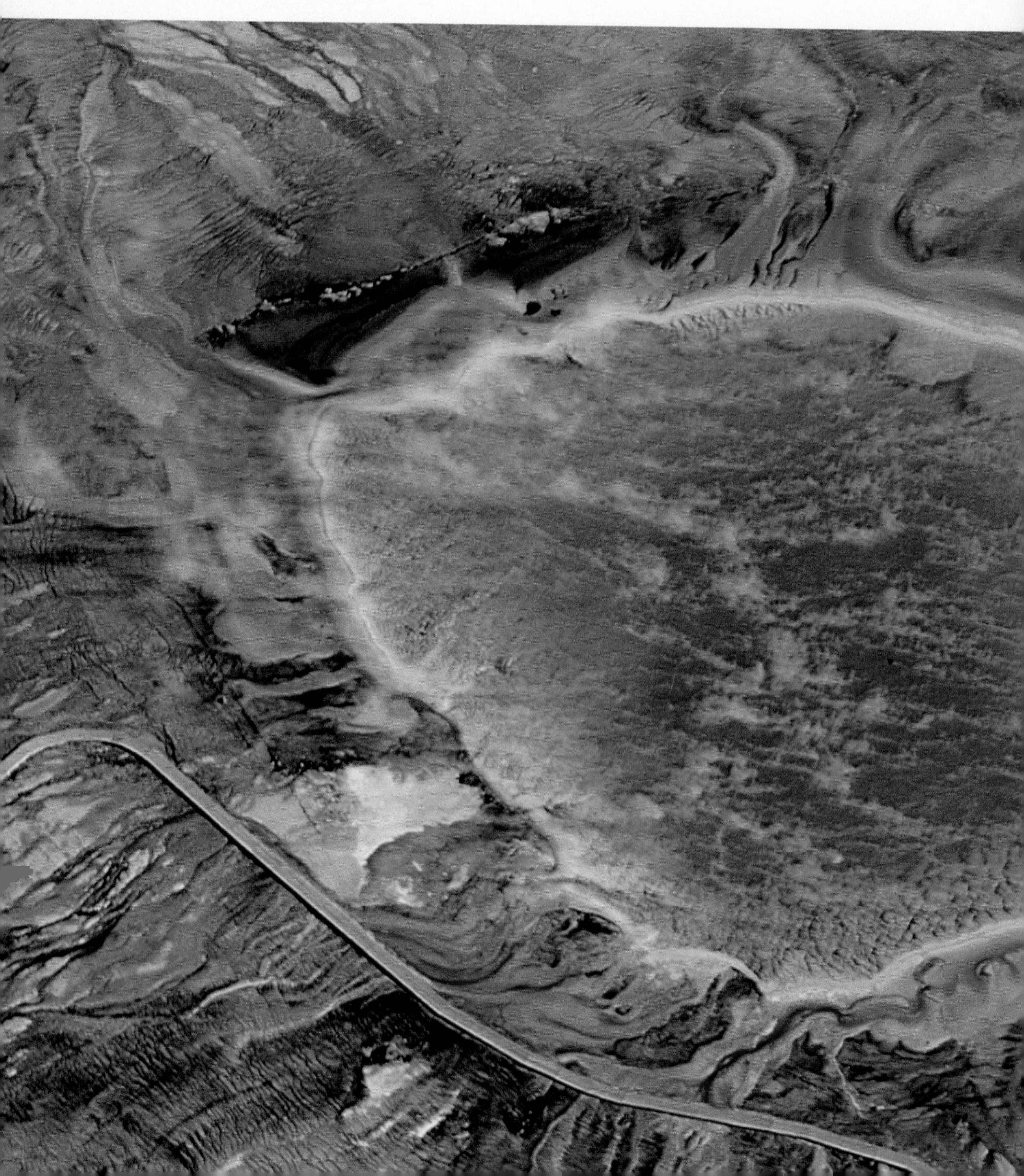

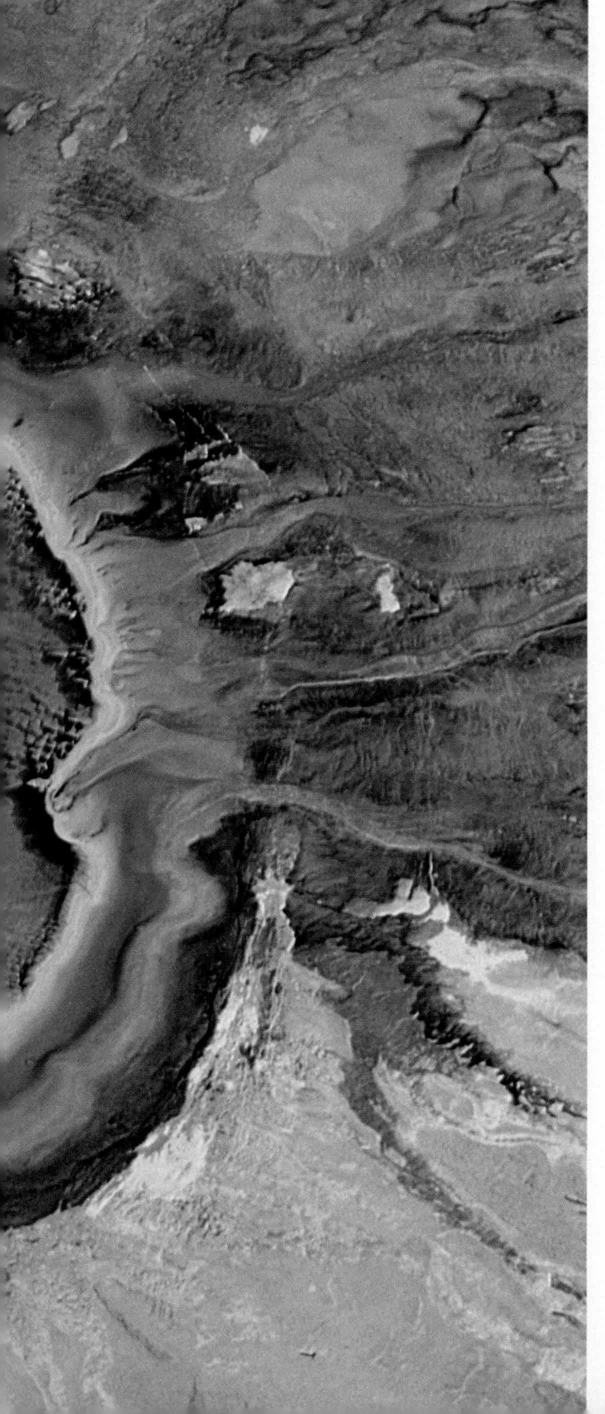

guide and trapper who knew the Rocky Mountains as well as anyone of his time.

Though Bridger liked to embellish his stories, sometimes stretching truth to the vanishing point, his first reports of Yellowstone were accurate. He did see a "mountain of transparent glass"—we know it as Obsidian Cliff, a mass of black volcanic glass—and bodies of water "boiling hot." But few believed him.

Another trapper, John Colter, is thought to have been the first white man into Yellowstone country. He too told of marvelous and eerie features, and he too was ridiculed.

Yellowstone's myriad marvels center around Old Faithful. I first saw the geyser perform on a Sunday afternoon—along with 2,000 other people. As the tower of hot water surged from the earth, I looked around and saw wonder reflected in nearly every face. An elderly couple next to me held hands, as if the hissing waters were pronouncing a benediction of happiness and good health for their late years. From the crowd I heard only one voice—a rasping whisper urging the geyser to "Go, boy, go."

What makes a geyser go? Water seeping deep into the ground near molten rock, or magma, is heated to temperatures as high as 400° F. Unable to boil at normal temperature (212°) because of the weight of water above, it becomes superheated. Steam forms. Pressure builds. Bubbles rise. More steam forms until the pressure suddenly forces a spout of hot vapor and water to the surface and high into the air.

Old Faithful erupts on an average of once every 65 minutes. Geyser experts concede that the complicated system of subterranean plumbing may one day cease to function. Chances are, though, that when Yellowstone's second century rolls to a close, Old Faithful will be working its sorcery as usual.

One of the park's most picturesque thermal areas greets visitors arriving at the north

entrance from Gardiner, Montana. Here they see Mammoth Hot Springs, as well as park headquarters and the site of old Fort Yellowstone. Tour buses load up for evening excursions to see elk and other creatures venture into the open to feed. Many people stop to watch Terrace Mountain turning itself inside out. Hot springs welling from subterranean limestone beds carry the dissolved mineral to the surface, depositing it in huge, terraced pools. At the base of the lowest terrace emerges Boiling River, the underground stream that drains this eccentric mountain of light, porous rock.

After the Civil War, with civilization moving closer to Yellowstone and prospectors verifying some of the early reports, expeditions were dispatched to explore the area. The first set out in 1869, but not until the following year was national interest stirred by the findings of a party headed by Henry D. Washburn, surveyor-general of Montana Territory. One member of the group, Cornelius Hedges, is credited with being among the first to propose that the region be made a national park.

In 1871 an expedition under Dr. Ferdinand V. Hayden of the U. S. Geological Survey visited Yellowstone. A photographer named William H. Jackson went along, and his pictures survive as classics that capture the splendor of the country and the drama of its exploration. Members of Congress found his pictures on their desks when they assembled to debate the establishment of Yellowstone as a park. The impact of his studies in black and white no doubt helped the proposal pass in 1872.

At first Yellowstone was a park in name only. Trappers and hunters continued to operate there, and various schemes—including a proposed railroad spur line into Upper Geyser Basin and over to Canyon—were put forth to exploit the park's natural wonders. The threat of desecration became so bad that in 1886 the Army was put in control. But in 1916, with establishment of the National Park Service,

Pausing amid the lodgepole pines of Grant Village Campground, a pair of mule deer seem puzzled by civilization's clutter. During the summer 2,400 campsites usually fill before noon. Crowding extends to roads, where anything from a construction crew to a wandering bear can cause monumental tie-ups.

SAM ABELL

Yellowstone came under its administration.

In the early years of this century, most visitors to the park traveled in horse-drawn carriages. Those arriving by train were transported from the station at Gardiner in double-deck coaches locally called tallyhos. The first engine-driven vehicle officially permitted in the park was a Model-T Ford. The year was 1915.

I spent many hours in the library at park headquarters, browsing through superintendents' reports and uncovering such morsels as, "On September 7, 1927, Col. Charles A. Lindbergh was seen circling over the Upper Geyser Basin in the *Spirit of St. Louis,* at about 2:30 p.m." He was barnstorming the country after his historic transatlantic flight that May.

To my surprise I also discovered that Yellowstone's thermal pools have accounted for as many serious injuries as have its bears.

In August 1927, for example:

- A doctor from Oklahoma was seriously burned when he backed into a pool. He remained in critical condition for ten days.
- A woman from Brooklyn stepped into a pool and received first-degree burns.
- A man from Salt Lake City died after falling into a pool near Firehole Lake.

Shades of a bygone era linger at Old Faithful Inn, "world's largest log hostelry." Built of fir and lodgepole pine with a cavernous lobby that soars more than 90 feet, it has awed guests since 1904. Jouncy ride in an old coach highlights a trip to Tower Junction, followed by a chuck-wagon cookout.

JONATHAN S. BLAIR. OPPOSITE: SAM ABELL

With thousands of thermal features, Yellowstone is indeed hazardous country. In 1970 a 9-year-old boy died when he fell into the bubbling waters of Crested Pool in the Upper Geyser Basin, not far from Old Faithful. Following this tragedy a railing was built to protect sightseers from the pool's 200° waters.

There are similar pools scattered over a large area of the park. Were all to be enclosed by barriers? Or were they to be left as is, without alteration to their settings, but with access rigidly controlled? The park has moved to meet the problem by relocating boardwalks so that they angle past the pools rather than approach them head-on, and by putting up guard rails on the pool side. But visitors still must exercise caution—common sense argues that a teetering perch atop the rails is a risky way to take a picture.

Covering 3,472 square miles mainly in the northwest corner of Wyoming, Yellowstone is too far from large urban centers to be plagued by groups of young people on weekend sprees. Also, troublemakers seem drawn to parks in areas blessed with more sun and warmth. Thus Yellowstone has been spared some of the more serious problems that beset parks near big cities.

"A lot of footloose youngsters come to Yellowstone, but relatively few give us trouble," a ranger told me. "Unfortunately, many of the young people in the park expect to be harassed when they see a ranger. That's why we must know how to communicate, to let the kids know they'll be treated fairly."

The surge of young people into Yellowstone began in the mid-1960's. Some arrive by motorcycle, others in anything from old hearses to stand-up-drive vans once used for milk and mail delivery. But many hitchhike. On almost any summer day, the roads of Yellowstone are fringed with uplifted thumbs.

I talked with many men and women of college age and found that, with few exceptions, they share a keen appreciation of the gifts offered by this giant among national parks. Shouldering packs, they stride out along the more than 1,000 miles of trails with the exuberance of frontiersmen. And seldom does a summer night pass without the plunking of a guitar heard somewhere in the hinterland.

Except for these young people, not many visitors venture away from the roads and established campgrounds. Rather, they concentrate their activities within an area covering no more than five percent of the park.

"You hear it all the time, that crowds have ruined the park," said a middle-aged Californian with whom I shared a table in the dining room of venerable Old Faithful Inn. "But the people who say that forget one thing: It's not ruined for those who like crowds."

Still, park officials try to disperse the visitors over a larger area of the preserve. In 1974 more than 26,000 visitors hiked off the main roads to camp out at least one night. And that, as the superintendent put it, "is what the future of Yellowstone is all about." One-way and bypass roads now ease congestion around such attractions as Old Faithful, where crowds gather to watch an eruption. For motorists passing by but not wishing to stop, delays have been reduced.

Veteran visitors to Yellowstone won't see as many begging bears as they used to. No traces of the nearly 2,000 tons of garbage generated by summer crowds are found along the roadway, and animals that scavenge in the night may greet the dawn with empty stomachs. In a program to wean the bears from the artificial feeding which generations of Yellowstone animals have enjoyed, the Park Service has closed garbage dumps and has cracked down on tourists who violate the regulations

Sunrise works its timeless magic on the Yellowstone River, summoning fish and fishermen to the challenges of a new day. In recent years some areas have been closed to anglers to preserve spawning sites.

DEAN CONGER, NATIONAL GEOGRAPHIC PHOTOGRAPHER

against feeding the wildlife. Campers and picnickers may receive a citation for leaving food on tables.

Not everyone is happy with this policy, which has resulted in fewer bears to be seen. I remember one comment that seemed to sum up the sentiments of many: "Do you realize I came all the way from New Jersey to see two things—Old Faithful and a real, live bear in the open? I mean, look, buddy, seeing a bear running free may not mean much to you, but when you live in Weehawken, it can be a big thing in your life."

When I raised this matter with the superintendent, he told me, "Of course it's great to see a bear, but in his natural habitat, not under conditions in which the animal is degraded by being fed scraps along the road. We were averaging 75 to 100 injuries a year to people trying to feed bears. Now we have less than a dozen."

Naturalists estimate that between 550 and 800 bears—black bears and grizzlies—live in Yellowstone. But since the park's founding in 1872 only three people have been killed by grizzlies within its boundaries. Provocation of the animal was involved in all three cases, as it usually is when a bear does bodily harm. Stressing that the grizzly is basically shy, the superintendent said, "If he *enjoyed* conflict, we'd lose a lot more people."

"We used to have names for many of the grizzlies," Ranger Wayne Replogle told me. "Caesar, King Henry VIII, and one named Ickes, for the Secretary of the Interior at that time. And Old Scarface—he must have weighed 1,000 pounds—ruled the park for a long time."

In search of unspoiled wilderness, backpackers crossing Specimen Ridge join the growing numbers who venture from roads to reap the park's full bounty of beauty. A nylon tipi fashioned from the panels of a parachute goes up beside a good climbing tree—a wise precaution in grizzly country.

SAM ABELL

Grizzlies huddle to discuss . . . Goldilocks? How to outwit rangers? The closing of park garbage dumps? Naturalists estimate that 250 to 300 grizzlies and 300 to 500 black bears roam the hinterlands, along with 13,000 elk, most numerous large animal. Park behemoth is the bison, weighing up to a ton.

Wayne has seen many changes during the more than 40 years he has served here as a seasonal ranger. "When I first came," he told me, "there were so few visitors that we'd hail down a car just to say 'Hello!' "

Wayne takes walks in the late evening, when the hush of that hour breathes life into happy remembrances. And he doesn't have to walk far to be where no change has come, where the awesome bigness of the land overwhelms the visitor of today as it did Jim Bridger more than a hundred years ago.

The Grand Canyon and falls of the Yellowstone River rank as popular scenic attractions. Viewed from the rim of the canyon, whose depth varies from 800 to 1,200 feet, the river flows like a swirl of frothy confection.

I walked along a trail that descends 600 feet in less than half a mile to reach the Lower Falls. There the water tumbles more than 300 feet to a foaming crash and then moves on through a screen of spray.

Of all the stretches of water in the park, the one that holds the most appeal for me is Yellowstone Lake. Sitting at an altitude of 7,733 feet, the lake collects snowmelt from the serried peaks of the Absaroka Range pressing in from the east. Far to the southwest, but still visible, rise the Tetons.

Of this lake with a shoreline of more than 100 miles, a member of the Washburn expedition wrote: "It was like the fairest dream which ever came to bless the slumbers of a child. How still it was! What silence reigned! How lovingly it laid its hush upon you!"

That same hush was laid upon me one afternoon when I took a small boat out onto its jadelike waters, and sat for hours while cutthroat trout played soccer with the lure on my line. Silence in our time, however, can be perishable even in the remote reaches of Yellowstone. High overhead, a military jet sent down a sonic boom that fell on the lake like a burst of divine rage.

YELLOWSTONE NATIONAL PARK

Area 3,472 square miles

Features: *World's most spectacular thermal area, with geysers, hot springs, pools, steam jets, mud volcanoes. Yellowstone Lake, largest mountain lake in North America (elev. 7,733 ft.). Grand Canyon of the Yellowstone. Upper, Lower, and Tower Falls. Obsidian Cliff; standing petrified trees. Black and grizzly bears, moose, deer, elk, pronghorn, bighorn sheep, coyote, bison; some 240 species of birds.*

Activities: *Visitor centers. Grand Loop Road (142 miles) connects major features. Sightseeing bus trips; 1,000 miles of hiking and riding trails. Campfire programs, guided walks. Trout fishing, boating, wilderness camping. Winter: Old Faithful visitor center—snow-coach tours, cross-country skiing.*

Season: *May-Oct.; most park facilities open from June to mid-Sept.*

Weather: *Warm, sparkling days, cool evenings (average elev. 7,500 ft.). Winter: −40° F. to 30 above.*

How to get there: *Major highways converge on Yellowstone's five entrances. See insert map. Consult touring services on routes and snow conditions in high passes during May, June, September, and October. Park buses connect with trains and buses. Write Yellowstone Park Co., Yellowstone Park, for schedules. Northwest, Western, Frontier, and United Airlines serve nearby cities; surface connections to park.*

Accommodations: *Make reservations early; opening and closing dates for each place vary; write Yellowstone Park Co. for list. Hotels: Old Faithful, Lake, Mammoth Hot Springs. Cabins: Old Faithful, Lake, Canyon, Roosevelt. Camp and trailer grounds.*

Services: *Main centers provide restaurants, stores, and garages. Hospital at Lake; clinic at Mammoth, nurse at Old Faithful. Religious services in park; chapel at Mammoth.*

Park Regulations: *Camping in designated areas only. Campfires outside campgrounds by permit only. No feeding or molesting animals or defacing natural features. Daily maximum two fish; fishing license (free) required; ask for fishing regulations. Boat permits required; no boat over 40 ft., no sailboats because of squalls. Pets allowed on leash, but not in boats or on trails.*

For further information write Supt., Yellowstone National Park, Wyo. 82190

FRANK AND JOHN CRAIGHEAD

Frank and John Craighead

Grand Teton

NATIONAL PARK, WYOMING

French-Canadian trappers more than a hundred years ago gave the Tetons their name. Gazing in awe at that spectacular granite skyline, they dubbed three towering summits the "Trois Tetons," for their fancied resemblance to women's breasts.

Later explorers thought "Tetons" a misnomer. "He indeed must have been long a dweller amid these solitudes who could trace in these cold and barren peaks any resemblance to the gentle bosom of a woman," wrote Nathaniel P. Langford on an expedition to nearby Yellowstone in 1872. But to us and to all who visit Grand Teton National Park today, the special appeal of the Tetons lies in the way they rise so precipitously from the lake-studded valley of Jackson Hole, the tallest peak clawing the sky at nearly 14,000 feet.

Our own first glimpse of this game-rich valley in the Wyoming Rockies, back in 1934, fired us with its promise as an outdoor laboratory for wildlife research. From Togwotee Pass on the east we let our eyes sweep the snow-flecked crests of the Teton Range. At its base shimmered broad Jackson Lake, through which flows the upper Snake River. Repeated visits to the Jackson Hole country won us completely to its sagebrush flats and timbered slopes.

One winter we came from warm oceans and hot tropical forests to Jackson Hole and canyon roads of snow, to a dazzling whiteness scarcely toned down by forest green, to nightly subfreezing temperatures.

During the following weeks the spring sun slugged it out with snow flurries that roared down the Teton canyons and tried to spread over the valleys. As if by magic, hot sun burned the snow blanket until fence tops showed, then the tips of the sagebrush. The porous glacial soil absorbed the melt and slowly released it to

Grand Teton peak, park's highest, towers above skiers crossing Blacktail Butte. Climbers reach its summit each summer but few dare the 13,770-foot monarch when winter swathes it in windswept snow and ice.

DAVID HISER

the Snake River. Almost overnight in early May, spring finally came to the valley, and winter slowly receded up the mountains.

Buttercups turned the first bare ground to a glistening gold. Shaggy, ill-tempered moose dragged out of the Snake River willow bottoms, waded into the unfrozen beaver ponds, and daily grew warier as they gained strength from the slimy green algae. Grouse drummed in courtship day and night. A lonesome saw-whet owl called monotonously for a mate. There were swirls of feeding trout, and then the aspens turning green and the willows red.

From the sagebrush of the valley and the blue waters of Jenny Lake we followed a trail over glacial moraines cloaked in lodgepole pine, and climbed Cascade Canyon into the subalpine zone of fir and spruce. Above tree line on the Skyline Trail towered a tremendous stratified limestone wall contrasting with the crystalline rocks of the Teton peaks. And above the cliffs and peaks, birds of prey soared and wheeled while scanning the meadows below.

Cross-country skiers halt for lunch and a wax job near Bradley Lake. Winter sports flourish amid Teton snows that average 16 feet annually—though blizzardy whiteouts may stall travelers for days.

DAVID HISER

February cold quick-freezes lake trout as fast as Jackson Lake ice fishermen reel them in. Ranger Rob Wallace checks the catch. In winter he uses a prop-driven, ski-fitted snowplane to patrol the 18-mile-long lake, largest in the park.
DAVID HISER

The Tetons can be moody as well as magnificent. During one of our summer climbs, storms that had been milling around all day fused at last in a rumbling mass of clouds and searing flashes. Thunder broke directly overhead. Lightning struck close by, leaving a strong ozone smell in its wake. Rain and hail flailed us as we crawled into timberline lean-tos, natural shelters where mountain sheep and elk bed down beneath the roofing of gnarled firs.

The elk in summer move to the high country of Teton National Forest and the timbered, grassy vales of the Yellowstone plateau. There they fatten, raise their calves, and frolic in cool alpine meadows. On clear September days, when aspens glitter golden on the hills, it is a tingling thrill to hear a bull elk bugling. Frequently we glimpse him on a hilltop in proud pose, his many-pointed rack silhouetted against the sky. This is the season of the rut, and the great bull is in his splendid prime.

With the first heavy snows in late October or early November, a herd estimated at 7,500 to 10,000 drifts down to winter in the lower Jackson Hole valley. During these weeks rifle fire echoes among the hills and on the flats, for the Park Service grants special licenses to hunters to cull surplus animals. Hunting helps keep the herd about the right size for the winter range available on the National Elk Refuge.

Many of our sharpest memories of life in Jackson Hole focus on adventures with its mammals and birds. We always had wild creatures around our cabins: ground squirrels, chipmunks, magpies, ravens, horned owls, prairie falcons, even white-footed mice. Kali, a female coyote, we raised from a pup. She played with the children, chewed up shoes, came at our call, and acted like a well-behaved dog. And like a good dog she assumed responsibilities. Once her excited barks brought John running to an irrigation ditch into which his infant son had

Hikers cut frigid tracks across Colter Bay, arm of Jackson Lake, on snowshoes furnished by the park. Teton Range, youngest in the Rockies, began nine million years ago as faulted rock thrust high above Jackson Hole; ice and water whittled the peaks.

DAVID HISER

crawled. The coyote's warning probably saved the child from drowning. Kali later ate four of our laying hens; we merely reprimanded her.

Since our first visits, Jackson Hole has been invaded by paved roads, motels, service stations, and a swelling tide of tourists. But the glorious semi-wilderness backcountry happily remains intact. Some areas within the park are nearly as wild as when John Colter, mountain man and trapper, set foot here in 1807.

After trappers and hunters of the last century took heavy toll of its animals, Jackson Hole lapsed into neglect. The westward trek of settlers washed around it to the Pacific, for the Hole was not farming country. Much of the valley, therefore, still held wildlife. Beaver boldly cut aspen trees and cottonwood for their dams, and rising trout rippled the waters.

Years before we found our way to Jackson Hole, the recreational value of the area and its potential as an "unfenced zoo" had been recognized. In 1897 Teton National Forest was created. In 1912 Congress set aside land in the valley for a National Elk Refuge, and in 1929 established Grand Teton National Park. The park area was tripled in 1950 by including lands formerly in Jackson Hole National Monument and in private holdings; 30,000 of these acres were presented to the American people by the late John D. Rockefeller, Jr.

"Conservation today means far more than just preserving our natural resources," said his son, Laurance S. Rockefeller, a National Geographic Trustee. "It means their wise use and full protection so that more and more people may enjoy and benefit by them."

Colter Bay was developed as a model for park accommodations envisioned in the Park Service's Mission 66 program. Campgrounds, trailer sites, and scores of cabins nestle amid tall pines. The community includes a visitor center, general store, service station, cafeteria and grill, laundromat, a beach, and a marina where you can rent boats or launch your own.

FRANK CRAIGHEAD

Summer sleigh ride: Youngsters run the Snake River in kayaks.

Bull elk, lord of the Teton high country, surveys his sanctuary. When autumn comes, he and rival bulls challenge for mates with whistling bugle calls, finest of mountain music. The Grand Teton elk herd, one of the world's largest, winters in Jackson Hole, where supplemental food stocks help the elk survive.

When you arrive in the park, we suggest you first drive up Signal Mountain for its commanding view of the valley and range. Later you may wish to exchange the driver's seat for the saddle. Whether you take a short horseback ride, join an overnight pack trip, or hike, you have 200 miles of park trails from which to choose.

A favorite is Cascade Canyon Trail, winding between crags to Lake Solitude, an 18-mile round trip. And ever beckoning the skilled climber are those towers of naked rock—Grand, Middle, and South Teton, Teewinot, Owen, Moran. Each crag offers a challenge. For the unskilled, guide services and a mountaineering school are available. Two days' instruction can ready a novice for a try at "The Grand."

Float trips down the Snake, whispering in its gravelly bed, are a delightful way to see the park. You can join an organized trip or launch your own rubber raft. The fast-flowing river stays open even through winter's coldest weather, and we have pioneered winter rafting on it to study big game and Canada geese.

It was one of these trips that showed us a rare woodland drama. We had tied our raft to the bank and snowshoed up a side canyon. High above us on an open slope we saw a band of mule deer lunging forward, belly-deep in snow. Panting with exhaustion, they reached a snow cornice that overhung a cliff.

Hardly had they paused when a golden eagle swooped down and attacked; it struck the deer with its wings, raked their backs with its talons. Evidently the bird was trying to panic its prey into lunging over the cliff to death on the rocks below. But the deer held together, fending off attack by rising on their hind legs and flailing at the eagle with their forefeet. The air-ground combat continued until the eagle soared off to find an easier meal.

Even when snow crunches underfoot in Jackson Hole everybody plays outdoors—taking their choice of skiing, snowshoeing, ice fishing, snowplane trips, or visiting the elk herds on horsedrawn sleighs. Then on summer nights valley folk look across sagebrush flats at a thousand-eyed dragon writhing along beneath the Teton ramparts—the procession of cars carrying visitors to this enchanted landscape.

People en masse, of course, could destroy the fragile beauty of this wild land. But we've found today's Americans increasingly responsive to the idea of preserving their national parks. Their cooperation and the efforts of the Park Service and other conservation agencies ensure, we think, that Grand Teton National Park will be available to the future's millions of visitors in all its unspoiled grandeur.

GRAND TETON NATIONAL PARK

Area 484 square miles

Features: *Teton Range, one of world's boldest, most majestic mountain fronts, rising 7,000 ft. above wildlife-rich Jackson Hole.*

Activities: *Visitor centers at Moose and Colter Bay. Scenic drives, 200 miles of hiking and bridle trails. Pack trips. Boating, trout fishing; float trips down Snake River. Scenic flights. Cross-country skiing, guided ski tours, snowcoaches through park; downhill skiing nearby; rental equipment.*

Season: *Road through park open year round; most activities June 15-Labor Day.*

Weather: *Warm, sunny days, cool evenings in summer. Near-freezing days, below-zero nights in winter.*

How to get there: *Major highways intersect in park. See insert map. Wyo. 22 over Teton Pass steep, not for trailers. Air service to Jackson.*

Accommodations: *Lodges at Jackson Lake and Jenny Lake; cabins at Colter Bay; write Grand Teton Lodge Co., Moran, Wyo. Signal Mt. Lodge; address, Moran. Write park for dude ranch list, winter facilities. Camp, trailer grounds. John D. Rockefeller, Jr., Memorial Parkway between Grand Teton and Yellowstone offers camping at Snake River and Huckleberry Hot Springs; summer lodging, trailer hookups at Flagg Ranch—plowed road ends here in winter.*

Services: *Stores, garages; car rentals at Jackson or Jackson Lake Lodge. Nurse at lodge, hospital in Jackson. Religious services in park.*

Park regulations: *Camping in specified areas only. Climbers must register at Jenny Lake; no solo climbing. Boat permit; Wyo. fishing license.*

For information write Supt., Moose, Wyo. 83012

MAURICE G. HORNOCKER

Donald J. Frederick

Rocky Mountain

NATIONAL PARK, COLORADO

Jagged streaks of lightning stabbed at Trail Ridge Road and hailstones ricocheted off my car. I pulled into the parking overlook at Rainbow Curve as the hail turned to snow and began slicking the highway. Around me rose the raw beauty of the Front Range that distinguishes Colorado's Rocky Mountain National Park—a dazzling array of snowy peaks, rugged ridges, and massive cirques. Far below, mist shrouded the "parks"—grassy meadows that sprawl between the peaks.

A car with Florida license plates slid into the slot next to mine. The driver motioned to me to roll down my window.

"Better stay put until this storm blows over," he shouted. "It's wild up ahead. The road's covered with snow. I can't believe it's July!"

Abruptly, the low-flying clouds scudded away; unmasked, the sun quickly melted the snow on the road. The highest continuous paved highway in the United States, 44-mile Trail Ridge Road tops 12,000 feet as it crosses the Continental Divide, from Estes Park on the east to Grand Lake on the west. Indians once followed a trail on the same ridge to cross the mountains, giving the road its name.

I was anxious to get back on the highway. Ahead lay one of the most dramatic stretches in the park, the sweeping expanse of tundra that borders 11 miles of the road above timberline. Arctic tundra, a region of cold wet soil supporting dense growths of herbs and shrubs stunted by drying winds, is common to Alaska and northern Canada. Under the name alpine tundra, similar vegetation leapfrogs southward to frigid, windswept heights here in the Colorado Rockies. For most of the year the tundra seems dead. But from June to August, blossoms burst forth and at times the brilliant crazy quilt spreads over entire mountainsides. I found it impossible, from a car window, to distinguish the tiny, ground-hugging blooms. "Belly plants," one botanist calls them.

"Stop at Rock Cut for a close look at the tundra," a park ranger had advised me. "There's a half-mile path there with small signs identifying exactly what you see."

The highway rose to a dizzying 12,110 feet at the Rock Cut overlook. To the west, snow draped the slopes of a massive range appropriately named the Never Summer Mountains by the Arapahos. More than 2,000 feet below, a canopy of green covered Forest Canyon, realm of deer, elk, coyote, and beaver.

I tore myself from the view and concentrated on the tundra. Dense tufts of yellow, five-petaled alpine avens pushed through patches of melting snow. Tiny pink moss campion basked in the sunlight. Brilliant blue sky pilots seemed to spring from the rocks. For an hour I lost myself in a Lilliputian garden of delights.

The park, of course, has a lot more to offer visitors. Anglers cast for trout in sparkling lakes and streams. Climbers tackle giants such as Longs Peak. Hikers toughen up on more than

Daisy-like rydbergia spangles a slope near the Never Summer range. Overleaf: *Trail Ridge Road cuts through tundra above the 11,500-foot tree line. Longs Peak looms in the background.*

DAVID MUENCH. OVERLEAF: DAVID HISER

Wild vistas and the 11,716-foot altitude make visitors catch their breath at Forest Canyon Overlook on Trail Ridge Road; one denizen of the realm, a marmot, poses for a picture. Sweeping views wait atop Longs Peak, where a sign warns inexperienced climbers away from a difficult route.

KENT DANNEN. OPPOSITE: DAVID HISER

300 miles of trails. And a permit system allots space to about 2,000 backcountry campers a night in the summer.

"Rocky Mountain is essentially a day-use park," the superintendent told me. "Many people from Denver and the surrounding area come up for the day just to unwind. Maybe they'll spot a bighorn sheep on Specimen Mountain. Or hook a brook or brown trout in the Big Thompson River. A lot of them just want to get away from it all by a little waterfall. In winter, cross-country skiing is the big thing."

I decided to seek out the varied attractions of the rugged quarter-million-acre preserve by following the advice of a veteran ranger. "To really know this park," he said, "you have to suffer a little. Lose your breath, develop a blister, endure a little wind, rain, or snow."

I broke in my boots on a hike that started in Beaver Meadows, only a mile and a half by car from the visitor center on the east side of the park. Guided by a ranger naturalist, I toiled up a narrow, rocky elk trail guarded by a huge boulder. An advancing squadron of storm clouds made fitful sallies at the sun.

As the path climbed from scattered trees into thick stands of pine and quaking aspen, the ranger turned to me. "Not a word now," he said. "This is my zone of silence. Walk slowly and just listen. . . ."

Somewhere a stream gurgled cheerfully. Trees whispered in the wind. A storm approached. Loud sighs and groans greeted the wind and rain that suddenly lashed their branches. Grumbling, the storm finally moved off. A ruby-crowned kinglet warbled the all clear, and a pair of mountain bluebirds suddenly took wing.

My companion motioned me forward and we scrambled to the top of a wooded moraine. Far below, the Big Thompson River wound through the wide, green meadows of Moraine Park.

"When I was a boy," he said, "two ranches and a golf course cluttered that beautiful valley.

Quaking aspens, turned autumn gold above Beaver Meadows, offer toothsome morsels and building material to beavers abundant in the park. Their dams and lodges are especially numerous in the Moraine and Horseshoe areas. If patient and quiet, you may spot them at work in the early evening.

Now all that's changed." After a short pause he added needlessly, "And for the better."

Since the park was established in 1915, a land acquistion program has reclaimed thousands of acres of private in-holdings. Only a few foundations and rotting log cabins remain of the mining camps and settlements that flourished during the 1880's within what are now the confines of the park.

Backbreaking climbs up precipitous slopes in search of the big strike tormented the miners in the late 19th century. Now, thousands of climbers—novice and expert—gather in the park each summer to tackle the mountains for pleasure. There are plenty of challenges—107 of the park's peaks exceed 11,000 feet.

The highest of these, 14,255-foot Longs Peak, pulls the largest crowds, which is unfortunate for the mountain. About 3,000 people make it to the summit each year, most of them in the summer and up routes that can be managed without ropes and other special equipment. "You might say it erodes the experience," sighed a park official, "when you find 200 people milling around up there."

Winter snows still hung on the mountain, making it a hazardous climb for a beginner. So I decided to "challenge" Flattop Mountain and Hallett Peak instead. I set out early one morning on my expedition with Charlie Post, a young backcountry expert. From the Beaver Meadows entrance we drove up to our starting point at Bear Lake above 9,000 feet.

"Flattop's only 12,324 feet, and Hallett's a few hundred feet higher," Charlie explained. "Just a short haul from one to the other."

Perky ground squirrels and chipmunks scurried among ponderosa pines and aspens on the lower stretches of the trail. At timberline the trees were dwarfed and distorted by their fight for survival. Century-old trunks reached no higher than our waists. Some sprawled like vines, bent low by countless snowdrifts; others, shaped by never-ceasing winds, had streamers of branches sweeping leeward.

Higher and higher we climbed. My heart began to pound wildly and my lungs seemed ready to burst. A throbbing headache gave way to dizziness. I felt miserable.

"A touch of mountain sickness," Charlie explained. "Your body's not accustomed to the high altitude yet and can't get enough oxygen. But don't worry. You'll make it."

Much to my surprise, I did make it—all the way to Hallett Peak. My reward was an unforgettable view. Glittering Tyndall Glacier filled the head of a steep valley at our feet. Gemlike lakes flashed with sunlight. Through distant haze I could make out the Great Plains stretching eastward into infinity.

That night back in my hotel room, I felt as though I had conquered Everest. Then my thoughts turned to Enos A. Mills, the naturalist whose lectures and writings led to establishment of the park. He once wrote: "He who feels the spell of the wild, the rhythmic melody of falling water, the echoes among the crags, the bird songs, the wind in the pines ... is in tune with the universe." I knew what he meant.

ROCKY MOUNTAIN NATIONAL PARK

Area 412 square miles

Features: *Scores of lofty peaks. Moraines, lakes, conifer forests, some 850 plant species, bighorn sheep. Adjoins Shadow Mountain National Recreation Area. See insert map.*

Activities: *Moraine Park and Alpine visitor centers. Two-mile-high Trail Ridge Road winds through tundra meadows. Backcountry hiking and camping. Nature walks, campfire programs, trout fishing, climbing. Winter camping, ski touring.*

Season: *Chiefly June-Sept. Park open all year.*

Weather: *Crisp (elevation 7,800 to 14,255 ft.).*

How to get there: *From east or west, U. S. 34. Air, rail, bus via Denver.*

Accommodations: *Campgrounds, trailer sites in the park. Hotels, lodges near the park. (Write chamber of commerce at Estes Park or Grand Lake.)*

Park regulations: *Permit for backcountry camping and technical climbs. Colo. fishing license.*

For information write Supt., Estes Park, Colo. 80517

DAVID HISER

CHARLES STEINHACKER

Runoff from a sudden rain gnaws crookedly through hills scoured by millenniums of erosion.

Badlands

NATIONAL MONUMENT, SOUTH DAKOTA

A tiny, three-toed horse roamed the swampy grasslands east of the Black Hills and there – 25 million years ago – he met his death. Perhaps a saber-toothed cat killed him, or he simply got mired. Layers of silt covered his bones; water-carried minerals petrified them.

Then the climate changed. The region dried up. Rare but violent rains cut into the earth, and ancient sediments again were on the move. Finally a thunderstorm washed the last bit of clay from the horse's bones. They rattled into a gully and came to rest among other fossilized relics in what is now Badlands National Monument in western South Dakota. Famed for paleontological treasures, this 40-mile-long swath of eroding clays lies between the White River and high, grassy plains to the north.

"A no-man's-land of unimaginable desolation," a visitor once wrote, and so it seems at first. Ragged pinnacles crowd the highway. Parking turnouts survey a sea of buttes, battlements, haystack hills. Fancy sees in them the Pyramids, the Great Wall of China, Aztec temples. Through them all runs a palette of color: pastel blues, pinks, greens, and tans arranged in banded layers. Their kaleidoscopic patterns shift as evening shadows lengthen.

But all is not desolation here. On high ground, the prairie dog, cottontail, and coyote scurry through the grass. Deer, antelope, and bison feed in lowland meadows. In spring, wild flowers bloom in frenzied profusion.

More than a million people a year travel U. S. 16A through the Badlands. Most content themselves with stops at the Cedar Pass visitor center and scenic overlooks along the 30-mile park highway. But others stretch their legs in fossil-rich ravines that have lured the world's scientists for more than a hundred years.

Travelers stay in the lodge or campground at Cedar Pass, or at the Sage Creek primitive campground. Often the next stop is the School of Mines and Technology in Rapid City, where a museum displays long-gone Badlands beasts. *Write Supt., Box 72, Interior, S. D. 57750*

Devils Tower

NATIONAL MONUMENT, WYOMING

You come upon it in the northeastern corner of the state where the Black Hills dwindle into plains. Suddenly the rolling land is rent by a solitary, massive tower of rock, almost shocking in its impact. Devils Tower, a weird volcanic pillar, thrusts like a nubbin of the underworld through the gentle soil. In 1906 President Theodore Roosevelt declared the Wyoming wonder our first national monument, one of nature's legacies to be protected by law.

Devils Tower, soaring 857 feet over the parking circle, rises 1,267 feet above the Belle Fourche River flowing nearby. Geologists debate the tower's origin. Most agree that molten rock welling up within the earth intruded surface layers, possibly 50 million years ago. Erosion washed away the enfolding soil, leaving the monolith to stand alone.

Encircled by majestic stands of ponderosa pine, Devils Tower seems itself like the petrified stump of some gigantic prehistoric tree. Flutings resulted from crack patterns that shot through the buried magma as it cooled and shrank. Indians claimed a giant grizzly clawed the formation, and some called it Mateo Tipi—Grizzly Bear Lodge. To others it was The Bad God's Tower. When Col. Richard Dodge helped survey the area in 1875 he picked up the Indian appellation and named it Devils Tower.

Prairie falcons nest among its columns, which average ten feet across, and chipmunks scurry through the sage on the flat 1½-acre top. At the base, prairie dogs entertain visitors—some 150,000 a year. Hiking the 1¼-mile trail around the tower, you can see the talus built up by fallen columns, broken loose by water freezing and thawing in crevices and joints. Don't try to climb the pillar unless you have experience, proper gear, physical qualifications—and the superintendent's approval. A parachutist who gained the summit the "easy" way in 1941 had to wait a week to be rescued.

Reached via State 24, the monument is open all year, though snow may close campsites.
Write Supt., Devils Tower, Wyo. 82714

Theodore Roosevelt

NATIONAL MEMORIAL PARK, NORTH DAKOTA

Darkness hid the badlands of North Dakota as the train panted to a stop. A bespectacled Easterner stepped to the platform of Little Missouri depot and gathered his hunting gear. Theodore Roosevelt, not yet 25, planned to shoot a buffalo in this frontierland of 1883.

He got his buffalo. But the starkly eroded, freakishly painted hills and the rugged ways of a ranch captured him for life. Within 20 days of his arrival, Teddy Roosevelt bought 400 head of cattle. Thus began his love affair with the West. He became a champion of the wilderness, a guardian of its resources.

T.R. would have been "dee-lighted" to know that his Elkhorn Ranch and two huge areas nearby now form a national memorial park. It takes in 110 square miles joined by the Little Missouri River—a North and a South unit, with T.R.'s Elkhorn Ranch site between. None of the original buildings remain at the site, which can only be reached over a rough, unmarked dirt road—a trip that should not be attempted without first making inquiry at park headquarters.

Enter the South Unit at the town of Medora on Interstate 94. Here visitors camp and hike among weird buttes, sagebrush plains, grassy bottomlands, cottonwood groves, and scatterings of petrified wood. They walk on reddish clay turned into bricklike rock—called scoria—by the heat of smoldering lignite beneath the surface. The lignite formed millions of years ago when vegetation, growing on sediments that washed into streams, was deposited in layers, creating beds of soft, impure coal.

Buffalo were disappearing when Roosevelt came to hunt them. Now in the protection of his park, they thrive along with deer and antelope.

Drive up U.S. Route 85 to the North Unit to see the meandering river in action, moving silt from one bank to another where cottonwoods have not yet taken hold to anchor the soil. You can camp here too and wander the self-guiding nature trails. But heed the warnings in park leaflets about prudence in approaching wildlife.
Write Supt., Medora, N.D. 58645

Devils Tower loomed as a landmark to westering pioneers.

ROBERT W. MADDEN, NATIONAL GEOGRAPHIC PHOTOGRAPHER

Bart McDowell

Mount Rushmore

NATIONAL MEMORIAL, SOUTH DAKOTA

The President placed a drill in the hands of a stocky, energetic man. The tool bit deep into granite. Thus in 1927 did Calvin Coolidge, self-conscious in a ten-gallon hat, launch the work of sculptor Gutzon Borglum upon the face of Mount Rushmore in South Dakota.

For 14 summers mountain foliage—spruce, pine, silver birch, aspen—shuddered to the blast of dynamite, the chatter of jackhammer. When the last stone fragment tumbled from the mountain, stillness settled over the valley. Carved from this Western Gibraltar stood the world's most heroic sculpture.

"Trained but not tamed," men said of Idaho-born Borglum. A famed disciple of Rodin in Paris, he was a man of many enthusiasms—writer, engineer, an impatient patriot. "There is not a monument in the country as big as a snuff box," he said in 1916. America demanded "an enlarged dimension—a new scale."

Borglum found that scale, and a challenge for all his talents, when South Dakota State historian Doane Robinson suggested a monumental sculpture in the Black Hills. Robinson had considered carving such popular Western figures as Kit Carson, Jim Bridger, and John Colter, but Borglum saw greater national significance in memorializing Presidents. Near the town of Keystone the sculptor examined an exposed granite core—5,725-foot Mount Rushmore—that commanded the surrounding countryside. Its southeastern face, bathed in sunlight most of the day, offered the greatest promise. With private funds, then Federal appropriations, the engineering feat got under way.

Borglum fashioned plaster models, measured them, then dropped proportionate plumb lines from the mountaintop. Faces would be 60 feet tall—as high as a six-story building. Dynamite shots probed reliable rock beneath the deeply

Granite giants of history, George Washington, Thomas Jefferson, Theodore Roosevelt, and Abraham Lincoln stare stonily on eternity. Eyes measure 11 feet across, mouths 18 feet wide, and noses 20 feet long.

ROBERT W. MADDEN, NATIONAL GEOGRAPHIC PHOTOGRAPHER

fissured surface, removing some 450,000 tons of granite before the project ended. Nine times Borglum remade his models to conform to solid stone. He climbed scaffolds to train miners helping him; he darted about the canyon to test the effect of shadow on cheek or chin.

First face to be completed was, appropriately, George Washington's. Next emerged Thomas Jefferson, eyes fixed on the horizon his Louisiana Purchase had assured. Brow-first, Abraham Lincoln took shape, melancholy in his mission to keep America intact. Last, with a square jaw fittingly in granite, Theodore Roosevelt's image evoked the vigor of 20th-century America. But Gutzon Borglum did not live to see his masterpiece complete; in March 1941 he died at 74, leaving seven months' work to the son he had named for Lincoln.

"I don't intend that it shall be just a three-day tourist wonder," Borglum once said. Two million tourists a year testify to his success. They stop in hotels and motels in Rapid City and Keystone. They picnic and camp in nearby Black Hills National Forest or feast in the restaurant near the Rushmore visitor center.

They come not merely to gaze at a giant curiosity but to observe a monument as large and permanent as the dream these four men made real. Some return time and again to watch morning light move across the faces, to see the figures backed by a sunset, to attend the nightly summer ceremony as floodlights whiten the granite against a black sky.

At whatever hour, the setting inspires awe. Architect Frank Lloyd Wright left aside all his barbs when he saw Rushmore: "The noble countenances emerge as though the spirit of the mountain heard a human plan and itself became a human countenance." Vacationists, freshly conscious of the meaning of citizenship, say even more by their reflective silence. *Write Supt., Keystone, S.D. 57751*

Instant replays of the sculpturing of the Presidents roll across two TV sets mounted high on a picture window in the visitor center, enabling viewers to watch a film history of the carving while gazing on the finished colossus. Riders of the annual week-long Black Hills Trail Trip (left) stop in at the shrine.

ROBERT W. MADDEN, NATIONAL GEOGRAPHIC PHOTOGRAPHER

Wind Cave

NATIONAL PARK, SOUTH DAKOTA

Tucked in a gully on the southeast flank of South Dakota's Black Hills lies a whistling barometer. This rare phenomenon is a hole in the ground, ten inches across, opening to a cave below. As atmospheric pressure changes, air sucks into or blows out of its rocky throat, sometimes with bush-rattling force.

In 1881 a Black Hills pioneer discovered the cleft 20 miles south of Custer. Indians probably knew of it long before, for Sioux legends tell of a sacred cave of the winds through which their forefathers entered the West.

Today hundreds of visitors step into this happy hunting ground of geology. They see few stalactites or stalagmites, but Wind Cave's walls and ceilings of calcite fins arranged in a honeycomb pattern called boxwork are the world's most extensive. Electricity lights nearly two of the 30 miles of explored passageways that descend some 326 feet.

From April through October, ranger-led tours examine the Model Room, Blue Grotto, Garden of Eden, and Monte Cristo Palace. In the Fairgrounds, ultraviolet light sets aglow the calcite fantasies of frostwork—clusters of tiny crystals resembling ice and snow. Visitors may sign up in advance for a cave-crawling tour into a more primitive section—no experience necessary.

You needn't be a spelunker to savor the cave's setting. When the elevator surfaces with visitors, sweatered against the underground chill, the warm hills seem charged with blues and greens to eyes attuned to reds and browns. The rolling plains, laced with ponderosa pine, once stretched like a sea of grass for a thousand miles. Then came cattle to graze and plows to break the virgin sod. But Wind Cave National Park preserves a treasured remnant of the Great Plains where buffalo still roam.

About 350 of the prairie monarchs live in the 44-square-mile park. In winter they swing massive heads from side to side, battering through snow to find forage. A buffalo can weigh a ton, run 30 miles an hour, and turn on a buffalo nickel. And he's unpredictable. The park highway usually provides a close enough view, and a safe one. Never approach buffalo on foot.

The great shaggy beasts share their domain with elk, deer, pronghorn, and thousands of prairie dogs. These bustling rodents maintain more than a dozen colonies here. Each hummocky town is clear of long grass, for the little fellows insist on an unobstructed view. A coyote or eagle sends them diving for a burrow.

The visitor center is open all year, a campground from May to September. Guided hikes and campfire programs are held during summer. *Write Supt., Hot Springs, S.D. 57747*

Jewel Cave

NATIONAL MONUMENT, SOUTH DAKOTA

A subterranean sparkler in rocky terrain 14 miles west of Custer, Jewel Cave is a spelunker's paradise. From its natural entrance in the depths of Hell Canyon, ladderlike steps lead to a rugged trail where the adventurous climb, stoop, and crawl, following the labyrinth to glittering treasure on the Primitive Tour.

For the less adventurous, an elevator in the visitor center is the starting point for a Scenic Tour by way of a paved and lighted trail.

Jewel Cave was carved when underground streams dissolved Black Hills limestone. The water's calcium carbonate spangled the chambers with crystals called dogtooth spar. Sparkling like jewels, they gave the cave its name.

In galleries and along tunnels, an underground feast is spread: clusters of cave coral or "popcorn"; helictites protruding like pretzels; petrified "bacon and eggs"; and mounds of silver "bubble gum," found only in this cave.

Spelunkers have explored some 50 miles of tunnels in the 1,275-acre national monument. The visitor center is open April to September; guided tours are offered only during summer. *Administered by Supt., Wind Cave.*

Lanterns light a niche on Jewel Cave's Primitive Tour.

SOUTH DAKOTA DIVISION OF TOURISM

David S. Boyer

Glacier

NATIONAL PARK, MONTANA

The car had Midwestern license plates, and as the driver dug the entrance fee out of his wallet, he peered at the snow-capped Rockies starched against the blue sky.

"About how much would you say one of those highest mountains weighs?"

The ranger at the gate managed not to flinch. He turned and followed the driver's gaze upward to the heights.

"Well, that depends," he replied. "Do you mean with or without snow?"

The answer was not quite as facetious as it sounded. A million or so years ago only the highest of these peaks rose above great overburdening glaciers that were grinding out the broad, bathtub-shaped valleys of western Montana's Glacier National Park. The total weight of ice may have amounted to more than that of the mountains themselves.

But the ancient ice sheets are gone now. Only half a hundred mini-glaciers remain, all born within the last 4,000 years. Seldom seen, seldom visited, even most of these have retreated in the last century to hidden corners of the highest cirques and valleys. Glacier Park, stretching from Canada 60 miles southward along the Continental Divide, owes its name more to the past than to the present. It is the garlanding beauty of snow, not ice, that each year draws more than a million visitors. Snow, and the wilderness experience offered by 700 miles of trails through lakelands, forests, and soaring alpine meadows. With pack on back, in a day or even an hour, a hiker can be alone in some of the most dramatic, unspoiled outdoors on the continent—as alone as he may want to be on trails where he could meet a grizzly.

Meeting or watching or photographing wild animals is part of the Glacier excitement—the deer, the elk, the moose, the bighorn sheep and

Carved by glaciers that gave the park its name, Cut Bank Valley spreads a tapestry of autumn color near U. S. 89. Mount Stimson, its peak an almost perfect pyramid, looms beyond Triple Divide Pass.

DAVID S. BOYER, NATIONAL GEOGRAPHIC STAFF

Snow lingers through summer on lofty slopes, to the delight of youngsters gamboling on the flank of Clements Mountain, overlooking Going-to-the-Sun Road. A churning plow opens the cliff-hanging two-lane highway by mid-June; storm and avalanche usually close it for the winter as October wanes.

DAVID S. BOYER, NATIONAL GEOGRAPHIC STAFF

mountain goats, the coyotes, sometimes a bobcat, even a cougar. Most excitingly the bears—Glacier's ultimate encounter.

Many people, myself included, wouldn't know a grizzly from a black bear: both can be large and brown. But one evening along a tumbling glacial stream near Kintla Peak, I heard an old saw for the first time.

"There's one sure way to tell," my guide remarked, smiling. "If he comes up the tree after you, he's a black bear. If he tries to shake you down, you can bet he's a grizzly."

Bears, of course, are no joke. On one terrible night in 1967, two girls camping in the backcountry 20 miles apart were fatally mauled by grizzlies—a curious coincidence of tragedies and the only such deaths since the park's establishment in 1910. Since then there has been only one other serious bear incident—the victim a photographer who had too closely pursued a mother grizzly to take movies of her cubs. In the hospital, he admitted he knew better than that. Even so, a person can hike the park trails for weeks and never meet a grizzly, or even see one.

Sometimes I hiked alone. More often I hitched along with backpacking families or joined one of the ubiquitous and irrepressible groups of youthful Glacier devotees.

They come here from all over the nation, to scrounge jobs making beds or waiting tables in lodges, living for their weekly one or two days off, when they can sling packs on their shoulders and sail off over the trails to touch the world of wilderness and bed down by a campfire beneath the stars.

Others pay their dues in advance. Beside a little tent at Gunsight Lake one morning, when dawn had turned to coral the highest battlements guarding Gunsight Pass, I met a youth from California. Behind a beard, beneath a guitar, and against a rock, he was sitting, softly serenading the moment.

"I worked as a janitor and car washer for

Bighorn sheep gather on the heights above Many Glacier Valley for the winter mating season. Rams that have run with bachelor bands during the summer will duel for flocks of spike-horned ewes, battering one another with massive horns. Visitors to Granite Park Chalet often see these animals.

STEWART CASSIDY. OPPOSITE: DAVID S. BOYER, NATIONAL GEOGRAPHIC STAFF

Cycle club huffs and puffs through Logan Pass on Going-to-the-Sun Road. To ease congestion and lessen danger on the narrow, twisting highway, rangers limit pedalers to light-traffic hours of morning and evening, and ban long car-trailers.

DAVID S. BOYER, NATIONAL GEOGRAPHIC STAFF

seven months so I could come here hiking," he told me. "I'll stay till my money runs out."

Walking and taking pictures. This is what I found most visitors doing. Trails fan out in all directions from lodges, chalets, campgrounds. Avalanche Lake Trail, an easy two-mile walk from Avalanche Campground, leads to a basin tasseled by six waterfalls, a superb setting for a picnic. Another short, easy trail leads from the Logan Pass visitor center to breathtaking panoramas of Hidden Lake.

For the more ambitious, a daylong guided trek winds along the spectacular Garden Wall to Granite Park Chalet perched on a mountaintop 6,700 feet above sea level. Another guided walk takes visitors to the park's largest and most accessible glacier—Grinnell—named for the explorer, naturalist, and author who roamed these parts in the 1880's and '90's.

Other trails wend the Continental Divide, pushing northward past Mount Cleveland—at 10,466 feet the park's loftiest peak—to fjordlike Waterton Lake, and to the remote reaches of Boulder Pass and Kintla Lake in the far northwest corner of the park.

Visitors may also swim in Lake McDonald, cast a fly into Two Medicine River, sizzle a steak over a wood fire at Rising Sun Campground. Or ride a horse, rent a canoe, even cruise a lake in a large, comfortable motor launch.

Once, with crampons strapped to my boots, I climbed a glacier with Howard Snyder and his wife Michèle. Both are avid mountaineers. From their living-room window on the plains outside the park they can count most of the major masses of the Glacier Rockies and many of the cathedral spires of adjoining Waterton Lakes Park in Canada. The two preserves, separated only by a line on the map, form International Peace Park.

"These are the true temples of God," Howard said as we watched his international mountains. Whether neophytes or people whose religion is mountains, visitors to Glacier experience

much the same feelings. The environment gets to everyone. Stepping on a flower—even by accident—soon seems a sacrilege.

When you come to Glacier, don't expect to find highways cleared of snow until early June or high-country trails open until early July. And if you are one of 25,000 hiker-campers who each year venture into the backcountry, you may find yourself slogging out through an ankle-deep snowfall even in July and August. Far more likely, you'll find warmth and sunshine for weeks on end.

All of the thousands of motorists who each summer day pass through the park coax their cars or campers over Logan Pass. Going-to-the-Sun Road over the pass is Glacier's only crossing for wheels—50 miles of twisting, climbing, switchbacking, precipice-hugging rampway. From St. Mary, on the park's eastern edge, the road skirts glistening St. Mary Lake, climbs over the 6,646-foot pass, then drops down, down, down to McDonald Valley.

No one who drives Going-to-the-Sun Road ever forgets its sheer beauty—or the white-knuckle driving. Here, even in summer, you could be engulfed by a rolling black thunderstorm or trapped for hours by an instant blizzard. Ten to one, though, you'll take pictures of mountain scenes against clear blue sky and find yourself delayed by nothing more untoward than stupendous vistas—and traffic jams.

Even here, far from any major population center, overcrowding is a problem.

"If the explosion of traffic continues," I was told by Ranger Robert Burns one night across

Stately Prince of Wales Hotel commands a majestic view of Waterton Lakes on the Canadian side of Waterton-Glacier International Peace Park. On the American side, Glacier rangers (opposite) ride over Gunsight Pass during annual trail inspection. Overleaf: *Mount Fusillade, high on the Continental Divide, scrapes the clouds above St. Mary Lake.*

DAVID S. BOYER, NATIONAL GEOGRAPHIC STAFF (ALSO OVERLEAF)

Countless streams like this tumbling creek near Logan Pass drain snowmelt to feed Glacier's 200 lakes, water alpine meadows, and nourish forests rich in wildlife. Mutual curiosity leads a mule deer and a young visitor to an amicable confrontation.

a backcountry campfire, "private automobiles may have to be restricted and other types of transportation substituted. We've already shut Logan Pass to large trailers and motor homes."

And the surge of interest in backpacking could bring problems, too, he continued. "In the future, park visitors may have to make computerized reservations to spend a few nights out here in a sleeping bag."

"Couldn't you open more hiking trails and wilderness campsites?" I asked, "and still keep a few corners reserved for grizzlies?"

"A few more trails, yes," Bob replied. "A few more campsites, sure—but each site has to be picked to protect park resources. That's why Adrian and I are out here—to find some."

Adrian Hatfield, backcountry manager, kicked a log into the fire. I had ridden horseback behind him for 30 miles that day, and would survive 50 more. Up Snyder Creek we had come, over Gunsight Pass, along St. Mary Lake, and up Triple Divide Pass, whose waters flow to the Pacific, Atlantic, and Arctic Oceans.

Lean, furrow-faced mountain men like Adrian were commonplace here in the 1920's and '30's, guiding wealthy sightseers through the glories of Glacier. Now the packtrains and the mountain men and the dudes are almost gone and Adrian Hatfield, mounted man of the mountains, was scouting trails and campsites for a new breed—ordinary Americans sore from backpack straps and chafing boots.

Several days later, along a stream and trail called Boundary Creek, I hiked on a border patrol with Ranger Jerry de Santo and Canadian Park Warden Brian MacDonald. Brian's walkie-talkie began to sputter. A garble of words came through. It was Max Winkler, chief warden of the Canadian park. Trouble.

"Brian, I'm sending the chopper for you. Get downstream to some place where it can pick you up. We've got a missing 10-year-old boy

ED COOPER. OPPOSITE: DAVID S. BOYER, NATIONAL GEOGRAPHIC STAFF

up around Mount Lineham. I'm going in on the ground. Maybe you can spot him for me."

We double-timed down the trail, and 50 minutes later Brian was airborne. I didn't see him again till night, back at Waterton.

"I found him," Brian said. "And we brought him out. Dead. Fell off a cliff, a thousand feet. Got separated from his group. Spent the night out alone, with a little thin sleeping bag, and nothing to eat in 24 hours but one sandwich.

"Guess he was exhausted, and scared. He probably tried to get down off the mountain because he'd seen a tent somewhere below."

It was the same old story, according to Max. "They come up here with inadequate equipment and inexperienced leadership. The oldest leader in that party of 20 kids was 18."

I knew that two seasons earlier the wardens had spent an anxious night climbing through a 12-inch snowfall to save seven boys who had become lost and nearly frozen on the upper reaches of Boundary Creek. Their leaders had returned to Waterton without them.

"We can only try to reason with people who think they can climb anything and survive anywhere," Max said. "But some of them won't change their plans no matter what you try to tell them. Think they're Davy Crockett. They act as if you're questioning their manhood."

About all an American Park Service ranger or Canadian warden can do under those circumstances is to sign a party out under protest, and provide them with maps and advice. And a couple of other things: They can keep themselves toughened up, and keep abreast of the latest mountain rescue techniques.

For Glacier, the people problem is only three months long—one of the shortest seasons of all national parks. The land has nine months in which to heal its man-made abrasions.

I have seen the park in all its seasons, and feel sorry for those who haven't. The summer visitor has missed the springtime thrill of ten thousand extra waterfalls, of glacier lilies nodding yellow in the snow. He can only imagine how the foothills come alive with color in the fall, and what it means to hear moose and elk bugling their mating calls across the valleys.

When winter comes, the peace is deep and quiet. The wilderness is impenetrable, except to those on skis or snowshoes. In this silence only the sounds of human movement are heard, and they are easily hushed by wind or snow whispering across the frozen land.

GLACIER NATIONAL PARK

Area 1,583 square miles

Features: *Superb glacier-carved mountain wilderness similar to central Alaska in climate, flora, and fauna. Some 50 glaciers, 200 lakes; conifer forests, flowered alpine meadows. Moose, deer, bear, coyote, bighorn sheep, mountain goat, cougar, fisher.*

Activities: *Visitor centers at St. Mary and Logan Pass. Sightseeing along 50-mile Going-to-the-Sun Road. Some 700 miles of trails. Day and overnight saddle trips. Boating, trout fishing; wilderness camping. Campfire programs. Guided bus, launch, and trail trips. For all-expense tours write Glacier Park, Inc., East Glacier Park, Mont. 59434, or (Oct.-May) Box 4340, Tucson, Ariz. 85717*

Season: *Normally June 15-Sept. 15.*

Weather: *Bracing; occasional rain and snow squalls. Elevation at hotels 4,500 ft. or less.*

How to get there: *From east or west, U. S. 2; south, U. S. 93 or 89. See insert map. Great Northern Railway. Buses from Missoula, Shelby, Kalispell, or Great Falls, Mont. Hughes Airwest and Frontier Airlines serve nearby cities; surface connections to park.*

Accommodations: *Hotels, motels, cabins: Glacier Park, Many Glacier, Lake McDonald, Apgar Village, Swift-current, Rising Sun; write Glacier Park, Inc., for reservations. Chalets: Granite Park and Sperry reached by trail; write Belton Chalets, West Glacier, Mont. 59936. Trailer and camp grounds at Rising Sun, Many Glacier, Two Medicine, Apgar, St. Mary, Avalanche, Fish Creek. Eight remote campgrounds.*

Services: *Cafeterias, stores, garages; car rentals at East Glacier and Whitefish. Religious services in park.*

Park regulations: *Fishing by rod only (no nets); no live bait; no license needed. Backcountry camping permit. Vehicles wider than 8 ft. and longer than 30 ft. not allowed on Going-to-the-Sun Road.*

Write Supt., West Glacier, Mont. 59936

DAVID HISER

The Great Plateau

Wind and water carve monuments to nature in Utah's Canyonlands.

Louis Schellbach

Grand Canyon

NATIONAL PARK, ARIZONA

Many years ago, the story goes, a cowboy emerged from a forest to find the colossal abyss of Grand Canyon yawning before him. "Wow!" he exclaimed. "Something sure happened!"

Averaging nine miles in width throughout its 217-mile length, the incredible mile-deep chasm staggers human senses. Its spectacle of colors shifts every hour. Dawn gilds its sculptured pinnacles but leaves the depths in blue shadow. Noon exposes a pitiless desert. Evening sets rock spires afire with alpenglow. Moonlight tints the gorge with mystery, and morning's fog fills it with a river of cotton.

"Something sure happened" to create Grand Canyon. Several million years ago northern Arizona stood barely above sea level. At some unknown later time, the land rose into an immense plateau, and the Colorado River scoured out its channel with silt, sand, rocks, and boulders. Erosion ate away the chasm walls: Wind carved caves in soft cliffs; pelting rains washed away soil; water ran into cracks, froze, and split off fragments; runoff undercut ledges, which eventually tumbled down. The Colorado carried the debris away. Relentlessly, the eroding action of weather and water still goes on.

Rain on the plateau to the north drains into the canyon; as a result the North Rim has been cut back two times as far as the South Rim, where water drains away from the canyon.

Because of the marked southward slope of the plateau, the North Rim rises 1,000 feet higher than the South Rim. Snows close the North Rim in winter, but roads and facilities on the South stay open all year.

One summer I joined a mule trip into the canyon. People who take such a trip swear there's no better way to see the great gorge. As if to prove them right, the mule trains are always

December snow stripes the ramparts of Grand Canyon, clinging to banks and ledges, leaving scarps bare. Cool forests, broiling deserts, raging rapids, quiet chasms vary the canyon's magnificent panorama.

WALTER MEAYERS EDWARDS

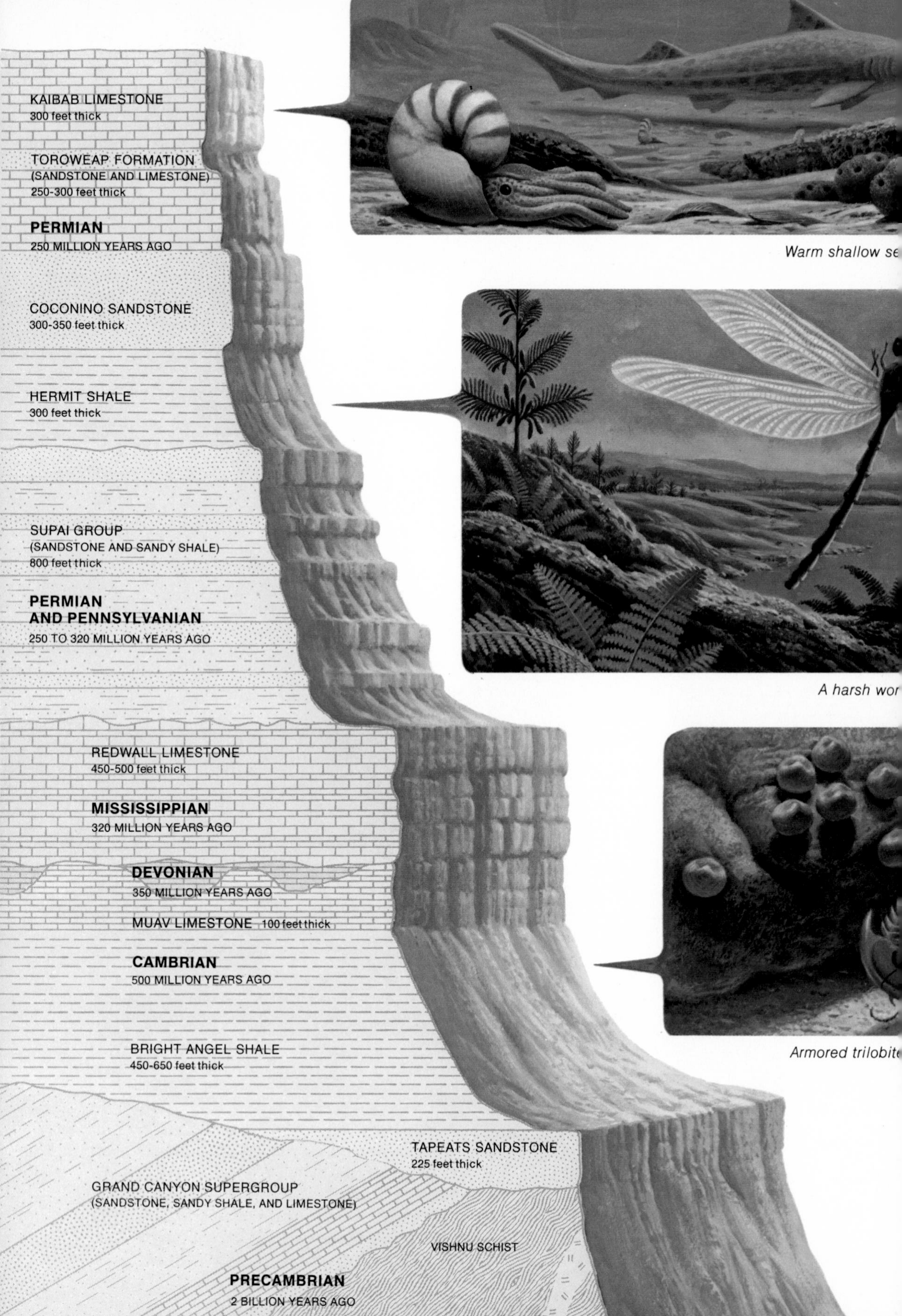

Warm shallow se

A harsh wor

Armored trilobit

rtured the creatures whose shells and bones slowly built up Kaibab limestone.

burning sun, droughts, and periodic floods characterized the epoch when Hermit shale formed.

minated the undersea realm whose remains lie embedded in Bright Angel shale.

Geological cross section of Grand Canyon depicts the stairway that life climbed through this museum of the ages. Erosion has erased traces of several periods—strata from the Age of Dinosaurs once towered above the present rim. Paintings show the life of three earlier formations. Upper: A two-inch nautiloid extends its tentacles; a primitive shark ghosts past sponges, spiny brachiopods, cup coral, and leaflike bryozoans. Middle: Dragonfly with ten-inch wingspread hovers over a semi-arid world of ferns and conifers and early reptiles. Lower: Trilobites, shown life-size, skitter past a brachiopod-encrusted rock; eocrinoids, distant relatives of starfish, wave many-fingered crowns.

PAINTINGS BY NED M. SEIDLER, NATIONAL GEOGRAPHIC STAFF ARTIST

Binoculars at the South Rim's Yavapai Museum bring the awesome gorge to the visitors; surefooted mules on Bright Angel Trail bring visitors to the gorge. Seen thus, or from lodges on North Rim (overleaf) and South, the canyon arrays an infinity of mood and hue.

WALTER MEAYERS EDWARDS (ALSO OVERLEAF)

booked up far in advance. The guide's advice is simple and reassuring: "Keep the reins in your hand at all times. Keep your feet in the stirrups and your mind in the middle. Never dismount unless I am at your side. Obey those rules and your mule will take care of you."

We rode off the brink of the South Rim and down Bright Angel Trail, taking a trip back through the ages when the earth's layer-cake sediments formed. But most of our party thought not of geology, only of mules and heights. They had never ridden a mule in their lives.

As long as the mules headed straight, the trail seemed a comfortable four feet wide. But then we halted for the traditional group photograph. Without hesitation, each mule did as he was trained: He put his tail to the wall and let his head hang out over space. Nothing but mule loomed between rider and thin air. Frightened tenderfeet clutched saddle horns and leaned back toward the rock.

Riders were scarcely adjusted to saddles when we entered a series of switchbacks cut into sheer cliffs. At each turn, the mules would lean far out over the precipice; then, so slowly the seconds seemed to last forever, they pivoted, one foot after another. In more than sixty years, Grand Canyon mules have been deserted by fearful customers, but rarely have they lost any riders to accident.

A thousand feet below the rim, riders turned in their saddles to see the fault line that Bright Angel Trail follows; the broken and shifted rocks on the west side stand 180 feet above matching strata on the east. Confidence partly restored, greenhorns began to enjoy the marvelous view as earth's strata changed colors before their eyes, the gray-white of sea-formed limestone giving way to the buff-colored sandstone of an ancient desert.

At last we reached the 550-foot Redwall, a magnificent limestone facade stained by iron oxides. On the trail down this cliff—another alarming series of switchbacks—our mules

displayed their legendary appetites. They stuck their heads way out over the trail's edge for a nibble on any clump of greenery they thought they could reach.

"Yank his head up," said our guide. "If you let him, your mule will eat anything. Sticks, straw hats, ropes. . . ."

We riders were hungry enough to eat anything by the time we stopped for lunch and a leg-stretch at Indian Gardens, a cottonwood oasis about halfway from rim to river. Long ago the Havasupai Indians drew water from these springs to irrigate their farm plots; today the freshets add their bit to water piped from the North Rim's Roaring Springs to supply Grand Canyon community, site of park headquarters on the South Rim.

We were standing on the Tonto Platform, a broad tableland that looks as if it should be the canyon floor. But down the middle of this plateau knifes the Inner or Granite Gorge, deep enough to swallow the 1,472-foot-high Empire State Building, with only its television tower sticking out.

Leaving the Tonto Platform, we followed another zigzag trail cut into the rocks of the Inner Gorge until we reached the Colorado River, 7.8 trail miles from our starting point. Here we stood 4,500 feet below the South Rim and 5,700 below the North.

Held between sheer walls only 300 feet apart, the river roared in fury. When the wind is right the torrent's mighty voice carries to the South Rim. Living up to its Spanish name, *colorado* (red), the river seemed as much mud as water. Thousands of tons of soil a day were moving before our eyes. "Too thick to drink and too thin to plow," say old-timers.

Conqueror of the Colorado was Maj. John Wesley Powell. He left Green River, Wyoming, on May 24, 1869, with nine men and four boats. Mile after mile the boats twisted through whirlpools and crashed against rocks. The men endured skimpy rations, damp clothing, and weary

"People of the blue-green water," Havasupais enjoy the creek that gave the tribe its name. A grin belies a youth's plight: nine months a year at faraway boarding school. Summer visitors must travel eight miles on foot or horseback in 100°-plus heat—yet 15,000 come each year. Overleaf: *Three men in a tub challenge the Colorado's muddy chaos.*

TERRY EILER. OVERLEAF: WALTER MEAYERS EDWARDS

portages. Early in August the voyagers entered the Grand Canyon. On the 28th three men gave up; making their farewells, each party felt sure the other had chosen certain death.

Powell and his remaining boatmen triumphantly emerged from the canyon the very next day. The three who quit were killed by Indians.

The 1,450-mile-long Colorado with its hundreds of dangerous rapids still poses something of a threat, even to the best boatmen. But now Glen Canyon Dam northeast of the park regulates the river's once violent caprices, and parties boat down in relative safety.

Kaibab Suspension Bridge, just wide enough for a mule, led us to the north bank and on to Phantom Ranch for dinner and sleep in a guest cabin. Bright Angel Creek, clear as the Colorado was muddy, made the ranch an oasis.

We were in another climate, 20° warmer than on the South Rim. It can be snowing on the North Rim, raining on the South Rim, and merely misting at Phantom Ranch. Daylight

GRAND

Stone chalice holds a golden dram at Shinumo Wash in Marble Canyon, once a national monument but now part of Grand Canyon National Park. Enfolded by marble-smooth limestone walls, visitors may find a more intimate grandeur here than farther downstream: narrow rapids, a ferned oasis, an archeological ruin.

is shortened by canyon walls on every side. Pack trains keep the ranch supplied. Food, fuel oil, even mail come in by mule express.

As our party rode on from Phantom Ranch to the North Rim we climbed through four life zones—all in 14 miles. To pass through these zones at sea level would take us from Mexico's shimmering Sonora Desert to the cool conifer forests of southern Canada.

The marked climatic differences in the canyon make it a barrier to many animals. In a few cases, those on one rim are of different species or subspecies from their relatives on the other. Classic examples are the Kaibab squirrel, found only on the North Rim, and its South Rim counterpart, the Abert squirrel. Both have tufted ears and a chestnut stripe down the back. But the Kaibab has a black belly and white tail; the Abert, a white belly and gray tail.

Grand Canyon deflects north-south highway and rail traffic too. By muleback, the trek from rim to rim takes two days. By car via Navajo Bridge is a day faster but 190 miles longer.

Sheltered in a red-walled side canyon is the most isolated Indian reservation in the United States. Supai is an enchanted land, a green valley where some 300 Havasupais tend family gardens and small peach orchards. Rodeos, card games, sweat baths, and friendly conversation fill their days. Some Havasupais, as well as neighboring Hopis, Walapais, and Navajos, find jobs in the park.

In 1540, decades before Englishmen settled Jamestown, Virginia, Hopis guided Don García López de Cárdenas and his 12 Spanish followers to the South Rim. Instead of the fabled Seven Cities of Cíbola, Cárdenas—a lieutenant of Coronado's expedition—found a mighty canyon. Some of his band ventured into the gorge and reported that rocks which from the rim looked "about as tall as a man" were "bigger than the great tower of Seville." Like visitors today, they did not appreciate the canyon's size until they descended into it.

Gazing from one rim across miles of clear Arizona air brings an uplifting of the spirit and a deep sense of humility. All who savor Grand Canyon's majesty find endless freshness in what naturalist John Burroughs called "the world's most wonderful spectacle, ever-changing, alive with a million moods."

GRAND CANYON NATIONAL PARK

Area 1,875 square miles. (Includes two former national monuments—Marble Canyon, Grand Canyon.)

Features: *One of world's mightiest gorges, cut by the Colorado River. Finest open record of earth's history. Varying color moods. Four climatic and plant-life zones from canyon bottom to the North Rim.*

Activities: *South Rim—Visitor center at Grand Canyon Village, interpretative talks at Yavapai Point. Rim drives, mule rides, bus tours, scenic flights. North Rim—Bus and saddle trips, nature walks, evening programs. One-day and overnight mule trips into the canyon start from the North Rim's Grand Canyon Lodge and the South Rim's Bright Angel Lodge.*

Season: *South Rim open all year. North Rim, mid-May to mid-October.*

Weather: *South Rim (elev. 6,900 ft.) bright, warm days, pleasant nights. North Rim (elev. 8,100 ft.) cooler. Snow in winter. Canyon floor 20 degrees warmer than South Rim.*

How to get there: *See insert map. South Rim—Ariz. 64 from U. S. 89 or 66. Hughes Airwest, Scenic, and Cochise Airlines to South Rim airport. Frontier Airlines to Flagstaff. Buses from Williams and Flagstaff. North Rim—Ariz. 67 from U. S. 89 Alternate. Hughes Airwest to Cedar City, Utah, and Page, Arizona.*

Accommodations: *South Rim—El Tovar Hotel, Bright Angel, Kachina, and Thunderbird lodges, Phantom Ranch in canyon (all open year round), Yavapai Lodge, auto lodge (both summer only); write Fred Harvey, Inc., Grand Canyon, Ariz. 86023. Camp and trailer grounds. North Rim—Grand Canyon Lodge (May-Oct.), write TWA Services, Inc., Cedar City, Utah 84720. Camp, trailer grounds at Bright Angel Point.*

Services: *Clinic on South Rim, nurse on North Rim. Restaurants, stores, service stations, post offices, religious services on both rims.*

Park regulations: *Some campgrounds require reservations. Hiking on trails only. Don't overestimate your endurance; the hike up from the canyon floor is strenuous. Pets not allowed in canyon.*

Write Supt., Box 129, Grand Canyon, Ariz. 86023

WALTER MEAYERS EDWARDS

Nathaniel T. Kenney

Zion

NATIONAL PARK, UTAH

By pressing the speed limit, the people with the back-East license plates managed to drive all Zion National Park's paved roads in a single Saturday. On Sunday they hiked the most popular trails—the easy and well-manicured Weeping Rock, Emerald Pool, and Gateway to the Narrows.

Monday morning they hitched on their trailer and made ready to leave for the next stop on their vacation schedule.

"Best park yet. Beautiful!" I heard the father tell a ranger as the family checked out of the campground. "And just think, we saw it all in one weekend."

But I, after many a trip beyond the pavement, know they didn't. Some of the best of 229-square-mile Zion in southwest Utah's glorious red-gold-orange canyon country lies deep in wilderness, little visited, unspoiled.

The soaring eagle, not man, is king of this wilderness. There are parts of it I am sure no human has ever seen, not the Indians of old nor those incredibly tough Mormon pioneers who settled Utah.

For me, with no head for heights, the worst of it is that old Mother Nature has stood the Zion landscape on edge. It is a perpendicular country of deep canyons, sheer cliffs, and dizzying elevations—and all the trails up to the greater part of the wilderness would tax the nerves of a mountain goat.

Take the West Rim Trail, for example. It starts on the floor of Zion Canyon, the beautiful gorge carved by the North Fork of the Virgin River, and leads to wild Horse Pasture Plateau 3,000 feet above. For a good part of the way, the trail clings precariously to the sides of cliffs.

Everything was lovely as my daughter Joni Greenough, dude wrangler Candy Jack Goodwin, and I set out on a sunny morning. Birds

Cliffs of Zion dwarf man's works. White serpentine in a russet rockscape, Utah Highway 15 from the park to Mt. Carmel Junction climbs the walls of Pine Creek Canyon. Sunset mists distant peaks.

SAM ABELL

sang. Cotton clouds sailed across a blue sky. Bridles jingled, leather creaked.

We splashed across the river into gently rising scrub country. A band of mule deer took off across a clearing. I love to watch these long-eared beasts run. There is always one in the crowd who bounces away stiff-legged, all four hoofs hitting the ground together.

We entered a small canyon and rode securely along its floor, albeit climbing steeply. Then abruptly everything changed. The trail left the defile at a sharp angle, meandered briefly through a jumble of great boulders, and ended, apparently, above a 500-foot-deep abyss.

I froze in horror. But the horse calmly turned left, and there we were on a ten-foot-wide ledge cut into the side of a 1,500-foot cliff. I dropped the reins and took a firm grip on the horn.

"I'll always remember you by that saddle," Candy Jack was later to remark. "It has your fingerprints in it, an inch deep."

I also closed my eyes. That way I didn't see the worst part of the trail, a stretch called Walter's Wiggles (left) built by custodian Walter Ruesch in 1919, about the time that Zion became a national park.

Candy Jack offered encouragement. "Never lost anybody here yet," said he. "Of course," he added, "this is the first time I ever saw the Wiggles. I only started this job two days ago."

We topped out at last on Horse Pasture, a cool windswept world 7,000 feet above sea level. Big trees grew here—white and Douglas firs, quaking aspens with leaves shimmering in the breeze, gnarled ponderosa pines a-scurry with squirrels chattering displeasure at human intrusion.

The trail angles across the plateau to meander along the rim of Great West Canyon. As large, deep, and beautiful as Zion Canyon, Great West would be equally renowned were it more accessible. Sam Abell, whose photographs grace these pages, is one of the few ever to enter it. He traveled with a small group led by Tom Brereton of Las Vegas, Nevada, a Zion hiking concessioner.

"We had to use alpine techniques," Sam told me. "Going up, we nailed pitons into the soft cliffs; we rappelled coming down. I slipped once and hung head down, helpless, until Tom rescued me."

One hiker sank to his hips in quicksand. In a section of canyon only three or four feet wide, the party negotiated a stretch of black water on an air mattress. They tried to sound for the bottom of the pool but their poles were not long enough to reach it.

I have seen Great West Canyon only from its brink—the time I braved the West Rim Trail. In the depths below, the colors of the great rock formations changed subtly as the sun descended. Gold turned to orange, and red to purple; the brown desert varnish on the rocks became rich chocolate, then ebony.

Returning the fearful route I had come, I walked most of the way, leading the horse. This settled my nerves but caused Candy Jack to have some doubts about my intelligence.

"The horse has got four feet to hold the trail," he said. "You only have two."

Next day rangers smiled when I described my great adventure.

"That trail's safer than the park highways on a crowded weekend," one of them said. "To me, none of the high places are as scary as the canyons in summer, when thunderstorms can cause flash floods."

Zion Canyon is the best known of all the park's gorges. Its lower reaches hold park headquarters and visitor amenities; here also are rock sculptures with fanciful names—the Great White Throne, the Three Patriarchs, the Temple of Sinawava. Zion Canyon can be hiked fifteen miles or so from the park's northern

"Following a Walter's Wiggles switchback, a horse goes both ways at the same time," Zion rangers swear. Only a low stone wall guards the verges of this awesome trail out of Refrigerator Canyon.

SAM ABELL

SAM ABELL

Shaped mainly by water's incessant toil, Zion's deep canyons cleave through faulted sandstone plateaus formed of sediments left by ancient seas and lakes. Begun in ages past, the task nature gave hurrying waters yet goes on. In time they will destroy the park by flattening canyons and highlands into sweeping, sea-level plains.

Man, meanwhile, enters this workshop of the rivers at his peril. Fording the Virgin River—a stream that a distant storm can swell 25 feet in a quarter-hour—a girl scrabbles for a grip on a slippery rock. Quicksand mires a hiker in Great West Canyon. His party became rock-climbers to bypass a thundering rapid, while guide Tom Brereton blazed a woodsy trail around another obstacle. Deep in Zion Narrows, a father gives his daughter a hand, and a hiker wishes she had worn sturdier shoes. Hiking here requires a park permit—and a weather check.

boundary down the Virgin's North Fork to the roadhead at the Temple of Sinawava.

But it isn't all easy going, for in the upper section lurks a series of fantastic gorges called The Narrows. Here the Virgin River sometimes squeezes to a torrent 20 feet wide, racing through slots of smooth rock that tower a thousand and more feet above the water.

When I decided to attempt the hiking trip, I went with Tom Brereton. Ranger Nick Lundstrom came along on a busman's holiday. We started in the ranch country outside the park and found easy going for the first few miles. Then the cliffs, looming steadily higher, closed in. Seeking shallow water, we waded the stream at every bend.

We lunched on a gravel bar under a cliff of purest white rock stained with streaks of red and rich brown.

"That's the Navajo sandstone, 2,000 feet thick," said Nick. "It's our most noticeable formation. Zion and its neighbor national parks, Bryce Canyon and Grand Canyon, form a remarkable geological museum. The rock strata reveal the changes in this part of the earth during the past two billion years.

"Once all the southern Utah and northern Arizona canyon country was sea or river bottom. About 13 million years ago the sea floor rose and became a 10,000-foot plateau. Then erosion set to work—canyon-cutting rivers and lesser waters and winds that carried the earth off in horizontal sheets.

"Up at Bryce the erosion has been less severe. There we see land more like it was when it rose from the sea. At Grand Canyon, on the other hand, there has been so much erosion that the strata we see at the bottom are among the oldest rocks known on earth.

"Zion lies in between, a sort of middle step in a great staircase of eternity. Here we can look at rock strata formed in the Mesozoic, or middle, period of geologic time. This was the era of the dinosaurs, and if you look hard enough, you'll find dinosaur footprints at several places in the Zion rocks."

Deep in the canyon the day ended early, and we made camp beside a pool in which a family of water ouzels were hunting aquatic insects and tiny fish. These slate-colored birds are avian submariners, able to dive as deep as 20 feet and walk the bottoms of the cold pools as happily as frogs.

Deer came to the river at dusk to drink. Judging from tracks in the sand, the place also was favored by raccoon, fox, coyote, and the raccoon-like ringtail of the dry country.

We woke to the songs of cañon wren and gray warbler, and breakfasted on bacon and flapjacks cooked over a fire of fallen pine branches. Then we took to the river again.

The last part of the hike is the best, also the toughest. The cliffs loom ever higher and the river drops ever more sharply, swelled by tributaries and many springs.

These pleasant freshets, which run even in dry season, jet from the cliffs all at one level known as the spring line. The upper strata of Zion's rocks are porous, and water seeps through until it strikes the hard stratum at the spring line, where it emerges. The wetness has encouraged hanging gardens of columbine, shooting star, and monkey flower, for which the park is famous.

Finally we climbed out of the riverbed and stepped onto the asphalt-paved trail that leads a mile into the wilds from the Temple of Sinawava. This is a beautiful and pleasant walk in the cool shade of maple, box elder, and willows; it is the park's most popular trail, and thousands have taken it on ranger-led hikes.

We were wet, ragged, and disheveled, and

The Virgin River's trickle belies the power that carved The Narrows. Here the gorge, only ten feet wide, looms 1,500 feet above the man. Overleaf: *Caught in a time exposure, tines of lightning rake plateaus behind Great West Canyon. Mesa on right is West Temple, a park landmark.*

SAM ABELL (ALSO OVERLEAF)

Dancing tongues of a campfire brighten a cave at the head of The Narrows. Generations of hikers and explorers have sheltered in the grotto; floodwaters do not reach its sandy floor. Artist Tom Blaue (right) sketches golden asters, one of the park's many species of wild flowers.

SAM ABELL

when we met a band of tourists, they stared. A lady said, "Gracious, you look like you've been fighting bears. Should we turn back?"

A century ago, bears—including grizzlies—lived in lower Zion Canyon. But they've been gone for years, and we assured the group there was no danger on that score.

Zion Canyon played only a small part in the park's human history, and that was a recent one. The first explorers of the region, the Spanish priest Juan de Escalante in 1776, then the fur trader Jedediah Smith in 1826, probably never saw it.

Even the local Paiute Indians avoided the place, although in the 1850's white settlers found them cultivating crops in the wide lower reaches where the Mormon towns of Springdale and Rockville now stand. Indians feared The Narrows as the abode of evil spirits.

There is another canyon, however, in which humans lived from prehistoric times until early this century. This is Parunuweap in Zion's southeast corner, desert country compared to lush Zion Canyon. It's a dry land in which many sorts of lizards thrive, and where stands of various cacti grow.

For a final trip into the Zion backcountry, I rode into Parunuweap to see a cliff dwelling dating back to Basketmaker Indian times, around A.D. 500. It is only a small place perched on a ledge high above the foaming East Fork of the Virgin River. If ever there was an easy path to it, it is long gone now, and the way is a near-vertical climb up broken cliff. I went there with, among others, Buster Jiggs McBroom, a rollicking cowboy out of West Texas.

Where the river's gravel banks first became cliffs, Buster pointed out Indian paintings on the rock, still legible.

"An old signpost," he said. "The wiggly line means a river—this one. The animal at the upper end is a bighorn sheep. It tells hunters they'll find desert bighorns if they keep going up the stream."

April snow dapples eastern Zion's Checkerboard Mesa. The photogenic landmark was formed from ancient sand dunes compressed into cross-bedded layers of Navajo sandstone millions of years ago. Vertical fractures caused by uplift of the land create a cobblestone effect accentuated by erosion.

Diseases brought in by domestic sheep and intense hunting wiped out the wild sheep of Parunuweap years ago. The Park Service has a plan to put a flock back in.

More and more we had to ride in the shallow bed of the river. It was hard going for the horses: The Virgin is a powerful watercourse, dropping 50 to 70 feet every mile on its way to the Colorado, and toting more than a million tons of rock wastes each year.

We turned into a tributary canyon before we reached the difficult upper sections of Parunuweap, so I leave the description of that part to Maj. John Wesley Powell. Famed explorer of the Grand Canyon, he walked down Parunuweap in 1872. He wrote: ". . . . we are in a canyon 2,500 feet deep, and we come to a fall where the walls are broken down and huge rocks beset the channel, on which we obtain a foothold to reach a level 200 feet below. Here the canyon is again wider, and we find a flood-plain along which we can walk, now on this, and now on that side of the stream."

We rode up the side canyon until the panting horses slipped in the loose shale of the steep hillside and could go no farther. We tied them in a grove of jack pines and went on afoot.

Finally we reached a shelf on which stood the little adobe houses and tall granaries of a community that was hundreds of years old. This was a high place, so high I could not go near the edge. It was hard to believe human beings chose to live here.

What if a man walked in his sleep, or a child toddled too far from his door? But at least the Anasazi, the Ancient Ones of that long-ago time, were beyond reach of enemies. With a pile of boulders, a man could hold off an army.

Among the rock paintings was the portrait of an elk, which could mean that this animal also once inhabited the canyon. Buster Jiggs found cow manure of recent vintage and was unhappy at this seeming mockery of our hard climb. But I suspect some previous visitor with a pixie sense of humor had brought it up in his pack!

Tired, we slid back down the cliff, saddled the horses, and rode downstream looking for a place to make camp. But black clouds raced in over the rimrock, and rain fell in solid sheets. In the great voice of the Virgin we sensed a new note of threat.

"If that river rises, we could be trapped here for a long time," I said. "What do you say we kick the horses up and roundtrip it back to the main highway tonight?"

So we did that, and we made it out of the valley with time to spare.

"Pshaw," sniffed Buster Jiggs, turning in his saddle to look back at racing waters now yellow with silt. "In Texas we got real rivers, the kind that wash whole counties down into Mexico. What'd this l'il old crick ever do but run off a few pore sodbusters that tried to put in a patch of beans too close to its banks?"

"Just built a national park, that's all it did," said I, and we jogged down the road in search of dry hay and hot baths.

ZION NATIONAL PARK

Area 229 square miles

Features: *Vertical-walled Zion Canyon cut from forested tableland by the Virgin River. Mile-long tunnel (car lights must work). Desert wildlife.*

Activities: *Visitor center at park headquarters. Scenic drives; 65 miles of hiking, riding trails. Climbing.*

Season: *Open all year. Roads snowplowed.*

Weather: *Summer days hot, nights cool (road elev. 4,000 to 8,000 ft.). Winter temp. 15-60°.*

How to get there: *U.S. 89 or I-15 to Utah 15. See insert map. Hughes Airwest to Cedar City; Sky West to St. George. Rental car to park.*

Accommodations: *Zion Lodge, May-Sept. (scheduled to close after 1975 season); write TWA Services, Inc., Cedar City 84720. Camp and trailer ground open all year. Motels in Springdale.*

Services: *Restaurant at Zion Lodge. Full services in Springdale.*

Park regulations: *Camping and fires outside campgrounds by permit only. No hiking or climbing alone.*

For information write Supt., Springdale, Utah 84767

SAM ABELL

Bryce Canyon

NATIONAL PARK, UTAH

On a thawing spring day you can actually hear erosion: the trickle of water, the rumble of rocks, the rattle of gravel. In the 36,000 acres of Bryce Canyon National Park, geology is as current as a newspaper, and far more sensational. For the traveler planning an easy three-park vacation—Grand Canyon, Zion, and Bryce—geologists promise a cross-section history of the planet earth. Rocks deep in Grand Canyon, formed some 1.5 billion years ago, are perhaps twice as old as life itself; the Canyon's youngest stones are about 180 million years old. Zion continues from there with strata documenting the Age of Reptiles. Bryce belongs to the present Age of Mammals, embracing the last 60 million years.

Bryce is not really a canyon; it is the cracked and eroded eastern face of southern Utah's Paunsaugunt Plateau. Its rocks, hardened from strata of sand and sediment laid down as ancient streams fed a huge inland lake, were lifted nearly two miles above sea level. The mass cracked, and in the fissures water and ice began their patient artistry.

Oxides of manganese and iron tinted the slowly emerging sculptures, here an eggshell white, there a pink or a flaming red so vivid it seems illuminated from within. Now from 9,105-foot-high Rainbow Point the plateau appears to shatter in endless fragments as it falls away to the Paria River half a mile below.

Capt. Clarence E. Dutton, an early surveyor, described a bewildering landscape of "standing obelisks, prostrate columns, shattered capitals, panels, niches, buttresses... the work of giant hands, a race of genii once rearing temples of rock, but now chained up in a spell of enchantment while their structures are falling in ruins." Today 400,000 visitors a year feel the spell of this enchanted place; from vantages such as Inspiration Point they gaze over a ghost city of Javanese spires and winding alleys.

Imaginations run riot as visitors descend into the fairyland on foot or horseback, searching among the giant chessmen for such oddities as the Three Wise Men, the Wall of Windows, and a Queen Victoria so real you can almost hear her stone skirts rustle.

Ranger talks and a visitor center tell a story of natural forces still at work on the architecture of Bryce Canyon. As if to confirm the lesson, now and then a boulder topples from its perch or an erosion-weakened arch caves in under its own weight. Several times this century the earth has trembled as nature gnashed her teeth along the Paunsaugunt Fault just to the east. Studies have shown that the rim retreats about a foot in 50 years.

It's not quite the same canyon it was when Paiute Indians gazed at the sculptured figures and decided they were evil creatures turned to stone—or when Mormon pioneer Ebenezer Bryce called it "a hell of a place to lose a cow."

BRYCE CANYON NATIONAL PARK

Area 56 square miles

Features: *Some of the world's most fanciful and richly colored formations, carved from 20 miles of southwestern Utah's Pink Cliffs. Bryce Canyon itself is the most spectacular of a dozen basins.*

Activities: *Visitor center. 17-mile rim drive (go first to Rainbow Point, stop at Bryce, Inspiration, Sunset, Sunrise, and other overlooks on way back). Some 60 miles of hiking and riding trails. Illustrated talks. Backcountry camping. In winter, snowshoeing and cross-country skiing.*

Season: *Visitor center open all year. Rainbow Point road, normally April-Nov.*

Weather: *Summer days warm, dry; nights nippy. (Rim elev. 8,000 to 9,100 ft.) Winters cold, snow.*

How to get there: *U. S. 89 to Panguitch, east on Utah 12. (Zion National Park is 85 miles southwest, Grand Canyon's North Rim 160 miles south.) Hughes Airwest to Cedar City, Utah; bus to park.*

Accommodations: *Lodge, May-Oct. (scheduled to close after 1976 season). Write TWA Services, Inc., Box 400, Cedar City 84720. Camp, trailer ground.*

Services: *Restaurant, stores, gas. Nurse at lodge, hospital in Panguitch. Religious services in park.*

Park regulations: *Do not disturb formations.*

Write Supt., Bryce Canyon, Utah 84717

ent witnesses watch the distant Sinking Ship.

D MUENCH

Cedar Breaks

NATIONAL MONUMENT, UTAH

Two miles above sea level, the Markagunt Plateau's green tabletop comes to a ragged edge. For 2,000 feet the "breaks," or cliffs, fall away in a fantasy of colors and eroded shapes. And on the rim, drivers can pull up at overlooks and enjoy a hawk's-eye view of formations even more colorful at a distance than Bryce Canyon offers at close range.

In this huge natural amphitheater, time has taken a great bite out of the Pink Cliffs that edge the plateau. Mineral-stained ridges radiate toward the cliff arc like the painted spokes of a circus wagon wheel. Between them, creeks and canyons converge at the hub and leave the monument as Ashdown Creek.

A campground, visitor center, picnic area, and often a committee of mule deer welcome summer travelers. The 9½-square-mile monument is open year round, but the visitor center closes from Labor Day to early June. Wise campers and motorists check road conditions and weather before risking off-season snows and freezes.

Where are the cedars? Mormon settlers in the mid-1800's thought they grew here in profusion. The "cedars" were actually junipers; today they thrive at the feet of the layered breaks and here and there climb partway to the rim. At the top, firs and spruces hold sway, sharing the subalpine environment with grassy meadows and splashes of wild flowers. And here in venerable grandeur stand bristlecone pines, some of them 16 centuries old.

Unlike the trails of Bryce Canyon, the roads and paths of Cedar Breaks do not descend to the scenery below. Instead they explore the rim, leading the visitor to vantage points and to flower-edged Alpine Pond. After touring the five-mile Rim Drive, motorists venture up Brian Head Peak, two and a half miles to the north in Dixie National Forest. There, at 11,315 feet, they walk to a shelter for unforgettable views of forests, meadows, and rainbows of rock.

For information write Supt., Zion National Park, Springdale, Utah 84767

WALTER MEAYERS EDWARDS

Rangers practice a rescue at Cedar Breaks; their skill guards hikers here and at Zion and Bryce.

Rabbitbrush offers its gold before a stone cathedral in Capitol Reef.

DAVID MUENCH (ALSO OPPOSITE)

Capitol Reef

NATIONAL PARK, UTAH

Prospectors called it a reef because its towering ramparts blocked passage, much as a coral bar turns away ships. Explorers called it "Capitol" for the graceful, fluted domes set amid the monumental architecture of erosion. Paiute Indians called it "Land of the Sleeping Rainbow" as they gazed at layers of rock in vivid reds and browns, subtle blues and greens. Each year more than a quarter-million visitors call this park magnificent as they hike and drive along a massive buckling in the earth's crust, a 100-mile scar called the Waterpocket Fold.

The fold angles northwesterly through central Utah; nearly all of it lies within the 397 square miles of the park (see insert map). A paved road follows a verdant canyon where Mormons settled; their schoolhouse is open to visitors. Petroglyphs and storage huts built in cliffside niches recall Indians who farmed and hunted amid this stark beauty 1,000 years ago.

Campers fall asleep to the hollow hoot of the horned owl—and endure the petty pilferings of the trade rat, who may drop a trinket if a brighter one catches its eye. Hikers stroll along easy trails or venture into country so rugged that they are urged to brief rangers so help can be sent if plans go awry.

Four-wheel-drive vehicles head northwest from Route 24 to wind among the weird spires of Cathedral Valley. In able hands, family cars can head south on dirt roads along the scarp to the Burr Trail cutoff. Some continue on to Bull Frog Marina on Lake Powell; others take the Burr Trail's steep grades and switchbacks through one of the few passes in the reef. Wise drivers ask about conditions before setting out.

Most visitors tour the scenic drive that begins near the visitor center in the northern section. Along its ten-mile gravel ribbon they capture in snapshots and memories the grandeur of layered cliffs, the loneliness of a uranium miner's shanty, and—with a lucky rain squall—a gauzy waterfall spattering into a canyon that will be dry and silent in an hour.

Write Supt., Torrey, Utah 84775

Natural Bridges

NATIONAL MONUMENT, UTAH

Every summer, thousands of travelers find their way off the beaten track at Blanding, Utah, to three huge bridges gouged from sandstone 225 million years old. Each spotlights a different phase in nature's bridge-building. Kachina, the youngest, seems at first glance to block its stream bed like a 206-foot-long dam. Waters that ate away its flank broke through only in comparatively recent times. Frosts and thaws still slenderize the 44-foot-thick span.

From Kachina, hikers follow a two-mile trail to the largest and most perfect bridge, Sipapu, a flat-topped spur of rimrock leaping its gorge in a 268-foot stride. Close by the monument's main road, a tendril of rock, Owachomo Bridge, stretches 180 feet. Oldest of the three, its span has weathered over the last ten million years to a fragile nine feet in thickness.

Write Supt., Canyonlands NP, Moab, Utah 84532

Owachomo Bridge defies the millenniums.

Walter Meayers Edwards

Glen Canyon

NATIONAL RECREATION AREA, UTAH-ARIZONA

Like a shimmering desert mirage, a vast new lake has grown in the West. Trapped behind Glen Canyon Dam, 75 miles upstream from Grand Canyon, a placid stretch of the Colorado rose out of its sheer-walled canyon to form an elongated lake twisting away to the northeast for 186 miles. To an astronaut, the nine-trillion-gallon reservoir looks like a forked thunderbolt splitting the Arizona-Utah desert. To visitors at 1,869-square-mile Glen Canyon National Recreation Area, Lake Powell looks like fun; its crystal water and abundant sunshine lure a million of them a year to a cliff-girt setting unrivaled by any other large lake in the world.

I first saw Glen Canyon in 1962, months before the lake began to fill it. Then a year's visitors were counted in the hundreds. Rafting down the Colorado, I saw this stretch much as John Wesley Powell knew it a century before: "Past these towering monuments, past these mounded billows of orange sandstone, past these oak-set glens, past these fern-decked alcoves... we glide hour after hour, stopping now and then, as our attention is arrested by some new wonder...."

Wearied by the rapids they had battled for two months, Powell's expedition found easy going here. The bearded Civil War veteran named the idyllic stretch Glen Canyon.

The choice was apt. Narrow tributary canyons tempted the explorer into fascinating glens. In secret fairylands, walls tapestried with desert varnish—the result of iron and manganese seepage—towered to thin cerulean crescents far overhead. Titanic chambers glowed in delicate hues of pink and orange.

Many such Edens beckoned to me, too. Others were inaccessible, unexplored. But years later, with the lake probing their twisting passages, the secret places had become accessible by boat.

So I took to the water again, this time with several college students as shipmates. On a scorching June afternoon we left Wahweap, five miles above the 710-foot-high dam and the spectacular bridge nearby, the world's highest steel-arch span. Before the dam and bridge were begun, 45 miles of jeep trails linked the site to paved highway; today U.S. Route 89 brings in cars—many of them towing boats incongruously through the desert—from Kanab, Utah, to the west and Flagstaff, Arizona, to the south. Child of the dam, the town of Page, Arizona, welcomes arrivals by air and bus and offers an array of accommodations and services. And far uplake, paved roads lead boaters and campers to marinas at Bullfrog Basin, Hall's Crossing, and Hite.

The bustle at Wahweap's marina-motel complex shrank astern as we steered our power boats—*Green Lady* and *Blue Lady*—toward Padre Bay, the lake's largest expanse of open water. Gunsight Butte loomed red and massive on our left, Dominguez Rock on our right, unnamed buttes all around like sentinels. Deep

Sketching silver signatures, boats thread a byway of Lake Powell. Snowmelt from the Rockies pools up behind Glen Canyon Dam, making waterways of gorges where lizards once sunned and hardy hikers tramped.

DAVID HISER

A lake is born, a desert dies around the feet of Gregory Butte. In 1962 the lofty rock looked down on the snaking Colorado River, fringed with tamarisks and locked on course by walls of its own making. In 1974 the river, like a genie unbottled, has made the butte an island in a glassy wonderworld where boaters explore nearly 2,000 miles of shore and glide over deeps that can plunge some 600 feet.

WALTER MEAYERS EDWARDS. BELOW: DAVID HISER

beneath our hulls lay the historic Crossing of the Fathers, once a ford on the Colorado; there in 1776 two Franciscans crossed, returning to New Mexico after a futile attempt to open a route to missions in California.

We beached our boats at Padre Point and dived into the water, clothes and all. The only way to beat the intense dry heat was to drink lots of water and get wet at every opportunity.

The next afternoon we entered Last Chance Bay and caught the lake in a dangerous mood. The weather in the canyon is capricious. Storms can be squally, and waves rising to six feet bounce off canyon walls to buffet a boat from all directions. Boating here requires competent crews and seaworthy craft at least 18 feet long.

A family in distress! The wind and whitecaps were toying with a couple and five youngsters in a homemade cockleshell of plywood.

"Can you take my children?" the father yelled.

"Too dangerous!" shouted one of our crew. "Head for shore! Over there!" We escorted the little boat to a sheltered beach, and soon the family was drying out around a fire.

After the storm, we continued uplake. On my raft trip I had hiked into many side canyons—clefts with names like Dangling Rope, Little Arch, Twilight, Hidden Passage. Powell had found Music Temple "filled with sweet sounds"; now these canyons lie under more than 300 feet of water. Others, like Cathedral and Forbidding Canyons, had lost only their outer defenses.

Cathedral had been one of my favorites. I had hiked and swum to only three of the reputed 30 "rooms" carved out of its gorge by millenniums of water-borne sand and gravel. This time we cruised in for two miles before its twisting channel became too narrow for our boats.

Six miles from Cathedral, 40 from Wahweap, stands Rainbow Bridge, a spectacular rock arch soaring 309 feet above the bed of Bridge Creek. Years ago I had labored five miles in broiling heat to see it, hiking up Forbidding Canyon past flower-decked dunes and occasional waterfalls, stopping often at cool pools en route. In those days only a determined few saw Rainbow Bridge National Monument. Today a marina floats in 300 feet of water in the canyon; thousands see the span with little effort.

The lake has already backed up beyond the bridge, and one day will form a reflecting pool 46 feet deep beneath it. But boats cannot go beyond a small dock; from there it's a quarter-mile hike to the span. Adventurers can come the old way, by foot or pony from Navajo Mountain outposts 14 and 24 miles away.

I saw something else new. Whenever the lake level drops, it exposes sun-cracked mud flats, driftwood, and the skeletons of dead trees at the heads of side canyons, and a white "bathtub ring" on the walls.

"We've known Glen Canyon for years," a Tucson couple told me, "and we still love it, though we liked it better the way it used to be." A houseboater disagreed; "This lake's the greatest thing that ever happened!" he exclaimed. Good or bad, Lake Powell is there.

One afternoon we perched on a cliff five miles uplake from the San Juan River. Our feet rested on a narrow ledge 700 feet above the water. *Blue Lady* floated below at the foot of a steep trail that led almost straight up a cleft in the wall to a narrow notch at the top, 200 yards to our right—the historic Hole in the Rock.

Here in the winter of 1879-80, some 250 Mormon pioneers faced a trek across almost impassable desert, crossing the Colorado, hauling their belongings 200 miles through some of the roughest country in the West. Only here could they cross without a long detour.

In six weeks of superhuman toil they widened the "Hole" with blasting powder, built a road three-quarters of a mile down to water's edge, assembled a raft, and on the far shore hewed a road up a 250-foot cliff. The first third of the way down was a 45-degree grade over rock that became slicker and more treacherous with the passage of every wagon. Incredibly, they *drove* their 80 wagons down, brakes locked, rear wheels wrapped with chains, a dozen men and boys—and sometimes women too—hanging on behind to keep them from barreling into the rocks below. Somehow, every wagon made the perilous descent safely.

After ten more weeks of road building through mile after mile of tilted and eroded rock, the pioneers halted and founded Bluff, Utah. There had been no casualties, and three babies were born en route, but the trek they thought would take six weeks had taken nearly six months.

Most traces of their heroic passage have weathered away. But in one stretch, where they had attached a road to a steep rock wall, we saw grooves cut to hold the inside wagon

Banking on a single slat, a wet-suited water skier adds a ragged fringe to a tapestry of lake and cliff. Summer skiers rarely need wet suits for warmth; the sun-warmed surface can hit 79°, the air 106°.

DAVID HISER

Rainbow Bridge flings a mighty arch over the slender creek that carved it. For ages the stream wore away its sandstone stumbling blocks—but dug through this one to leave a rib of rock. Water that wafts boaters near may weaken the span's abutments; geologists check regularly for signs of trouble.
DAVID HISER

wheels, and holes for beams to support a wooden roadway for the outside wheels.

Just north of Hole in the Rock, the lake is fed by the muddy Escalante River. Before Lake Powell drowned the quicksand at its mouth, few but plateau-roaming cattlemen knew the upper reaches of the Escalante or its deep tributaries—Fiftymile Creek, Davis Gulch, and Clear Creek on the west; Stevens, Cow, Fence, and Explorer Canyons on the east.

Now boaters crease the bays that fill the canyon mouths. In Fiftymile they float *over* Gregory Natural Bridge, which once towered 180 feet above the creek. In Davis Gulch the lofty triangular window of La Gorce Arch is now close to waterline, and a 100-foot panel of Indian pictographs, believed to be a thousand years old, barely escapes the lapping waves.

Much has been learned in these canyons about the Anasazi, the Ancient Ones whose cliff dwellings, storage cists, ceremonial kivas, and pictographs were the subjects of a flurry of scientific effort while the dam was being built. In Slick Rock Canyon, I had watched bronzed young archeologists measuring a ruin in a high alcove. That evening they sorted their finds: arrowheads, a chalcedony drill, a bit of cotton cloth, tiny corncobs, a size-13 sandal that made me wonder if the huge hands and feet in some petroglyphs were true to life.

"The Indians who lived here about A.D. 1250 probably covered the valley with fields of corn, beans, and squash," one researcher told me. "The stream level was higher then."

Another archeologist had told me about the exciting discovery of a 20-room pueblo in a Forgotten Canyon alcove. "Impassable falls above and below had sealed it off. We chanced on an ancient hand-and-toe trail pecked into the rock, bypassing the lower falls.

"Most of the roofs were still in place, and we found whole pottery vessels. Two perfect red

Ship of the desert ghosts through glinting waves on a dust-dry breeze. Arid canyons turned to bays echo the plop of the lure and thrash of the catch. But hikers still find challenge in side canyons and on the upper Escalante River. And boaters below the dam can meet the canyon the way it was.
DAVID HISER

bowls still had scraps of food in them. We named the place Defiance House, because on the cliffs above are pictographs of three men brandishing weapons and shields. The place had not been disturbed for seven centuries."

Though the lake has drowned many ruins, Defiance House, at the top of a steep talus slope, will always be well above the water. Vandalism has now become its greatest menace.

As we boated up Clear Creek, I felt a pang when I recalled my hike into the tapestried, vaulted glory of Cathedral in the Desert. Cruising over it now is interesting, with twists and turns and an impressive alcove in the rock. But I missed the towering dome, the green pool, the tiny crystal stream, and the delicate moss and maidenhair fern on the red sand floor.

Explorer Canyon is steep; the lake reaches into it only about a mile. We hiked to the far end, splashing through crystal pools, pausing to examine some aquatic creature or to drink from a cool, sweet spring. Here 500-foot-high walls merged in a gigantic alcove. Water trickled into an inviting pool. Vines entwined a chaos of rocks under the overhang. The great alcove acted like an orchestra shell, reflecting the chirps of swooping violet-green swallows and the sweet descending notes of cañon wrens. We left this glorious retreat reluctantly.

Hikers can still find this kind of scenery in side canyons of the Escalante and even in a few off the main lake—canyons much like those that have been drowned. But the big attraction these days is fishing; perhaps four boaters out of five in the upper lake come to wet a line for bass, trout, crappie, or bluegill.

Striped bass are the latest arrivals, introduced by the state of Utah in 1974. They grow two inches a month and can attain 40 pounds.

In 1883 Cass Hite triggered a gold rush. Now a marina far up the lake bears his name, and a buoy marks his submerged grave—perhaps the only floating gravestone in the West.

We fueled the boats at Hite Marina and soon roared under the bridge just uplake from the Dirty Devil River, the only highway span between Moab, Utah, and the dam. Here Glen Canyon becomes Narrow Canyon, and seven miles farther up it becomes Cataract Canyon.

The water by now was turbid. We would soon reach the rapids at the end of the lake. Between Cataract's high rugged cliffs, millions of years older than Glen's, we steered to journey's end.

The glens Powell knew are gone now. And silt must fill Lake Powell inevitably, if not in our time. Meanwhile, the lake has become a waterway to a galaxy of desert wonders.

Write Supt., Box 1507, Page, Ariz. 86040

Paul Jensen

Arches

NATIONAL PARK, UTAH

What's the difference between a natural bridge and an arch? "Simple," said the superintendent. "A bridge bridges a watercourse and an arch doesn't. Anywhere in Utah's red-rock country a canyon stream might cut itself a bridge. But the hundred arches here are on high ground away from streams. All were cut by weather from stone fins."

"Fins?" I asked. We had driven up from the visitor center, five miles from Moab, and stopped at Courthouse Towers. Park Avenue's sandstone skyscrapers stretched before us—only the doormen and poodles were missing.

"Fins," he said and pointed to a crease in my fender. The paint had cracked along lines of stress. "That's what happened to this whole area. Only here the 'paint' is a 300-foot-thick layer of Entrada sandstone. The earth humped and the sandstone cracked clear to the bottom in regular rows ten to twenty feet wide."

"And these isolated rocks?" I looked down Courthouse Wash snaking away to the west.

"Flukes of erosion," he said. "Over millions of years the elements have worn most of the fins away, leaving solitary formations like the Organ, Sheep Rock, the Three Gossips. Then there's Delicate Arch. But that's one you'll want to see alone. Some things are better without people talking all the time."

The West abounds in marvels of nature: the world's grandest canyon, its tallest and biggest trees. But Delicate Arch is not the world's biggest anything. It doesn't have to be. Alone, it would be lovely. Combined with its setting, it is incomparably beautiful.

Here nature's hand has chiseled a great amphitheater and on its rim left standing a spraddle-legged colossus. I saw not a speck of dust or even a lichen clinging to this pink stone arc or to the coliseum it embellishes, whose polished sides plummet to the valley.

The sun went down and an eerie pall fell over the lifeless scene. Wisps of a breeze hissed across the grainy surface. Swept by a sudden chill of loneliness, I hurried down the trail.

Whereas Delicate Arch impressed me with its weird beauty, Landscape Arch, carved from an enormous fin in the middle of Devils Garden, struck me as just plain impossible. Coming up the trail, I didn't see it at first, for it blended into the high wall behind. Then suddenly it seemed to snap into place—a 291-foot band of black and red stone, the world's longest natural span.

Mathematically speaking, Landscape Arch can't stay up. It's all wrong—far too long, far too flat. One end is only six feet thick, while in the center the arch humps its back, spreads 20 feet wide, and weighs thousands of tons. But there it stands. Park officials worry about the cracks that pierce Landscape. When it falls, as surely it must, it will be a sad day for all.

Go see it soon, and spend some time among the other marvels. Hike through Fiery Furnace, where slender fins, blazing red in sunset's glow, tower 200 feet above a labyrinth. It's rough going, but deep within the Furnace fresh water awaits in potholes and there are cool coves where the sun never penetrates.

Write Supt., Canyonlands NP, Moab, Utah 84532

Delicate Arch stands 85 feet high and 65 feet wide, a star attraction of the 114-square-mile preserve. Open year round, the park offers tent, trailer, and backcountry camping, and summer campfire talks. Visitors find full services in nearby Moab.

DAVID MUENCH

Rowe Findley

Canyonlands

NATIONAL PARK, UTAH

Our lead packhorse vanished before my eyes, a sure-footed beast seemingly gone clattering over the cliff with all our pots and pans. But it was only a trick of the terrain that made the pack trail into Horse Canyon look like a leap into space. When I got to the canyon rim I could see the trail looping in precarious switchbacks down the rocky slope to the canyon floor far below.

"Nobody rides this stretch," our packtrain master said. I slid off my horse and watched him vanish over the rim with the others. Down into their dust we nine humans clambered; at the bottom we mounted again.

The five-mile trail led toward a labyrinth of rust-red, off-white, and cream-striped chasms called the Maze, a place of pristine solitude and ancient pictographs, part of Canyonlands National Park in southeast Utah. Packtrains are common in this rugged, all-but-roadless park; so are jeeps, dune buggies, and hikers on foot.

As I roamed the park, I crossed the paths of Mormon missionaries and ranchers, mountain men and explorers. I walked with the ghost of John Macomb, who in 1859 gazed down on the spot where the Green and Colorado rivers meet—the heart of the park—and said, "I cannot conceive of a more worthless and impracticable region." I boated the rivers as did John Wesley Powell, who viewed the confluence a decade after Macomb and marveled at "ten thousand strangely carved forms... and beyond them mountains blending with the clouds." I crossed the trail of Butch Cassidy, who robbed turn-of-the-century trains and banks with blasting powder and good humor. I roamed where the wild uranium hunters of the 1950's staked claims that sometimes overlapped four deep.

That afternoon in the Maze we hiked to cactus gardens abloom in lavender, lime, and cream. Canyonlands in May is dotted and scented with flowers—pale and delicate evening primrose, sweet and yellow hollygrape, fields of globe mallow that stretch away into an orange blur on the horizon. A fetching cluster of purple marks the sinister locoweed, addictive and fatal to livestock. Horses will struggle on their dying legs to find it. *"Loco,"* the Spanish say, "crazy."

Stone shapes—stetsons, boots, Indian heads—loomed on our skyline. And I suddenly saw the sandstone all around me as separate bits, welded to each other grain by grain. If it could be broken apart again, there would be more sand in Canyonlands country than in all the Arabian Peninsula.

"Chiniago!" yelled our volunteer chef, borrowing from a Navajo word for "Come and get it!" We feasted on steak as sunset lit the sky.

At dawn, photographer "Toppy" Edwards and I rode up a winding chasm to the cadenzas of cañon wrens. We rounded a bend and faced huge pictographs on a sandstone wall.

In ancient inks of brown and ocher and black and white, an army of figures stood in ghostly array among desert sheep, flitting birds, and scurrying rodentlike animals. A six-foot man raised his right hand, one finger giving root to a graceful tree. A crouching figure held a pair of sticks; another wielded a sickle—the famed

Window on a weathered world frames visitors to the White Rim at a northern corner of Canyonlands. "Most up-and-down terrain in the world," a geologist described the park's dizzying vertical geography—virtually roadless except for miles of jeep trails. Far below loops the silt-laden Colorado River.

DAVID HISER

ROAD CLOSED
SCENIC
RESTORATION

A hike in Davis Canyon brings a family face-to-face with prehistoric Indians—or ritual beings—in the "Five Portraits" (below). A small smile (opposite) fills a portal built centuries ago; small hands reach for an airlift over Salt Creek and help a ranger tend scars of visitation. Nearby, the Needles jut nearly 500 feet over Chesler Park (overleaf).

DAVID HISER. OVERLEAF: WALTER MEAYERS EDWARDS

seed beater and reaper—proof that Indians hereabouts harvested wild grains in prehistoric times. A similar picture gallery is preserved in Horseshoe Canyon, a 3,178-acre annex just west of the main park area.

Legacy of landlocked seas, a salt deposit as big as Maryland and as much as 2½ miles thick underlies southeast Utah and part of Colorado. Under pressure of hundreds of feet of rock, the salt rises like putty into faults and weak spots, warping the surface upward. As the rock strata crack, water seeps in and dissolves the salt away, letting the surface drop. It is this heaving process, combined with erosion, that creates the land's fantasies in stone. Thousands of spires, buttes, arches, and balanced stones pepper the park with curious names: the Doll House, Druid Arch, Paul Bunyan's Potty, Land of Standing Rocks.

The salt's most awesome creation is a three-mile-wide pockmark called Upheaval Dome. Toppy and I hiked into its center, a tortured jumble that made us feel we had stepped onto the moon. Red cliffs towered 1,000 feet; curves in their strata told of warping under tremendous pressures. A huge column of salt pushed upward here, bulging the surface until it cracked open and eroded unevenly to form a crater of concentric strata, their jagged edges twisted aloft in a three-dimensional bull's-eye with a stone stiletto scoring a perfect hit.

One day I found a student taking samples of

Both boon and bane, water cools dusty throats at a desert font near the Doll House—and heats tempers at a gravelly ford on Salt Creek. Travelers equipped with four-wheel-drive risk breakdowns and quicksand to see the Molar take a bite of sky (opposite) as Angel Arch turns her winged back. Only hikers enter Upheaval Dome (overleaf); a road ends at its raw edge.

WALTER MEAYERS EDWARDS. OPPOSITE AND OVERLEAF: DAVID HISER

the water in potholes. I peered into one and found it alive with mosquito larvae, shrimp, water fleas, Mayflies, gnat larvae, whirligig beetles that zipped in dizzying spirals . . .

"The balance is acute," he said. "Kill the algae and you kill everything. In a small pool a bar of soap can do it, or a cigarette butt."

Springs keep some pools full, but others fill only when it rains. Ground-level temperatures, often above 140°, dry out the hollows and bake them for months, perhaps years. Yet even here, life persists. In egg form, or as dehydrated larvae or pupae, tiny creatures wait out broiling heat and winter's freezing cold in a brown, dusty crust on the rock. With new rains the crust wriggles into "instant life."

The desert soil has its own kind of crust, a crumbly dark amalgam of algae, fungi, lichens, and other tiny plants called cryptogams that benefit each other. Some tap the air for nitrogen, a boon to the desert soil. Others secrete a glue

Eyes stray from scenery to stewpot as a lowering sun turns campers to cutouts along the White Rim. Autumn snows drape 12,000-foot summits of La Sal Mountains. And between, red rock hides the Colorado River, ever deepening its awesome gorge through Canyonlands.

that helps cement the crust and retard erosion. One passage by cattle or humans can powder the crust, leaving it vulnerable to wind or rain. How fragile this rugged-looking land really is!

Three miles below its confluence with the Green, the Colorado becomes a churning sluice as it squeezes through Cataract Canyon. The muddy water boils over boulders fallen from sky-high cliffs and debris jetted in from side canyons by the incredible force of once-in-a-century super-storms. A dozen miles of frothing stairs offer raft riders as breathtaking a trip to Lake Powell as they could want.

"I hope you enjoy getting wet," Dee Holladay said as I piled my gear into his 17-foot inflatable raft. One man had a waterproof watch and camera; another sealed his wallet in plastic. We seemed to be rigging for a dive.

Snowmelt in the mountains had swollen the flow. "Forecasts say 40,000 cusecs," said Dee.

"What does that mean?" someone asked.

"Cubic feet per second. Above 20,000 we lose all control." Of course he was kidding—or was he? On a rock at Mile-long Rapid we read an inscription left by prospectors in 1891: "Hell to pay. No. 1 [boat] is sunk and down."

Mile-long is a chaotic prelude to three mighty cataracts known as the Big Drop. Many a boatman has gotten a rude dunking here. To express the demonic wrath of the Big Drop's final rapid, somebody named it Satan's Gut.

Above each rapid there comes an instant when the swiftening current grips the boat irrevocably and a once-distant roar now overwhelms your ear—like being in the birthplace of thunder. You try to see the rapid ahead, hidden by a shoulder of water that speeds ever closer.

Then the tossing rooster tails of spray, the geysers, the long smooth slides that end in splattering explosions, rise into view as your raft lips over the edge. Here and there you dodge horrendous sucking vortexes, holes in the river that can swallow you. Your raft lurches ever faster, rams into jolting walls, buckles, whirls, takes water. "Grab those buckets and bail!" shouts your boatman. And already you hear the next rapid's roar.

At last a turn in the canyon shot us from Satan's Gut into the stillness of man-made Lake Powell. Once there were sunlit rapids here too; now they are locked in the lake's blue silence.

We pitched camp in a side canyon. Next morning we awoke to find the 2½-inch paw prints of a cougar close by. It gave us a kind of joy to find a wild creature still uncowed by man.

I hope he enjoyed his drink from the lake.

CANYONLANDS NATIONAL PARK

Area 527 square miles

Features: *Surrealistic desert-wonderland of canyons, spires, and buttes cut by the Green and Colorado rivers. Bighorn sheep, bobcats, cougars, beavers; rich variety of birdlife. Ancient Indian pictographs.*

Activities: *In the north, dirt roads from the Neck lead to Grand View Point and Upheaval Dome overlooks on Island in the Sky. A thousand feet below, the White Rim Trail offers 100 miles of four-wheel-drive adventure. Rugged jeep trails lead to Chesler Park, the Needles, and Salt Creek in the south, and to the Maze and Land of Standing Rocks in the west. Camping, hiking, backcountry exploring. Ranger stations at the Neck, near Squaw Flat campground, and west of the Maze. Jeep tours, river float trips, scenic flights.*

Season: *Park open all year. Spring and autumn best for hiking and exploring.*

Weather: *Summer days hot, nights cool (elev. from 4,000 to 6,000 ft.). Other seasons generally pleasant, but dust storms and high winds common in spring.*

How to get there: *U. S. 163 south from I-70 to turnoffs near Moab or Monticello.*

Accommodations: *No rooms or meals in park. Campgrounds have no hookups for trailers. Bring own fuel—collecting firewood prohibited. Primitive campsites in four-wheel-drive areas.*

Services: *Lodging, food, and full services in Moab and Monticello; limited services at Canyonlands Resort near the main southeast entrance. Rental four-wheel-drive vehicles available.*

Park regulations: *Carry ample gas, water, tools, emergency supplies. For extended travel, obtain topographic maps. Permit required for private, unguided float trips through Cataract Canyon.*

For information write Supt., Moab, Utah 84532

WALTER MEAYERS EDWARDS

WALTER MEAYERS EDWARDS. OPPOSITE: DAVID MUENCH

Lehman Caves

NATIONAL MONUMENT, NEVADA

Pioneer rancher Absalom Lehman stumbled upon a small cave in 1885 and thus gave his name to an intimate, exquisite cavern system in the flank of 13,063-foot Wheeler Peak five miles west of Baker. Ninety-minute tours, conducted year round by park rangers, lead over a paved trail past "bacon-strip" draperies, terraced pools, and rare, geologically puzzling formations called shields or pallettes—thin disks of calcite that angle from the floor and walls. Fluted columns reach from floor to ceiling. Posed with special permission (visitors are not allowed to touch the fragile formations), the woman above indicates scale.

A café, open Easter through September, provides meals and refreshments; picnic facilities are available. There are no overnight accommodations in the 640-acre monument; campers can pitch tents in the adjacent Humboldt National Forest amid the aspens along trout streams. Drive in from U. S. Highways 6 and 50 ten miles north or from U. S. 93 forty miles west.
Write Supt., Baker, Nev. 89311

Timpanogos Cave

NATIONAL MONUMENT, UTAH

Leave high-heeled shoes in the car when you visit Timpanogos. The three small caves connected by tunnels lie at the end of a mile-and-a-half trail that switchbacks a thousand feet up the side of American Fork Canyon in Utah's scenic Wasatch Mountains. Keep eyes and ears open for rocks falling on the trail, and allow three hours for the round trip.

Don't forget a sweater—cave temperatures hover around 42°. But the delights of these little chambers, richly filigreed with sparkling translucent crystals, outweigh the chill. Stalactites are jeweled with drops of water, for this is a living cave, its formations still growing. Adding an inch to a feature may take hundreds of years. Nickel and other minerals in the calcium carbonate of the dripstone tinges with color the coral-like helictites, fragile structures whose crystals grow every which way.

The 250-acre monument, 35 miles south of Salt Lake City, is open all year, but its caves are closed November through April.
Write Supt., RFD 2, American Fork, Utah 84003

Craters of the Moon

NATIONAL MONUMENT, IDAHO

Youngsters expect moon men in pressurized suits and fishbowl helmets. Instead they find in this 83-square-mile monument west of Idaho Falls one of the world's most complete displays of volcanism. Here the earth's crust was weak, and for thousands of years lava bubbled from wounds along a zone of cracks we call the Great Rift. Hot magma lapped around living trees, turned them to torches, and left impressions of their burned-out trunks. Molten blobs, hurled from spatter cones, hardened in midair to teardrop shapes called bombs.

Today all is black desolation with an austere beauty of its own. Rivers of rock seem to flow around cinder cones and lava domes. Visitors gingerly touch ropy pahoehoe lava to see if it is still warm, and marvel at fantastically heavy-looking chunks of volcanic froth.

A seven-mile loop road and side trails explore these pockmarked wonders. A quarter-mile walk leads to the cave area, a series of lava tubes, or caves. The largest, Indian Tunnel, is more than 830 feet long and was once used by Indians as a waystop on journeys.

From April to October campers pitch tents near the visitor center and slake their thirst on water piped from mountains to the north. In winter, cross-country skiers and snowshoers sport on the cinder slopes.

Write Supt., Box 29, Arco, Idaho 83213

Hardy plants adorn the stark surface of Big Craters lava flow.

Colorado

NATIONAL MONUMENT, COLORADO

Dramatic and intriguing names hint at the fantastic sandstone formations embraced by this 28-square-mile park: No Thoroughfare Canyon . . . Cold Shivers Point . . . Devils Kitchen . . . Squaw Fingers . . . Coke Ovens . . . Kissing Couple. Cliff-lined canyons and monoliths carved from the northern edge of the Uncompahgre Plateau rise 1,500 feet above the Grand Valley of the Colorado River. Book Cliffs march across the skyline to the north; rugged escarpments flank Independence Monument, a free-standing colossus 500 feet high.

The colorful, still-eroding landscape tells a story which geologists read like the pages of a book. Sedimentary rock laid down during the Age of Reptiles is superimposed on crystalline rock dating from the earth's nearly lifeless infancy. But several chapters are missing. No strata exist between the two types to record the passage of nearly a billion years. The missing layers may have been stripped off during an intervening uplift of the earth's crust, when the elevated area would have been especially subject to erosion.

At the turn of the century John Otto, a dedicated outdoorsman, wandered into this majestic expanse four miles west of Grand Junction. He settled in Monument Canyon and began to build trails throughout the mesas and canyons. Believing these scenic wonders should be preserved, Otto began a letter-writing campaign that triumphed in 1911, when President Taft proclaimed the area a national monument.

Between the east and west entrances a 22-mile road, open all year, skirts the monument's western rim. From the east it climbs No Thoroughfare Canyon, tunnels through a cliff, and emerges at well-named Cold Shivers Point. Here visitors pause to view the chasm floor 500 feet below. Along self-guiding trails, hikers may glimpse bobcats and deer, or spot the monument's bison herd in the canyons.

The visitor center, with a campground and picnic area, is located near the west entrance.
Write Supt., Fruita, Colo. 81521

Black Canyon of the Gunnison

NATIONAL MONUMENT, COLORADO

Anglers seeking brown and rainbow trout in the gorge of the Gunnison River occasionally claim they can see stars gleaming in the strip of sky overhead—in full daylight. Fish stories, of course, but the exaggerations are understandable. Rangers do confirm that, except at midday, an eerie twilight shrouds the depths between these stupendous walls.

Knifing through the Colorado Plateau region in the western part of the state, the Gunnison has cut as deep as 2,400 feet through base rock in the last two million years. Black Canyon of the Gunnison National Monument, established in 1933, includes the deepest 12-mile stretch of this 53-mile-long chasm.

And black is the word for it. Other canyons may be longer or deeper, narrower or steeper, but no other combines all these elements in an atmosphere of such profound gloom. Cliff bottoms reveal ebonylike schist, millions of years old. Overhangs cast long shadows on frowning walls banded by coarse gneiss and granite that vary from somber gray to pink. Blocky "islands" and pinnacles of unevenly weathered rock loom above the canyon floor, especially at the park's eastern end. To stand in bright sun at the lip of the abyss and peer straight down at the tiny river below is enough to raise goose bumps on anyone.

Small trees crowd the plateau, among them piñon patriarchs whose 500 or so years are chronicled in the rings of their gnarled trunks. Coyotes, bobcats, and mule deer roam the 21-square-mile sanctuary and campers occasionally see a black bear or a cougar.

Visitors drive both rims of the canyon. A paved road along the south rim is reached via U. S. 50 from Montrose. An unpaved, summer-only route on the north rim is accessible over a gravel road beginning east of Crawford on Route 92. A campground on each side provides limited firewood and water. Nature walks and campfire programs are conducted near the south rim campground in the summer.
Write Supt., Box 1648, Montrose, Colo. 81401

Black Canyon's Painted Wall—a 2,250-foot dr

DAVID H

David F. Robinson

Dinosaur

NATIONAL MONUMENT, UTAH-COLORADO

"Where are the dinosaurs?" asks a small boy, camera at the ready. The ranger smiles. He's heard that one before—in jest, usually, but sometimes in dead earnest.

"Well, young fellow, you're about 140 million years too late. But they *were* here, lots of them. Come on up to the visitor center and take a look at what's left of them."

The scene has played many times at Dinosaur National Monument, a vaguely Y-shaped park of 326 square miles spilling from eastern Utah into western Colorado just north of U. S. Route 40. Most of its visitors know the last dinosaurs died long before humans appeared. But as the park's open-air jitney hums up the hill between the parking lot and the center, eyes peer from under shading hands at moonscapes of naked rock and eroded canyons, a vista that seems to say creation is not quite finished here.

An imagination free as a child's can almost see a great, grotesque *Stegosaurus* lumbering from behind a sun-broiled outcrop, its stumpy feet scuffing up puffs of dust as its spiked tail drags an undulating autograph in the sand. Armor plates jut like rows of leaning tombstones up and over the hump of its back. From beak to tail it spans 20 feet, yet its tiny head hides a brain no bigger than a golf ball. Wheezing noisily, it pauses before the rock's angled face. The tiny eyes glaze, the wheezing stops, the brute stands still as stone....

Then small hands pat its fiberglass head, rap on its haunches to see if it's hollow (it is), and click off snapshots of this life-size model, standing like a nightmarish watchdog at the entrance to one of the most striking displays of dinosaur remains in the world. On a balcony running the length of a building that's a cross between barn and greenhouse, visitors enjoy a grandstand view of a steep rock face strewn with an incredible array of fossil bones. Here are leg bones as big as a man, ribs like an archer's longbow, teeth like tent pegs in a skull the size of a garbage can.

A lifeless panorama? Not quite. Among the bones, leaning on a vertebra or braced against a pelvis, two technicians perch hour after hour, patiently chiseling away the sandstone around these wonders from the distant past. Who can guess what the next bite of the chisel may reveal for the first time to human eyes?

As I listened to the rangers' brief talks and chatted with quarry technician Tobe Wilkins, the real wonder of these fossil bones dawned on me. It is not just in their size or strangeness but also in the story they can tell—a story of fantastic landscapes, staggering forces, and unimaginable stretches of time.

In a distant age that paleontologists label the Jurassic period, this uptilted slab of sandstone was an ordinary sandbar in the curve of a river. Today's arid landscape of canyons and ragged peaks was then a steamy semitropical wetland. Sluggish rivers meandered in shallow channels; lakes and marshes sprinkled the land. Windblown ash sifted from volcanoes booming far westward, adding grain by grain to a layer geologists call the Morrison Formation.

Weird tree ferns towered nearly 100 feet; pine-like araucaria trees soared to 150. Mosquitoes buzzed about, and shy mammals no bigger than a house cat foraged in the rank undergrowth.

Close brush with a dinosaur: Technician Wilkins whisks away rock dust from the fossilized leg bones of a 70-foot-long Camarasaurus. *In Jurassic times such reptiles roamed a tropical marshland; today the park preserves this graveyard of gargantuans.*

DAVID HISER

BRONTOSAURUS

Big as a live one and just as ugly, a Stegosaurus *replica greets jitney riders at the quarry. The site was a knoll until scientists cut out its middle to mine skeletons for study and display. Bent by the lens (below), bones* in situ *jam a fantastic frieze.* Overleaf: *The twisting Yampa nears its confluence with the Green, carving one of many spectacular canyons known best to those who ride the rivers.*
DAVID HISER (ALSO OVERLEAF)

Over it all reigned the dinosaurs, "terrible lizards" whose kind appeared some 200 million years ago. They were a stupid lot, averaging a pound of brain to 40 tons of bulk. But they owned the earth for 140 million years, dying out about 60 million years ago.

Here the two-legged *Nannosaurus* scurried through the clearings, a harmless vegetarian the size of a chicken. Now and then the bogs trembled as an 80-ton *Brachiosaurus* lumbered out of the water, perhaps to stretch its long neck for a snack of treetop greens; as tall as a four-story building, it ranks as the biggest land animal of all time. Though the fearsome *Tyrannosaurus* had not yet thundered onto nature's stage, smaller carnivores stalked the land on powerful hind legs, their curved and serrated teeth well suited for tearing at carrion or stilling a struggling victim.

One day—so the bones suggest—the river bore a grisly burden: the bloated carcass of a *Camarasaurus.* Crocodiles ripped at the rotting flesh as it slowly rounded the bend and bumped onto the sandbar. There it stuck, long neck and tail trailing with the current.

For perhaps a century the river added to its

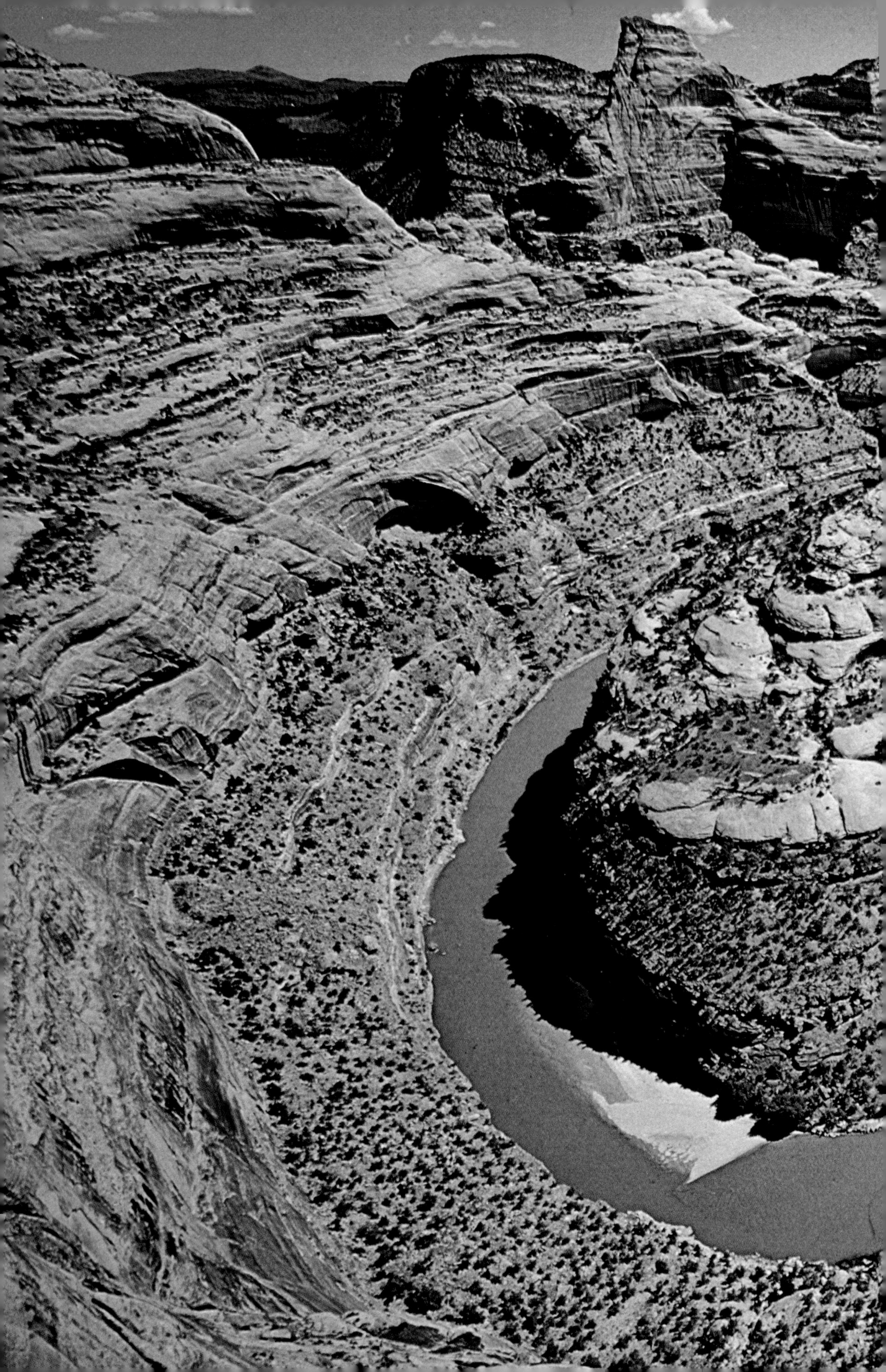

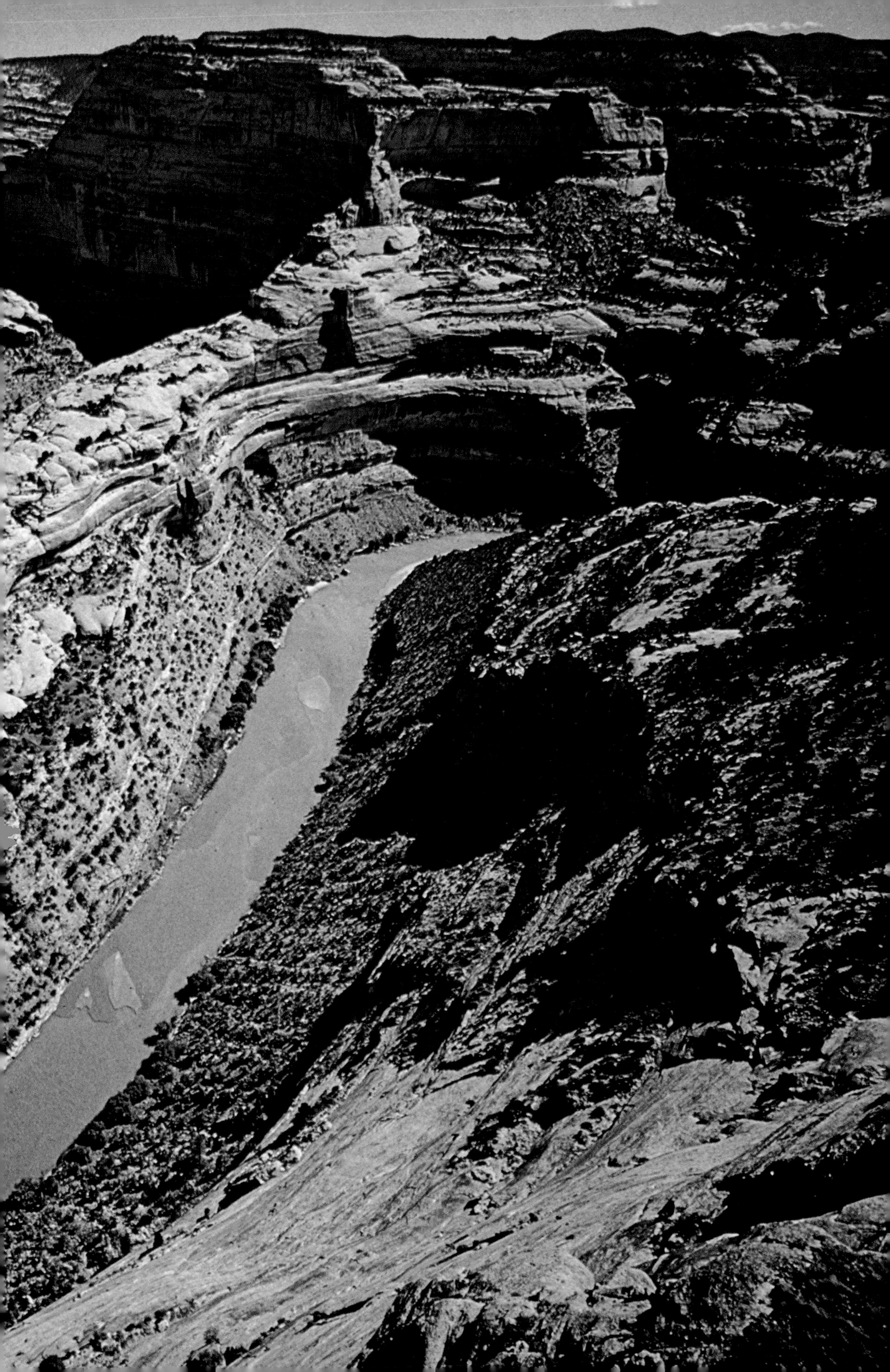

graveyard. Far upstream in drier lands a young *Stegosaurus* may have tried to ford, only to drown and ride the current to a last stop on the bar. Sometimes a single bone washed up, worn and rounded from tumbling along the bottom. Here a bone bore teeth marks of a carnivore; there a tail showed two fused vertebrae where, perhaps, one great beast trod upon the tail of another. As the current stirred the pile, some of the bones rolled away to oblivion. Others sank into the sand, each adding its statement to a time capsule of life in an era of giants.

Buried bones usually disintegrate. These did too—but as each molecule dissolved into the subsurface water its place was taken by a molecule of the minerals in the water. When the bones were gone, stone replicas lay in their place, often complete to the last tooth mark, the telltale injury scar, even the details only a microscope can reveal.

As ages wore on, a vast inland sea drowned the marshland, then gave way to a huge lake. Mud accumulated a mile thick, pushing the old sandbar ever deeper and squeezing its grains into stone. Then the earth's crust convulsed in mighty upheavals as the newborn Rocky Mountains shouldered the plain aside. Like a phone book ripped by a titan, the stratified rock was torn apart, exposing upturned edges of pages.

Far down inside one page lay the ancient sandbar. Water had littered it with bones; water had petrified them; water had buried them deep under layers of sediment. Now water would dig them out again, a raindrop at a time, slowly eroding peaks higher than today's Himalayas.

On a knoll in 1909 paleontologist Earl Douglass lay down his spade for his diary. "... I saw eight of the tail bones of a *Brontosaurus* in exact position," he wrote. His timing was perfect; a million years either way—a twinkling in geologic time—and the trove would have been too deep to find or gone to dust.

From the knoll, he and his colleagues mined a score of mountable skeletons and hundreds of separate bones. Hundreds more still lie in place, as one ranger put it, "like the leavings of an enormous turkey dinner." The technician's job is to "relief" the bones but leave them anchored in the rock face; a specimen is removed only if something more exciting lies below it.

The visitor center is more than a tourist attraction. It is a scientific laboratory. Below the balcony, visitors watch through glass as specimens are cleaned, studied, and squeezed of every drop of information they can yield about life and death in the Age of Reptiles.

I left the center for a look at the other face of the park—the canyons, rivers, and scenic drive that lure throngs of adventurers and snapshooters. A 30-mile drive takes them from headquarters at Dinosaur, Colorado, past scenic viewpoints to the Harpers Corner trailhead. Another mile on foot reaches canyon's edge for an awesome view of Steamboat Rock and the Green and Yampa rivers. It's a rugged realm; names like Starvation Valley, Hells Canyon, and Upper Disaster Falls weren't coined in jest.

Adventurers by the thousand ride the torrents each summer in neoprene rafts, overgrown inner tubes that buck like broncos in the ever-changing rapids. At Split Mountain Gorge I helped Wyoming Girl Scouts beach the black steeds that had borne them on ten days of excitement and discovery. They had seen Indian petroglyphs perhaps a thousand years old, and floated past canyon walls whose layers reach back to times before the dinosaurs. They were tired, sunburned, hot; their clothes were dirty, their trip was over. Worth it? One girl said it all with a grin as broad as the canyon.

In nearby Vernal, Utah, I bought honey in a plastic dinosaur, picked up a free "dinosaur hunting license," and toured a fine museum with three concrete dinosaurs locked in ponderous combat on its front lawn. The cheery leviathans grinned at me from signs, menus, T-shirts. Vacationists and "river rats" roam the land now. But this is still dinosaur country.

Write Supt., Box 210, Dinosaur, Colo. 81610

FARRELL GREHAN

The Southwest

Saguaro spines guard a screech owl's home in a dry and thirsty land.

Thomas B. Allen

Carlsbad Caverns

NATIONAL PARK, NEW MEXICO

As we hiked the switchback trail up the canyon wall, our shadows tagged along, small and playful as pups, rippling over sun-bleached rocks, weaving through patches of cactus. About 500 feet above the canyon floor the trail ended at an iron gate erected not by a troll but by the superintendent of Carlsbad Caverns National Park. We unlocked the gate, lit our lanterns, and entered New Cave.

So did our shadows, suddenly giants that danced on the vaulting walls to the rhythm of our swinging lanterns. It took a while to sort them out, they had grown so. The one with the cap was Charlie Peterson's. The park's cave naturalist and keeper of the gate, he throws a friendly shadow that obviously knows its way around in its kind of place. The two shadows that jigged as a lantern continually shifted from one carrier to another belonged to my son Roger and his friend Chris Koch. The fairest shadow of them all was owned by my wife, Scottie. And of course I'd recognize that one with the mustache anywhere.

Charlie and his shadow were leading us into the wild side of the park. A Cinderella long ignored, New Cave is finally getting callers. Nearly everybody knows about her glamorous sisters, the magnificent caverns bathed in electric lights and served by miles of paved trails. Now people can discover an underground wonderland where darkness reigns.

Blackness enwraps us as we follow Charlie into the heart of the cave. But, shyly emerging through the darkness, beauty glows by lantern light: massive, gleaming stalagmites . . . a shower of stalactite spears thrusting from the ceiling . . . draperies of translucent stone big enough to hide behind. And then—an apparition rising from an underground of demons.

An archeologist making the first report on

Spelunkers in New Cave warily pass a stone-masked denizen, The Clansman. Rangers lead parties on lantern-lit treks through this "wild" cave, 23 miles from the tame but magnificent Carlsbad Caverns.

DAVID HISER

A sunbeam spotlights visitors in the twilight zone at the natural entrance to Carlsbad Caverns. Others get briefed electronically at one of 43 information stations along the three-mile route. Slip-proof asphalt trails and handrails aid hikers. Those who take the plunge by elevator get a fast 750-foot trip. Pioneer visitors rode guano buckets down.
DAVID HISER

New Cave in 1938 abandoned scientific terms to describe this nightmare in stone: "Small stalactites hung from the bestial upper lip, giving the appearance of monstrous fangs. The jutting chin hangs slack, and stains at the sides of the mouth make the figure appear to drool." He dubbed the formation The Clansman.

Geology can explain goblins. (The Clansman's snow-white "hood" was produced by limestone that lacked mineral coloring.) But to appreciate a cave, you have to have a chance to put your own imagination to work. To give everyone that chance, park officials not only have opened New Cave but also have changed the way visitors see the vast caverns themselves. Soon after "the most spectacular underground wonder in America" opened as a national park in 1930, wonder-seekers were conducted by guides on mass tours. In time, as many as 2,800 persons surged through on a single tour. Sometimes it seemed there were more people standing around than stalagmites. "Visitors were not getting a quality experience," a park official told me. "Now they go through on their own, and each one comes away with a personal feeling about the caverns."

The same quest for a quality experience inspired the decision to open New Cave. For me, the experiences melded into one. In the cave I felt the awe of darkness. In the caverns I learned to cherish the magic of light. I came away with this: Man does not live by light alone.

I was glad to learn we wouldn't be entirely on our own when we explored the caverns. Not far from the entrance we met our first ranger, who ushered us to stone benches. She reminded us to stay on the paved trail and not to touch the formations, some so fragile that a knuckle's rap would shatter them. She told us what to expect: a 1¾-mile walk *(continued on page 175)*

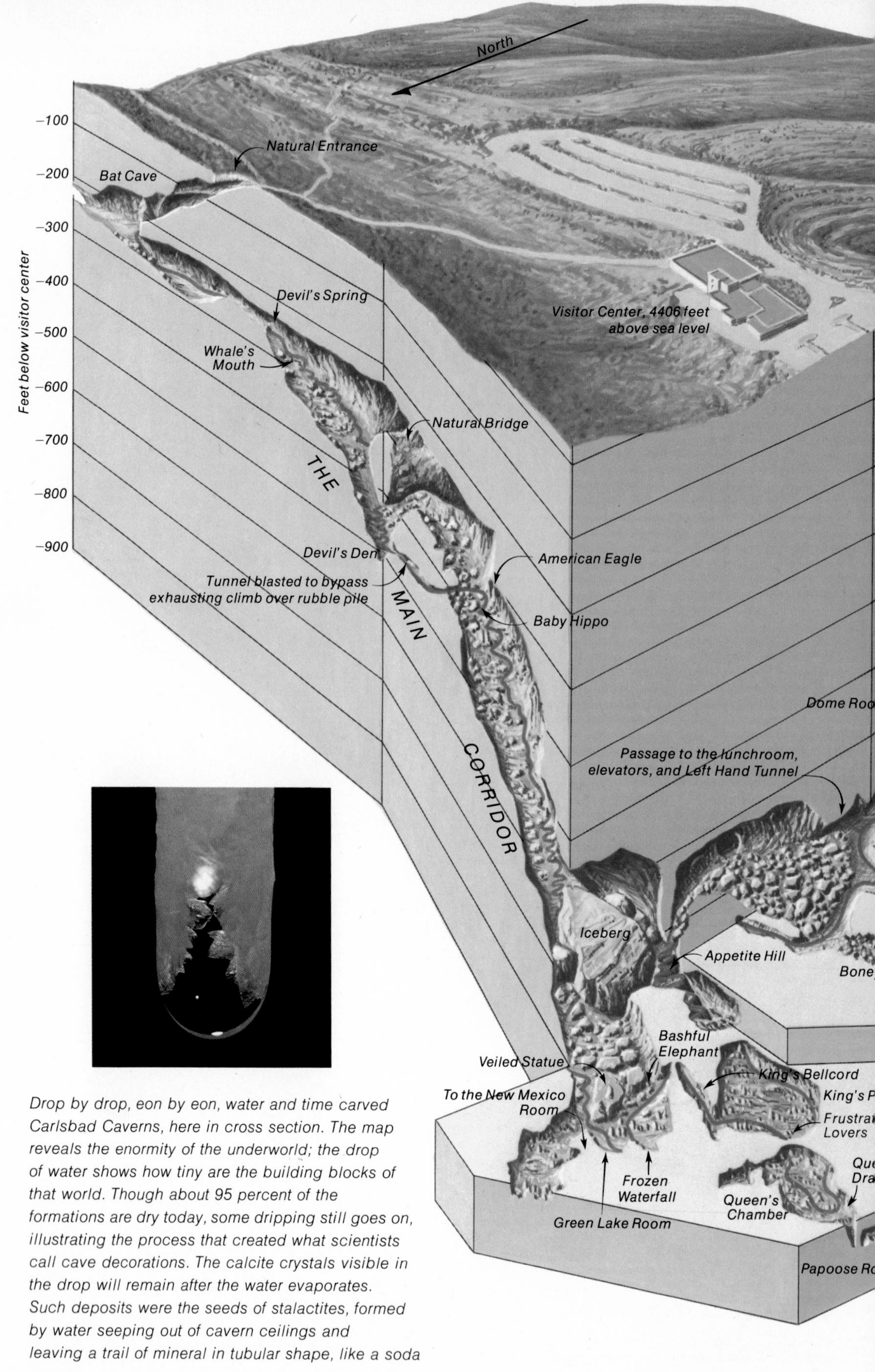

Drop by drop, eon by eon, water and time carved Carlsbad Caverns, here in cross section. The map reveals the enormity of the underworld; the drop of water shows how tiny are the building blocks of that world. Though about 95 percent of the formations are dry today, some dripping still goes on, illustrating the process that created what scientists call cave decorations. The calcite crystals visible in the drop will remain after the water evaporates. Such deposits were the seeds of stalactites, formed by water seeping out of cavern ceilings and leaving a trail of mineral in tubular shape, like a soda

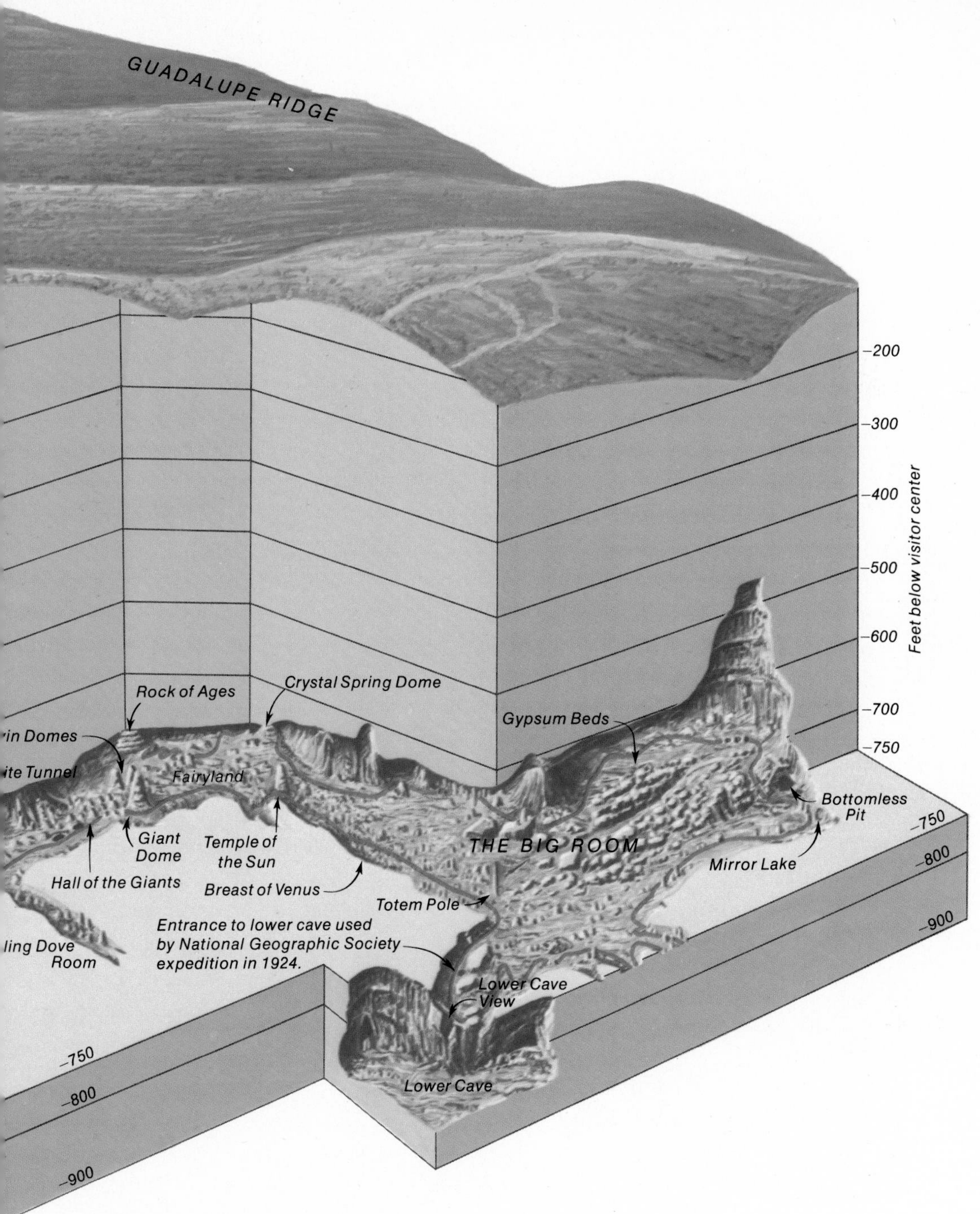

straw. Where the drip continued, droplets falling to the floor built a stalagmite growing upward. Sometimes stalactite and stalagmite met and grew together in a pillar or column. A pair that didn't meet but came tantalizingly close is dubbed the Frustrated Lovers. Many formations have achieved star status by earning such whimsical names.

A paved trail, bypassing Bat Cave near the natural entrance, leads a mile along the Main Corridor to the Green Lake Room, the first of the decorated chambers. Appetite Hill readies hikers for the lunchroom, welcome halfway point of the trip.

The trek continues into the Big Room, whose ground plan resembles a cross, with one arm some 1,800 feet long and the crosspiece 1,100 feet. A stroll through the Big Room takes about 30 minutes.

Everywhere, shutters snap. But our photographer, David Hiser, estimates that 90 percent of the pictures he saw being taken would be failures. His advice: "Rely on existing light, using a tripod for exposures of several seconds with indoor Type B film. If you use a small flash unit, pick subjects within ten feet."

Overleaf: *Glittering stalactites by the thousands drape the King's Palace, 829 feet deep.*

PAINTING BY TIBOR TOTH. OPPOSITE: DAVID HISER. OVERLEAF: ADAM WOOLFITT

Mountaineering in the dark, visitors clamber through New Cave. Others search for fossils in a wall of guano, once mined as fertilizer; its height reveals ancient bats' long tenancy. The reservations-only tour is rugged: one mile to the cliffside cave, 1 1/4 miles through it, 1 1/4 miles back to your car.
DAVID HISER

that would take us 829 feet down, then 80 feet back up to the lunchroom. From there we'd tread fairly level ground for a 1¼-mile circuit of the Big Room. She sent us on our way with the welcome news that rangers posted along our route would answer our questions.

They did more than that. One ranger flashed his light into the darkness to catch the sparkle of a drop of water as it fell. We saw it hit the point of a glistening stalagmite that eons of such drops had built. Another ranger stopped us as we passed under an arch. "We don't have many fossils that you can see," she said. "But I think I can show you one." She scanned the rock for a moment and pointed to the petrified remains of a solitary trilobite, a marine creature smaller than her fingernail and older than the caverns she knew so well.

"It seems so endless!" Scottie exclaimed as we walked once more around the Big Room. I knew she meant more than size. Our eyes could encompass the vastness of Carlsbad's chamber of superlatives: 14 acres, the largest area of any known natural underground cavity. Its Bottomless Pit isn't; with the aid of a ranger's flashlight we could see bottom, 138 feet down. And we could see Big Room's highest point, 285 feet above the pit. The 423-foot vertical drop is the longest in the caverns.

So, reckoned in feet, the Big Room is not endless. But the eye cannot fathom the room's panorama of splendors. Sweep your gaze across the room, and towering pillars merge with soaring domes in a vista of soft light and dense shadow. Stare up at the serried lances that bristle the ceiling, and a glint of white soon tugs your eye to a frozen cascade of dazzling stone; a little sign names the colossus, Rock of Ages. Other signs proclaim the Hall of Giants, the Sword of Damocles, the Temple of the Sun. The fanciful names only serve to emphasize that words become beggars here. "I don't need names for what I'm seeing." Chris said. And I knew what *his* words meant.

Rarely, though, does the handiwork of man intrude. The caverns' 27 miles of electrical cables snake unseen, linking 800 well-hidden lamps or bulbs (average life, 600 hours; brightest, 1,500 watts). People are surprised to learn there are no colored lights; the Park Service frowns on any gilding of Carlsbad's beauty.

Visitors have brought into the caverns the need for drinking water and waste disposal. Huge pumps send waste water to the surface. Air locks at the underground entrance to the elevators seal off the caverns' atmosphere. The temperature is kept around a natural 56° F. By confining in one place maintenance systems, rest rooms, souvenir stands, and a restaurant (which can serve 2,000 box lunches an hour), the park preserves a natural look elsewhere.

In the gleam of dripping water you sense that the caverns remain alive. But the main acts in the drama of creation have ended. It began when a Permian sea covered the area over 200 million years ago. At the edge of the sea, limestone-secreting organisms built a reef that geologists call Capitan. While the Rockies still

Naturalist Charlie Peterson's imported light bathes hidden wonders of the New Mexico Room, off the visitors' path. Cave "coral" fringes a pool of drip water. Crystal helicities grow in bristling clusters, the power of crystallization apparently surpassing the tug of gravity, which shapes normal stalactites.

DAVID HISER

were growing, this region was raised above sea level. Acid-bearing ground water entered the reef along minute cracks and started dissolving stone. When the Guadalupe Mountains were upthrust, air filled the hollows as the water table lowered. Finally, with seeping water came decorations. As the water evaporated, minerals remained, each tiny deposit the seed of a ceiling's stalactite, a floor's stalagmite.

The caverns lie beneath a rumpled, faintly green blanket of desert terrain—the backcountry, where on dim trails we walked the gantlet of cholla and other menacing cacti; where we flushed a mule deer and a roadrunner that acted out its name. Here the park offers another quality experience: backpack camping.

But you don't have to trek to the backcountry to experience the desert. Near the visitor center a one-mile, self-guiding nature trail loops you through a sampling of the "3-S" plants of the region: "In the desert most things for their own protection either stick, sting, or stink." We warmed up (the temperature hovered around 100° F.) on this trail for one of the longer, scheduled hikes led by rangers.

About 20 of us, straggling along between two rangers, filed down a trail to a hollow heaped with stones. "The Indians who were here before the white man came lived off this land," a ranger told us. We all looked around, wondering how they did it. "For a feast they would dig a pit like this—3 to 5 feet deep, 10 to 15 feet wide—ring it with rocks, gather wood, and keep a fire going for 24 hours to heat the rocks. They'd fill the pit with sotol and other desert plants, and cook them. We tried it once and all we got was a mash of stuff that wasn't very tasty." Later he found something that was: dark-purple fruit

Temple of the Sun, summoned from darkness by the caverns' lights, bestows beauty far below the park's desert realm. Iron oxides that tinge the limestone conjure the delicate shades of color.

gingerly plucked from prickly-pear cactus. He showed us how to peel away the skin, whose invisible needles can make a pin cushion of your fingers. You cannot pick, break off, or carry away any of Carlsbad's desert scenery. But the park allows adventurous gourmets to sample the cactus fruit (called "tunas").

Still surprised by this addition to the menu, Rog and Chris did a double take when Charlie Peterson invited us to the annual bat breakfast sponsored by the park staff. "You mean we'd have to eat. . . ?" Charlie laughed and assured them that we'd only watch for the bats; the menu was ham and eggs.

Carlsbad's bats, darkening the sky as they spiraled by the millions in and out of their cave, led modern discoverers to the caverns. Pictographs on the entrance walls attest to Indian knowledge of the black hole. But, beginning in 1901, white men explored it and soon began mining for nitrate-rich bat guano. Within 20 years their buckets had hauled out 100,000 tons of the valuable fertilizer. When the caverns became a park, upwards of 9,000,000 bats slept by day in Bat Cave.

Each night at sunset, from April to October, visitors lingered to see the bats pour out—18,000 a minute, more than 1,000,000 an hour—to feed on insects in distant fields. At sunrise, the bats returned in another spectacular flight.

We had watched an evening flight that numbered only in the thousands. But a ranger said that bats have been known to fool their watchers by flying out before the audience filled the amphitheater near the entrance. Now, ham and eggs consumed in predawn darkness, we awaited the morning flight. I was beginning to wonder whether anyone had remembered to invite the bats to the breakfast when someone shouted, "Look! There's one!" The sun rose high enough to etch the day's first shadows on the rocks. "I just saw one . . . Hey! There go three at once!" But where were the millions?

In recent years, I was told, rarely more than 1,000,000 bats have lived in Bat Cave at one time; the exit rate on a typical night flight has been around 5,000 a minute. Other estimates put the population far lower. Most experts blame the loss on widespread use of insecticides or point to anti-bat campaigns in Mexico, winter home of the Carlsbad colony. Scientists suspect insecticides may not only cut back the bats' food supply but also affect fertility or weaken the young so that fewer reach maturity.

As the bats fly off at night they vanish into the darkening horizon. There, to the southwest, looms a long, unbroken wall—the Capitan Reef. The same vanished sea that spawned the honeycomb of Carlsbad also left behind this immense limestone monument. There, in the Guadalupe Mountains, prow of the Capitan Reef, another national park beckons.

CARLSBAD CAVERNS NATIONAL PARK

Area 72 square miles

Features: *World's most spectacular limestone caverns; colorful stalactite-stalagmite formations in fanciful shapes. Big Room is world's largest known natural underground chamber.*

Activities: *Visitor center. Naturalist's talk on bats each summer evening. Elevator service. Desert nature trail. Lantern trips into New Cave.*

Season: *Park open year round.*

Weather: *Surface temperature varies from near zero in winter to above 100° in summer. Cave stays at about 56°. Elevation at entrance 4,350 ft.*

What to bring: *Sweater or jacket for cave; low-heeled shoes with rubber soles or heels; cameras allowed.*

How to get there: *U. S. 62-180 and 285. Major air and rail service to El Paso, Texas. Bus or rental car from El Paso to park.*

Accommodations: *None in park. Hotels, motels, trailer parks in Carlsbad, 27 miles northeast.*

Services: *Restaurant, curio shop, nursery, kennel adjoin visitor center. Lunchroom in caverns. Garage, car rentals, hospital, church services in Carlsbad.*

Park regulations: *No casual camping or fires; back-country camping by permit. Walking sticks in caverns by permit. Pets on leash, none inside.*

For further information write Supt., 3225 El Paso Road, Carlsbad, New Mex. 88220

DAVID MUENCH

TEMPLE OF THE SUN

Autumn gilds and crimsons McKittrick Canyon, oasis amid desert lowlands and stark cliffs.

Thomas B. Allen

Guadalupe Mountains

NATIONAL PARK, TEXAS

WALTER MEAYERS EDWARDS

The stream, so weak it merely grazes the rocks of its bed, steals through McKittrick Canyon with hardly a murmur. Yet this trickle bears a mighty burden: the ration of water that sustains an ecological crossroads in Guadalupe Mountains National Park. In this sanctuary of merging sere and green, prickly plants of the desert grow in the dappled shadows of the forest. The solitary spear of a sotol thrusts alongside a soaring ponderosa pine; knife-edged leaves of agaves cluster at the foot of a bigtooth maple. Here water—and life—is so precious, a visitor may not even wade lest an errant foot scrape a film of algae.

The canyon, accessible only by a cairn-marked foot trail, stems from the great Capitan Reef, a geological wonder. Built of limestone secreted by marine creatures over 200 million years ago, the reef here is mountain, including 8,751-foot Guadalupe Peak, tallest in Texas. About 35 miles to the northeast, the reef is the raw material of Carlsbad Caverns.

On our visit to Carlsbad (page 166) we camped at Guadalupe and found that the parks complemented each other. In one we descended to our reward; in the other we hiked and climbed to it. The hike took us to the oasis of McKittrick. The climb—a two-hour scrabble up rocky slopes—began at 5,695 feet, the elevation of our beware-of-cactus campsite, and ended on the ridge of 8,362-foot Hunter Peak. Here we found another oasis: the Bowl, a needle-carpeted, mile-wide catch basin whose moisture sustains ponderosa pine and Douglas fir, survivors of an ancient forest.

From the ridge we looked down upon the newcomers, which arrived thousands of years ago with a desert climate: creosote bush, yucca, lechuguilla (whose spikes can pierce a leather sole). Beyond towered the scarred wall of El Capitan. Once the 2,000-foot beacon for conquistador, stagecoach driver, and homesteader, it guards a 77,500-acre park that welcomes only those who cherish wilderness.

Administered by Supt., Carlsbad Caverns.

Bart McDowell

Big Bend

NATIONAL PARK, TEXAS

One summer, when my father was a venturesome teen-ager, he joined a posse of deputies and rode into the Big Bend to search for a gang of cattle rustlers.

"We never found the thieves," he told me years later, "but we sure found some wild country." He also found its folklore, and over the years he shared his Big Bend stories with me. We were a Texas family, running cattle, horses, and short-hair goats on our Rancho Chuparosa, a rocky spread on the Mexican bank of the Rio Grande. The river's ragged cliffs seemed monumental to me, but not to my father.

"You should see them upstream," Father would say. "In Santa Elena Canyon the cliffs are 1,500 feet—and straight up." When one of our trotlines snagged a really big catfish—a monster as long as a man's arm—Father would venture the opinion that "it probably swam down from the Big Bend." And he told me, too, about deer and bear and mountain lion—all the game was larger upstream, he said.

There were tales of lost mines and curative springs and old battlefields. When the river rose in muddy flood, Father showed me the Big Bend on maps, pointing out the 107-mile-long horseshoe turn in the Rio Grande, along with the Davis and Chisos mountains: "Probably a cloudburst on those slopes." And so my earliest boyhood imaginings came to endow the mysterious Big Bend country with heroic dimensions and almost mythic events.

Later, when I was a schoolboy, we Texans were urged by teachers and newspapers to give money so that Big Bend lands could be bought and presented to the U. S. as a national park. The state legislature responded with an appropriation. And before the park was established in 1944, I got to see Big Bend as it was: few roads and fewer people—a strange and

Bombarded by skybolts, Pulliam Ridge in the Chisos Mountains looms above a desert floor strewn with grama grass, creosote bushes, flowering prickly pear, and naked stalks of the treacherous lechuguilla.

JAMES L. STANFIELD, NATIONAL GEOGRAPHIC PHOTOGRAPHER

Hey, hay! Horse and rider strike up a friendship —with help from a pocketful of grub. Bridle trails and illustrated talks (right) each year acquaint 300,000 visitors with Big Bend. Chisos Mountains Lodge (bottom) offers overnight accommodations.

JAMES L. STANFIELD, NATIONAL GEOGRAPHIC PHOTOGRAPHER

haunted desert landscape, the most wildly western country I had ever seen.

I returned to the Big Bend time and again—until circumstances took me from Texas. Years passed. Then recently I promised my own son I would take him to see this awesome place. But I had misgivings: memory might have magnified the land and its wonders.

Thus it was that 10-year-old Rob and I drove the 40 miles from Marathon south along U. S. 385, one of two highways that provide access to Big Bend from the north. We entered the 1,106-square-mile park at Persimmon Gap.

"Comanche warriors trailed through this pass," I told Rob. "In the autumn they crossed the river and rode south to capture horses and slaves. They wintered in Mexico, then headed north again through the gap."

We chased a blue-black thunderstorm to Panther Junction, and then turned right to enter the fastness of the Chisos Mountains. These soaring peaks of upthrust volcanic rock stand all in a piece, a mixture of geology, sculpture, and pure theatrics. Our road wound upward, cooling us now with a mile-high altitude and the green-needle shade of juniper and piñon. We entered Chisos Basin, most comfortable place in the park—even in the fierce heat of summer. Wildlife, too, seemed to agree. On a nature trail next morning Rob and I walked head on into six Carmen whitetails, small, short-antlered deer found only in this region. The animals froze, watching us. We froze, too. The deer breathed first, then moved gracefully away.

Other forms of life make these remote mountains a biological island in the desert. Nowhere else in the country will you find the drooping juniper tree, for example, or hear the trilling of the Colima warbler, one of 382 kinds of birds that make the Big Bend a paradise for bird

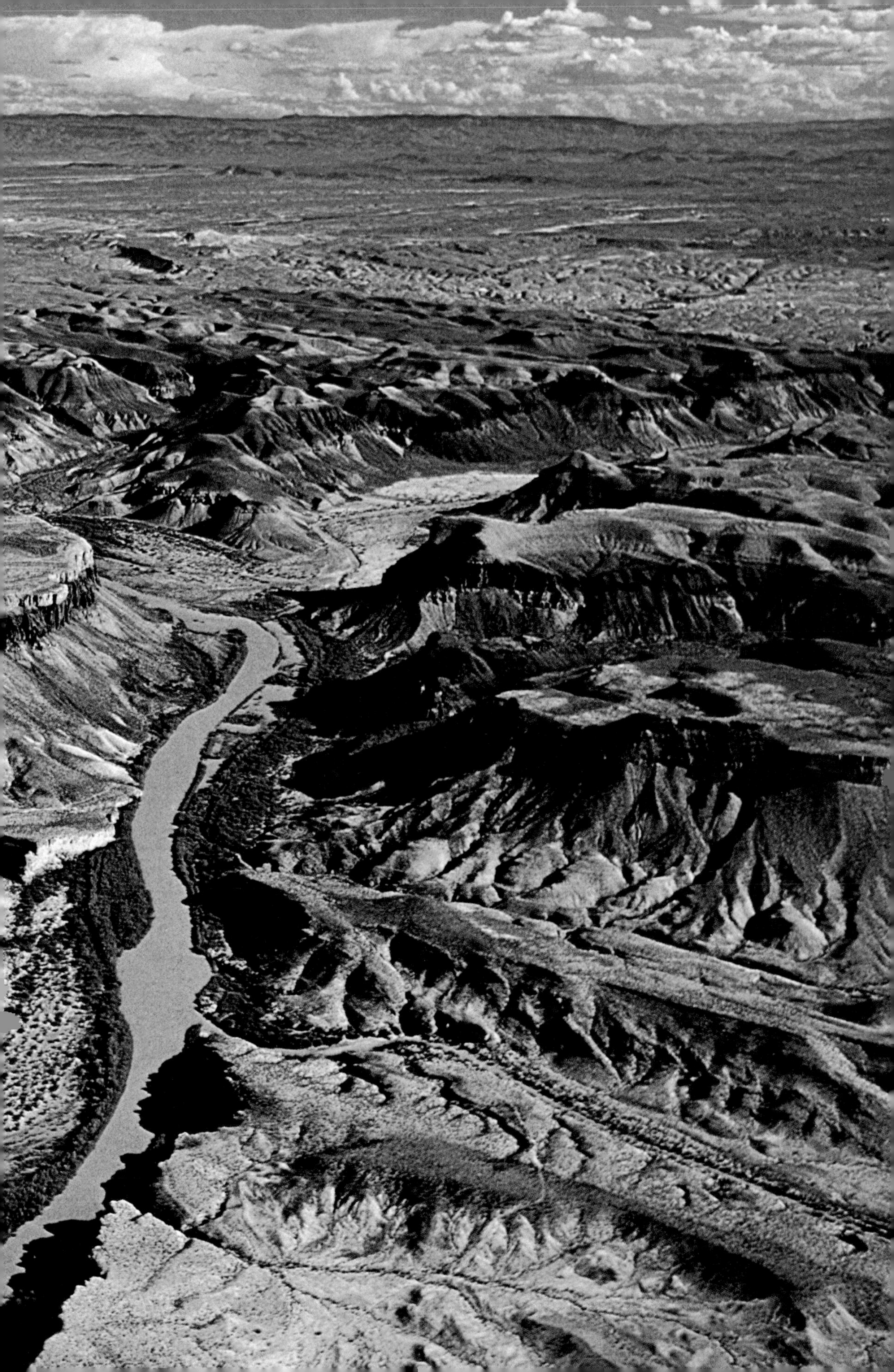

watchers. Mule deer, coyotes, badgers, bobcats, and an occasional cougar roam the parklands, as does the cranky, wild, pig-like javelina. And who but a Texan would boast of the park's 60 cactus species?

Ruggedness and isolation long have protected Big Bend's living things. Spanish conquistadors, fresh from triumphs in Mexico, never did succeed in exploring this part of the Rio Grande. Later adventurers failed too, until Robert T. Hill of the U. S. Geological Survey came along in 1899. Paddling ten hours a day, his party of six finally managed to penetrate the river's wildest canyons and gorges.

Violent men took refuge in these labyrinthine lands. Aside from Comanche warriors and the rustlers who escaped my father's posse, the Chisos offered sanctuary to train robbers, smugglers, revolutionaries—outlaws of all kinds. A gold mine lost, a damsel kidnaped, a rancher slain—such events are still remembered. Crusty Judge Roy Bean, "the law west of the Pecos," claimed dominion over Big Bend. Roving bands of Mexican desperadoes invaded U. S. territory here as late as 1916, looting a store and mine at Boquillas.

Times change. Rob and I found modern violence confined to a struggle of river against rock and to the colors of the high desert. For here nature balances upon contrasts. The great river nourishes a fertile strip along its banks; beneath cottonwoods, fishermen run trotlines for ten-pound catfish, and sometimes wade into Mexico. Lunarlike mesas nearby display the austere beauty of classic desert. And beyond stand the 7,800-foot Chisos peaks, abruptly cool and green.

Campgrounds in each environment give Big Bend year-round use. Roads and trails lead to places such as Burro Pass, Dagger Flat, Castolon, Green Gulch, and Santa Elena Canyon.

A sense of adventure endures here, too—on white-water float trips through echoing canyons; on rocky horse trails; along tree-shaded pathways. Those who trek into the backcountry are advised to carry drinking water and to watch for poisonous snakes. "There are no doctors or nurses in the park," visitors are warned. "Carry your own first-aid supplies."

Rob and I did whenever we hiked in dinosaur country north of Panther Junction. Paleontologists here recently discovered the remains of a reptile "with a pelvis the size of a Volkswagen," as one park interpreter put it. "He died on his back—with a tyrannosaurus tooth lodged in his ribs." Even then, it seems, this country saw its share of blood and violence.

On a big weekend, 2,000 or more people may crowd campgrounds from Rio Grande Village to Santa Elena. But few venture far beyond the roads. And if a water shortage someday curtails the number of visitors allowed in the park, Rob and I will gladly wait our turn to experience the backcountry solitude the park offers.

The moon rose full one evening—the true Comanche moon the Indians awaited for their regular river crossings. It had also risen full for geologist Hill and his exploring party during their river passage. From the canyon floor, he had watched the moonlight "gently settling from stratum to stratum.... I could never sleep until the glorious light had ... driven darkness from the canyon," he wrote.

Rob and I watched the same timeless shadow play. And we listened to an oldtimer who assured us, "Bright as the moon is tonight, you can bet your boots things are going on right now: smugglers, maybe some rustlers, and wetbacks crossing for sure."

I needn't have worried about coming back to Big Bend. It was as big and wild as ever.

Write Supt., Big Bend National Park, Tex. 79834

Fleet-footed roadrunner, a member of the cuckoo clan, holds its prize aloft. Mice, lizards, insects —even rattlesnakes—fall prey to this desert hunter that sprints to speeds of 15 miles an hour. Overleaf: *The Rio Grande sluices through a maze of sandstone hills at the park's western extremity.*

FARRELL GREHAN. OVERLEAF: JAMES L. STANFIELD, NATIONAL GEOGRAPHIC PHOTOGRAPHER

William Belknap, Jr.

White Sands

NATIONAL MONUMENT, NEW MEXICO

"Stay on the road, folks. Watch our speed limits," said the ranger as he handed us our permit, "and have fun!" We left the Spanish-style visitor center and set out to explore along the Loop Drive. The country looked flat and unpromising. Have fun doing what? I began to wonder if there would even be anything to photograph. My family and I, like most others who visit here, little suspected the breathtaking surprises in store.

But as we drove, my disappointment faded. Shimmering white dunes loomed ahead. Our 12-year-old son Buzz and our daughter Loie, 10, called a halt at the first drifts and shot from the car as if spring-ejected. They scampered up a slope, dropped to their knees, and scooped up great handfuls. Then the magic hit Fran and me. We ran our fingers through the incredibly soft stuff—cool, delightful. Off came our shoes and we raced up a snowy mound.

"I had no idea it could be this lovely," Fran said. "It's like fairyland!"

Enchantment, disbelief, puzzlement—ours were typical reactions to White Sands. We strolled along the roadside dunes, fascinated by the way desert plants—yuccas, sumacs, and even cottonwoods—fought to keep their heads above the sugary tide. Just sand? Not quite. It was like nothing we had ever seen, great rolling waves of it, white and fresh as a snowfall.

At the museum we learned that White Sands, located in a valley called the Tularosa Basin, displays a 228-square-mile deposit of gypsum sand. Utah and Australia have similar deserts, but neither rivals New Mexico's. Rain and melting snow dissolve gypsum beds in surrounding mountains; runoff collects in Lake Lucero, the basin's lowest point. Evaporation leaves selenite crystals, and the wind pulverizes and whirls them into gleaming patterns.

Moonlit sculpture carved by the wind enraptures visitors at White Sands. Composed of crystals from a dry lake bed and adjacent flats, spindrift piles to 50 feet in the world's largest gypsum desert.

CHARLES STEINHACKER

Surfers skim the dunes in New Mexico's mammoth sandpile, but plants dig deep and find a precarious foothold. Hardy species like the yucca grow tall—some to 30 feet—to escape the smothering tide. An earless lizard with lip scales to screen out the sand blends with its bleached desert domain.

ADAM WOOLFITT. OPPOSITE: WALTER MEAYERS EDWARDS

How does gypsum differ from ordinary beach sand? If you heat quartz sand, it melts into glass, but gypsum bakes into pure plaster of Paris. Soft gypsum rubs to powder between your fingers, and its transparent, wind-driven crystals will not pit the finish of your car. You can even taste the difference. Unlike sand, gypsum dissolves in water and has a definite flavor—mineral and unpleasant.

Late on our first day a windstorm arose, and we saw nature's construction force at work building the gypsum dunes. Curiosity sent us struggling up a powdery hillside. Amazingly, once on top we walked through the storm without getting sand in our eyes. The heavy gypsum travels as "bed load," rolling instead of flying. Braced against the blast, with heavy particles peppering our legs, we saw White Sands come to life. Wind undermined our foothold when we stood still, letting us sink slowly. Air turbulence started small dunes as we watched. Feet first, we slid down the steep dune—and got sandblasted as our faces passed the crest.

The park rangers have their hands full. Their job is a combination of protecting a natural wonder and helping visitors. "Traffic can be a problem," one ranger explained. "Some people disregard the no-dune-driving signs and get bogged down; others like to speed on the interdunal flats. It's best to stay on the road."

Perhaps the busiest Park Service man is the one who operates the road grader. The more the wind blows, the harder he works. "We used to fight the sand," he said. "Now we cooperate with it. If a dune wants to cover the road, we plow another route around it."

White Sands National Monument, completely surrounded by the White Sands Missile Range, lies 15 miles southwest of Alamogordo. The visitor center and picnic areas stay open all year. Sand surfboards can be rented, but bring your own water and wood or charcoal. Back-country campers must register.

Write Supt., Alamogordo, New Mex. 88310

Chiricahua

NATIONAL MONUMENT, ARIZONA

Rising abruptly from southeastern Arizona's golden desert, the Chiricahua Mountains look misplaced. Pine-oak forests on their flanks blend into spruce-fir woodlands on their crests; from a distance they resemble the purple-crested ranges of New England. And their tortuous canyons and grotesque rocks seem to belong to landscapes on the moon.

This 17-square-mile preserve is best seen up close. Then the pioneer name, "Wonderland of Rocks," snaps into focus as visitors drive the ten-mile Bonita Canyon Road to a sky-high view from Massai Point. Silent organ pipes of stone seem ready to echo a thunderous fugue along the way; the Sea Captain and China Boy look down in perpetual disdain. Imaginations can run wild among the sculptured rhyolite pinnacles, born of ancient volcanic ash deposits and shaped by countless centuries of erosion.

More than 15 miles of trails take hikers to such formations as Punch and Judy, a natural bridge, and balanced boulders that seem ready to crash from their eroded pedestals at a breath. Most trails wind through canyons where sharp-eyed visitors may spot the pig-like peccary and the unique Apache fox squirrel. The raccoon-like coatimundi forages in the deep gorges, and the Arizona white-tailed deer can be seen even around the Bonita Canyon campground, wandering through shady forests and open chaparral. Many plants and animals that abound in Mexico's Sierra Madre have established their northernmost outpost in the Chiricahuas, thriving aboard this rock-ribbed ark afloat on a sea of grass.

Once these canyons sheltered Chiricahua Apaches, fierce holdouts against land-hungry pioneers. Geronimo swept down with his raiding parties, then vanished among the stone hobgoblins. The Apache Kid and "Big Foot" Massai won respect as lone raiders. And Cochise Head, a mountaintop profile visible from the road, honors the clever chief who for years eluded troopers from nearby Fort Bowie.

Write Supt., Willcox, Ariz. 85643

Organ Pipe Cactus

NATIONAL MONUMENT, ARIZONA

The desert pulses with life as spring touches Arizona's Organ Pipe Cactus National Monument, a 516-square-mile preserve along the Mexican border. In March and April, if winter rains have been plentiful, Mexican goldpoppies, blue lupines, magenta owlclover, and a host of other wild flowers parade their colors with stunning brilliance.

Here, in an environment that encompasses three distinct desert ecosystems, flourish some 30 cactus species. They range from the giant saguaro to the miniscule fishhook and include the spiny plant from which the monument takes its name. The organ-pipe cactus, found in the United States only in south-central Arizona, may consist of 30 or more unbranched stalks clustered in a single plant that grows 20 feet high. In late May the tips of its fluted columns blossom with whitish, lavender-tinged flowers that open only at night. In midsummer its reddish, succulent fruit ripens, providing food for birds, small animals, and the Papago Indians whose reservation adjoins the monument's eastern boundary.

Bighorn sheep, mule deer, and the elusive peccary, a species also known as the javelina or musk hog, roam the stark, sun-blistered mountains, rocky canyons, and sweeping outwash plains called *bajadas*.

Gila woodpeckers drill nest holes in cactus boles and elf owls roost amid their spines. Coyotes howl—and campers feel that beyond the hiss of their cookstoves civilization, perhaps, has slipped centuries away.

From the visitor center, 17 miles south of the entrance on U. S. 85, two gravel roads loop into the backcountry. Twenty-one-mile Ajo Mountain Drive winds to the slopes of the monument's highest peak (4,808 feet) and offers outstanding views of cactus clumps. Puerto Blanco Drive, 51 miles, circles its namesake mountains and provides access to freshwater springs at Quitobaquito, where a desert pupfish species has survived since the close of the Ice Age.

Write Supt., Box 38, Ajo, Ariz. 85321

Sunlight haloes cholla (left), organ pipe, and sag

JOSEF M

Edwards Park

Petrified Forest

NATIONAL PARK, ARIZONA

As if dropped by a negligent giant, thousands of jewel-like logs lie scattered across the blistered, mile-high desert in northeastern Arizona. In the Triassic Age these were living trees. But 190 million years saw their wood turn to stone, glowing with rainbow colors. The world's biggest, brightest collection of petrified wood now clusters within the 147 square miles of Petrified Forest National Park.

The forest's northern section sits astride Interstate 40, tempting travelers to interrupt their journey for a look at one of nature's strangest revelations. I followed their lead. Like many visitors, I planned to spend an hour or two but ended up staying all day.

The shattered stone trees, like broken jackstraws, lie clumped in six areas. Paved roads lead to five of these forests, each with its special features. At Rainbow Forest, visitors wind through a garden of tumbled 160-foot trunks to snap pictures of Old Faithful, a sprawling monster that looks as if it crashed to the ground perhaps a dozen years ago. Actually, its gnarled trunk belongs to no familiar species—not even a dinosaur would recognize it. At Crystal Forest short logs seem to have been left for pulpwood. But no woodsman cut these glittering chunks. Petrified wood is as hard as steel.

"The only trees we don't have are upright ones, though we have found a few stumps," a ranger told me as I gazed at Jasper Forest's prostrate trees. He explained that they probably grew along a primeval river. Most were a long-extinct type of conifer. Falling from natural causes, they were swept off by floods and grounded here, in what was then a floodplain.

"These petrified trees have lost their branches and most of their bark," he added, "suggesting that they tumbled downstream and came to rest stripped of their boughs."

Stranded by an eternity of wind and rain nibbling the soft earth around it, a petrified log balances on a slender pedestal above Blue Mesa. In time it will topple and crash to the rocky ravines below.

DEWITT JONES

The stranded trunks were buried by sediments that in time hardened into a shale and sandstone layer called the Chinle Formation. The land sank. Then an upheaval, some 70 million years ago, produced the Rocky Mountains —and uplifted the 400-foot-thick Chinle high above sea level. Erosion laid bare some of the trees. But now they were stone.

The magic was performed by silica and other water-carried minerals that filled each wood cell, duplicating its structure like plaster in a cast. Over the centuries, details of the wood were retained. Traces of iron, manganese oxide, and carbon added color. At Rainbow Forest Museum, I saw cross sections of logs glowing with Arizona's brilliance: the deep reds and orange of sunrise, the purple of a thunderstorm, the blazing blue of the desert sky.

Where plain silica infiltrated the cells, the logs look exactly like yellowed trunks lying half-shattered and rotting. The scattered chips surely flew from an ax only yesterday. The grain stands out; splinters protrude. I picked up a sliver, expecting the spongy feel of old wood. But what I touched was cold stone, heavy, brittle, dry. Earthquakes caused the chipping and the fracturing that make many long trunks look as if they had been sawed.

Although in ages to come more agate wood will crop up as the Chinle wears down, the law imposes severe penalties for removing any of our present heritage of petrified wood. Rangers told me why. If each visitor should pick up just one piece and lug it home, there would be no Petrified Forest left for our grandchildren to see. But you needn't go away empty-handed.

Visitors frolicking on a fallen giant, one of the park's largest, discover in museum cross sections the petrified rainbows at the stony heart of these primal trees. Before protection came in 1906, gem hunters carted off whole logs, dynamited others seeking amethyst crystals. A proposed mill to crush the fossils into abrasives brought Government action.

WALTER MEAYERS EDWARDS. LOWER: DEWITT JONES

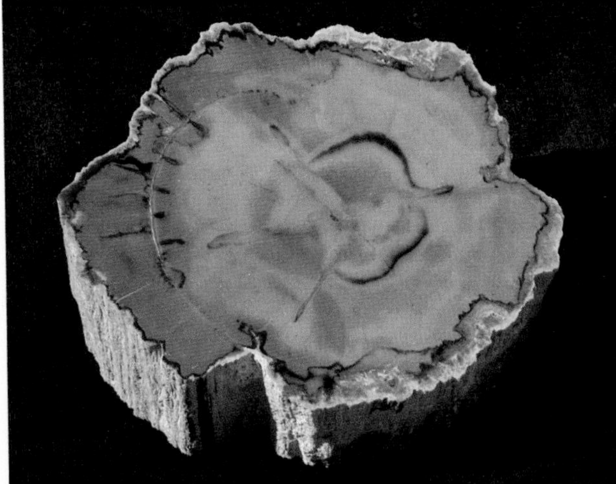

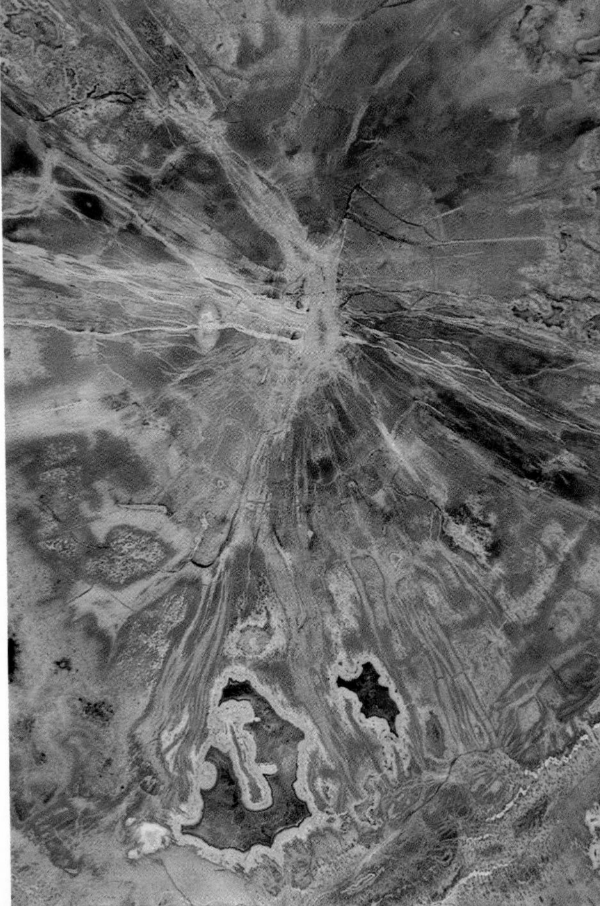

Petrified wood souvenirs from outside sources can be purchased at the concessions.

Part of the Painted Desert falls within Petrified Forest; a rim drive leads to views of eroded mesas extending to the northern horizon.

Indian ruins dot the park. Rainbow Forest's Agate House, made entirely of petrified chunks, once housed the ancients. On a hill overlooking the Puerco River stand the crumbling walls of a pueblo. Six hundred years ago it was a teeming village with 150 rooms. Nearby, petroglyphs cram Newspaper Rock.

Painted Desert Oasis and Rainbow Forest Lodge offer meals, gasoline, and souvenirs. You can picnic but not camp, and the road linking I-40 and 180 is closed at night. Nearest lodgings are at Holbrook, 26 miles west.

Write Supt., Holbrook, Ariz. 86025

Sunset Crater

NATIONAL MONUMENT, ARIZONA

The ranger pushed back his hat: "To get an idea why Sunset Crater is a national monument, put yourself in the year 1065. You're an Indian trying to farm these highlands east of the San Francisco peaks, Arizona's highest. You're worried by rumblings underfoot, so you and your family take off. Soon your farm blows sky high. The earth flames; rocks and cinders rain down. Lava oozes from cracks in your cornfield. When things cool off, you come back to find a newborn mountain—jet black."

The ranger swept his arm toward Sunset Crater, a 1,000-foot-high cone stained red and orange as though tinted by a setting sun.

"Many cornfields were smothered," he continued, "but the eruptions also touched off a land rush." Ash from the crater trapped rainfall. Returning Indians found new grass growing through the cinders. Soon others were arriving from all over the Southwest. Languages and customs mingled, dwellings and pueblos rose—like those preserved at nearby Walnut Canyon and Wupatki. But winds eventually stripped away the life-giving ash. Crop failures drove families from the again-barren land.

Today the crater looms above its lava field amid small spatter cones. Bonito Lava Flow curves from its base like an inky glacier. Knife-edged squeeze-ups show where hot lava was forced from cracks, then cooled upright. Ice formations within a series of crawlway-connected caves lure the adventurous (flashlights required) and are reached via the Lava Flow loop trail, an easy, 45-minute walk. The cone itself is closed to climbers.

Limited camping facilities are available adjacent to the five-square-mile monument, a half hour's drive north of Flagstaff.

To the northeast stretches the Painted Desert with its Navajo hogans and Hopi villages. The Hopis still look on Sunset Crater as the home of friendly spirits who see to it that Indian storerooms are crammed with corn—a legend easy to believe in this otherworld setting.

Write Supt., Flagstaff, Ariz. 86001

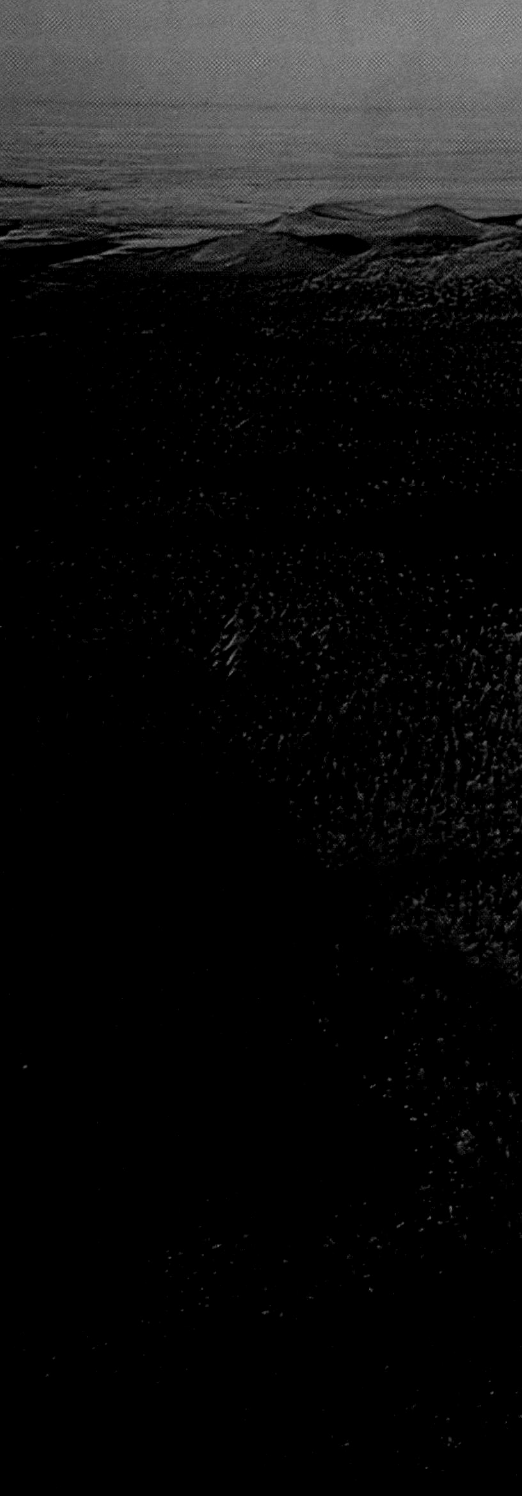

DAVID HISER

Sunset Crater, rising from a forest of pine, spewed ash over 800 square miles at birth.

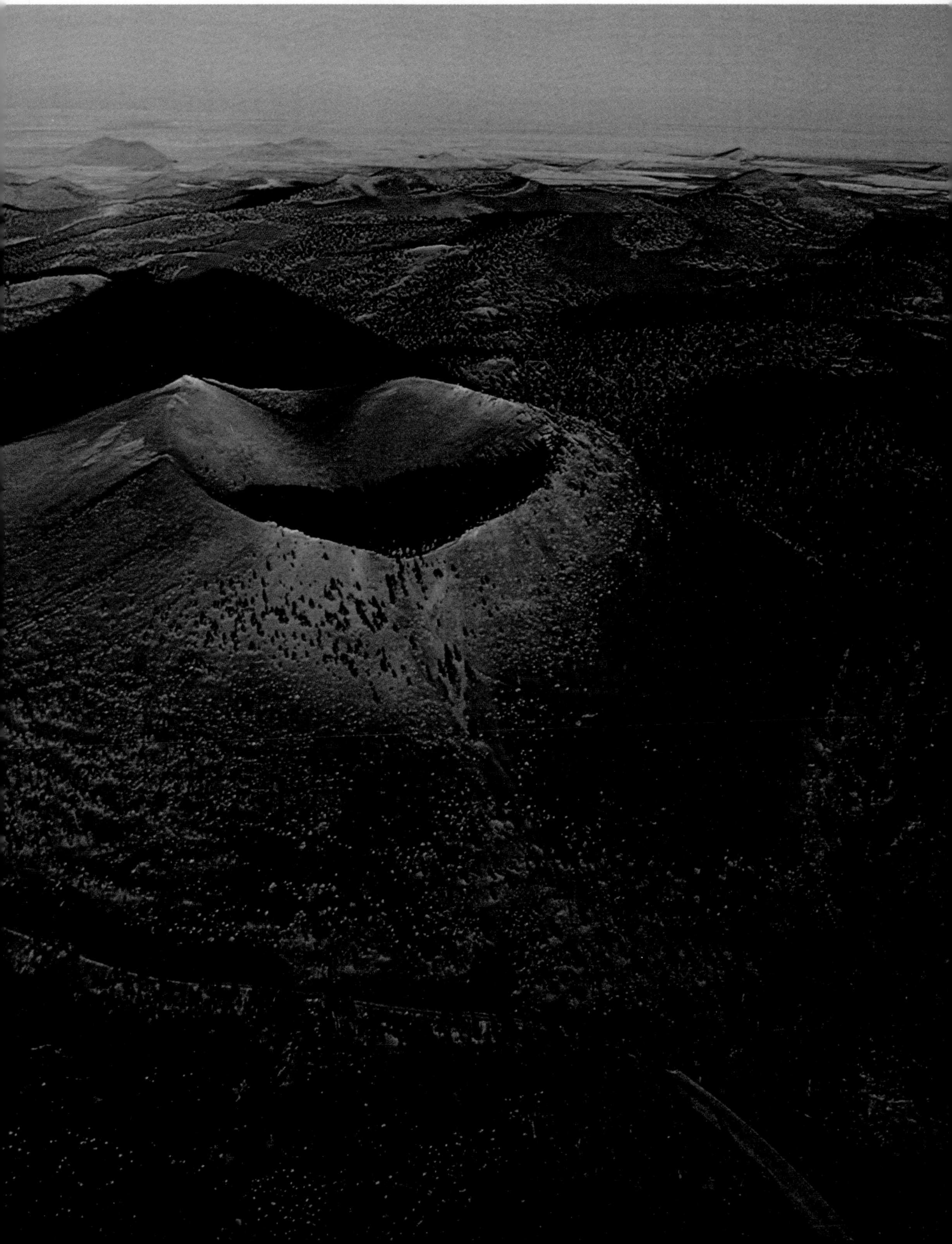

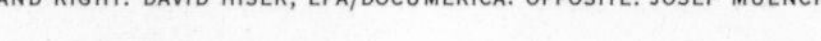

DAVID MUENCH. BELOW, LEFT AND RIGHT: DAVID HISER, EPA/DOCUMERICA. OPPOSITE: JOSEF MUENCH

Prickly-pear cactus

Hedgehog cac

Saguaro cactus

Saguaro

NATIONAL MONUMENT, ARIZONA

Strange armies of towering, gesturing figures stand rooted to the southern Arizona soil. For mile upon mile the majestic saguaros watch over the desert, brandishing their thorny arms above the 123-square-mile national monument that bears their name.

Mightiest of the nation's cacti, the saguaro—pronounced sa-WAH-ro—at five years of age is a puny pincushion. But it can grow 50 feet tall, sprout as many arms, and endure 200 years of heat, cold, drought, and downpour. After a rain its broad, shallow roots suck up huge quantities of water; its ribs swell like accordion pleats as spongelike tissue stores the moisture.

In the monument's two sections, these green giants stand in a patchwork carpet of cholla, prickly pear, and paloverde. Visitors to the monument's major area, 17 miles east of downtown Tucson, picnic amid a pastel desertscape abounding in wildlife or tour the nine-mile Cactus Forest loop road for a look at some of the area's grand old veterans. Hiking and horseback trails lead to a different world on 8,000-foot peaks robed in forests like Canada's. In a smaller section 16 miles west of Tucson, gravel roads cross a younger saguaro stand. Many visitors approaching this unit pause at the famed Arizona-Sonora Desert Museum for a close look at the plant and animal life for which the desert is home: lizard and deer, tortoise and coyote, cacti of every size and shape. The desert's story is told also in visitor centers in both sections of the monument.

For centuries Indians have foraged among the saguaro. Remnants of ancient campsites dot the desert, and here and there sharp eyes may spot petroglyphs. Today Papago Indians harvest crimson saguaro fruit as did their forebears; some they eat raw, some they make into cakes, syrup, candy, jam, and wine.
Write Supt., Box 17210, Tucson, Ariz. 85731

Giant saguaros stretch moisture-filled arms toward a sky that gives them little rain. In spring, cacti's colorful blossoms bless both desert and mountain.

Weather chiseled El Morro's buttress; centuries of wayfarers carved hundreds of inscriptions on its base.

El Morro

NATIONAL MONUMENT, NEW MEXICO

Rearing 200 feet above the western New Mexico plain, El Morro (The Headland) has beckoned generations of travelers, for at its foot gleams the desert's priceless treasure—a pool of water. Weary folk made camp beside it. Then they scratched their marks on the smooth face of this sandstone crest, scarring it with history in the raw. Indians cut pictures of hunts. Conquistadors carved haughty reports of triumph in the new land. Juan de Oñate, New Mexico's Spanish colonizer, left an engraved calling card dated "the 16th of April of 1605"—the oldest European inscription in the Southwest.

Today, signing El Morro is prohibited. But visitors to the 1,278-acre monument 58 miles southeast of Gallup may hike to the summit to inspect ancient Zuni ruins. Many search the rock for autographs of pioneer ancestors who reined up at the landmark, quenched their thirst, and gratefully signed the stone register.
Write Supt., Ramah, New Mex. 87321

Capulin Mountain

NATIONAL MONUMENT, NEW MEXICO

Some 7,000 years ago, northeastern New Mexico shook with volcanic eruptions. Frothy lava exploded from vents as trapped gases burst free. Blobs cooled to cinders as they landed around the vents, slowly building cones. Thus arose Capulin Mountain, a perfect example of one of these cinder cones, now preserved in a 775-acre monument 34 miles east of Raton.

Bluebells, daisies, and lupines paint the cone's black slopes, and near its 1,500-foot crest grow chokecherries, for which the Spanish gave Capulin its name. A good all-year road spirals to the top, where trails explore the rim and descend 415 feet to the crater floor.
Write Supt., Capulin, New Mex. 88414

Great Sand Dunes

NATIONAL MONUMENT, COLORADO

"This is one national monument where you can write your name all you want—in the sand, that is!" The superintendent of Great Sand Dunes enjoys dropping this remark to visitors whose graffiti-scrawling urges have been frustrated by "Do not deface" signs in other national park areas.

"Write it in letters a yard high! And put in your home town, if you like. The wind will erase it all by morning anyhow."

Here in southern Colorado, where desert meets mountain, the winds give and the winds take away. From the southwest, across the heat-hazed expanse of San Luis Valley they come, driving the loose sand along. As the winds funnel through a series of passes in the snow-capped, 14,000-foot Sangre de Cristo range, they lose velocity and drop their gritty burden at the base of the mountains.

After untold centuries, these sands of time have smothered some 50 square miles with crests soaring to 700 feet above the valley floor, highest dunes in the inland states.

The wind-sculptured sands are at their loveliest—and coolest—during the changing light of dusk or sunrise, when slanting rays cast shadows that dramatize the undulating troughs and crests. Visitors are encouraged to tramp and play to their heart's content—or to wade in Medano Creek before its waters vanish into the thirsty sand. A round-trip hike from the visitor center to the tallest dunes takes about three hours—sand-slogging is slow going! A visit during winter months may reward you with the added beauty of snow frosting the dunes.

Open all year, the 57-square-mile monument offers picnic and camping facilities. Guided tours and campfire lectures are held in summer. Alamosa, 36 miles to the southwest, provides overnight lodging for non-campers.
Write Supt., Box 60, Alamosa, Colo. 81101

Overleaf: *Waves of sand billow against the flanks of Colorado's Sangre de Cristo Mountains. Nomadic hunters ranged this remote valley 10,000 years ago.*

DAVID MUENCH. OVERLEAF: ED COOPER

David F. Robinson

Chaco Canyon

NATIONAL MONUMENT, NEW MEXICO

An insignificant turnoff led me out of the whooshing mainstream of Interstate 40 at Thoreau, New Mexico. East, north, east again, I followed a black stripe away from the world of man and machine. July heat in the 90's conjured a pond in every dip, but the thirsty desert drank each mirage before I could splash through. Ten brown miles of sand and sage blurred past. Twenty miles. Thirty. At forty a sign and pavement's end jerked my foot to the brake; from there a road that seemed little more than the scrape of a bulldozer blade led north for 25 miles to a broad, shallow canyon full of heat, silence, and emptiness.

I got out of my capsule of civilization and squinted through a veil of my own dust. The ride had seemed like anything but a pilgrimage to a great cultural center. But 1,000 years ago it would have been just that, a trip from the boondocks to the big city. Here before me lay the shell of Pueblo Bonito, the "beautiful village," a magnet for immigrants in the days of Indians we call the Anasazi—the Ancient Ones.

In the quiet of this haunted valley I could almost hear the bustle of the crowded pueblo in its heyday. Voices seemed to echo just ahead as I strolled through a doorway in its massive outer wall. They were discussing something....

"Cut!" someone called, and a here-we-go-again sigh rose from half a dozen throats. I had blundered into the filming of a television special by a station from faraway Boston. With proper good nature they accepted my apologies and invited me to watch—quietly—as the show's narrators resumed their discussion and the cameras devoured it all.

Some 70,000 visitors brave the bone-jarring roads to the canyon each year, many of them tarrying in a rather Spartan campground at the canyon's southeastern end. Tens of thousands

Pueblo Bonito spreads its ruined half-moon under Chaco Canyon's north rim. The desert citadel once sheltered about 1,000 Indians in 800 terraced rooms; its outer wall rose as high as five stories.

DAVID HISER

Tiny doorway in Pueblo Bonito's outer wall exacts a bow from entering tourists. Inside the massive rampart, they explore with ranger-guided groups or wander alone through the three-acre labyrinth. Adding on new rooms may have made old rooms stuffy; perhaps doors in line aided ventilation.

DAVID HISER

more would now visit from their easy chairs. Yet the stars of the show are absent; centuries before Columbus they played their last tragic scene. Then, exeunt—and no one knows why.

From the narrators, the exhibits in the visitor center, and the rangers conducting groups on tours, I pieced together the story of man in Chaco Canyon. Then I took a grandstand seat on the canyon rim and watched with mind's eye as the long tale unfolded.

Time's curtain rose on the virgin canyon of perhaps 7,000 years ago. It was a greener valley then; piñon and ponderosa were probably sprinkled about its floor, and a thin plant cover helped to hold the soil against the insistent surge of runoff from cloudbursts. Winters were cold, and ice in crannies of the canyon walls helped to lever away the great slabs of rock that now and then boomed onto the floor. But summers were warm and the soil was kind.

Enter the Indian. He probably came first in a small family band, wandering in quest of game and edible plants. But by the beginning of the Christian era the Indians of Chaco Canyon had settled down. Six or seven centuries later, new waves moved in; dim traces of their farming villages dot the long, low canyon and the mesa tops above.

Home to these sturdy planters was usually a round house of poles and mud over a sunken floor of earth. Basketry was their main craft; thus we call them Basketmakers. Gradually they began to build with stone, and to join one dwelling to another in apartment houses we call pueblos, from a Spanish word for village.

By the 11th century the culture of Chaco Canyon reached full flower. Corn was still the mainstay, but now the farmers tilled a new strain probably traded northward from Arizona and Mexico. And with the new corn had come the seeds of change. Architecture became more massive; ceremonial rooms called kivas grew from small hideaways to great round chambers of stone. Sprawling pueblos like Bonito dotted the canyon, each pulsing with life and always a-building. Lured by the promise of these growing centers, folk from the outlands flowed in. By the mid-12th century about 7,000 Indians peopled the area, perhaps the largest concentration in the prehistoric Southwest.

Suddenly they began to leave. The great pueblos echoed hollowly as room after room fell empty. By the end of the 13th century the canyon and its stone wonders were deserted. Drought, erosion, soil exhaustion, feud, disease —any might have quenched the flame once burning brightly here. But the Chacoans left no written records. And the stones speak no tales.

Enter the scientist, lured by the valley's promise as was the Indian of old. By his ingenious techniques and plain hard work he makes roof beams, pots, even stones reveal what they can of man in Chaco Canyon. The National Geographic Society began its excavations here in the 1920's, and today shares sponsorship

Its thumbprint chapped by time, a roof beam set in the stones of Pueblo Bonito links nature and history. Wide rings tell of good growth years, narrow rings bespeak years of drought or hardship. And the pattern they form fits only one time span, thus telling scientists when the tree lived and died.

Peering through a microscope, an expert at the University of Arizona's Laboratory of Tree-Ring Research measures the rings in a Douglas fir sample to the nearest hundredth of a millimeter. Patterns that stand out under high-intensity light are fed to a computer; from the printout a date can be given. To establish a continuous calendar, researchers matched the patterns in trees whose lifetimes had overlapped, working back in time by such comparisons until the record of a thousand years was laid out.

DAVID HISER. OPPOSITE: BRUCE DALE, NATIONAL GEOGRAPHIC PHOTOGRAPHER

Only in the Southwest have men built huge kivas like those of Chaco Canyon. Casa Rinconada dents Chaco's floor with its 64-foot-wide chamber. Resembling a giant keyhole, it defies experts to unlock secrets of ceremonies that unfolded inside.

DAVID HISER

of a project spanning more than a dozen years.

Dr. Thomas R. Lyons of the National Park Service was several years into the project when I talked with him after my visit. From his office at the University of New Mexico—a partner in the project—he spoke about what is called remote sensing, which may include photos taken by anything from satellites to hot-air balloons. Dr. Lyons and his colleagues have traced ancient flood-control canals and mapped some 200 miles of roads.

And what roads! They were only footpaths, since Chacoans had neither wheeled vehicles nor horses, yet some stretch 20, 30, even 40 feet wide. "A good guess," Dr. Lyons mused, "is that these were make-work projects to keep farmers busy during times of plenty. The Egyptians built pyramids; maybe the Chacoans built boulevards." And maybe some of the boulevards linked pueblos to other bustling centers up to 60 miles away—an Indian "interstate" of a thousand years ago. (When my visit ended I would wish for such a road as I jounced and fishtailed northward out of the monument on roads no better than those I'd endured coming in from the south.)

Enter the visitor. Most archeological digs offer us only a glimpse into a cross-section trench. But at Pueblo Bonito and more than a dozen other large ruins in this eight-mile stretch of canyon, we can stoop and enter rooms where Indians lived, see corncobs and stone grinding mills they left behind, peer into kivas and imagine the intricate rites they knew.

The sun was climbing down from its perch as I hiked down from mine. Shadows stretched across the plazas; roofless rooms and kivas yawned in bold relief. The camera crew had ended the day's intricate rites and were packing up their artifacts. Months later, back in Boston, they would make this day live again.

If only they could make the days of the Anasazi live again—now *that* would be a show.

Write Supt., Bloomfield, New Mex. 87413

David F. Robinson

Mesa Verde

NATIONAL PARK, COLORADO

On a snowy day in December, 1888, two cowboys rode across little-known Mesa Verde, the "Green Table" rising out of the southwest corner of Colorado. Canyons carve the broad tabletop into smaller mesas; on the edge of one we now call Chapin Mesa, Richard Wetherill jerked his horse to a stop.

"Charlie, look at that!" He pointed. Charles Mason's eyes went wide. Across the canyon a silent stone city lay sheltered by an enormous cave. Stone houses, piled story upon story, rose to the arched cave roof. It looked like a cliff palace, and thus the two men named it. If not for swirling snowflakes, they might have been amazed many times over, for nine more ruins lay cold and silent within their range of vision.

If Mason and Wetherill returned today—spurring four-wheeled steeds up a cliff-hung drive off U. S. 160 near Cortez—they would find the ruins preserved and partly restored. In a museum and a visitor center they could see what science has learned about the ancient residents through archeology, early accounts, and modern Indian traditions. They could clamber up and down steep trails, ladders, and timeworn toeholds cut in rock, to view the sites close up and fire queries at guides—some of them Ute Indians whose adjoining tribal park will preserve more ruins along the Mancos River.

If the cowboys could have stood here two and a half centuries before Columbus, quite a different scene would have unfolded—a scene recreated by former park archeologist Don Watson and other experts. Hundreds of Indians lived in Cliff Palace then, sheltered from enemies and elements. On courts and terraced housetops women bent over cooking fires. Old men and women toasted their aching bones and talked of bygone days when "things were better." Young women and girls reduced brightly colored corn to precious meal on grinding stones called *metates*. The constant rasping of stones was made bearable by the melodious grinding songs. At times, chanting priests in underground kivas added a deep undertone.

At Balcony House, an adobe-paved court spreads beneath another cave's vaulted roof. On three sides stand beautifully built two-story houses; along their upper stories run narrow walks, or balconies, that lead from one door to the next. Along the fourth side of the court runs a low wall that kept toddlers from tumbling 700 feet downslope to the canyon floor. In the rear of the cave a seep fills a pool of clear, cold water. Each family had a few simple, rectangular rooms for a home. Here Mesa Verdeans slept and stored their possessions.

The floors of these rooms seldom exceed eight by ten feet. Few dwellings have window openings. The doors average approximately 16 by 24 inches, and the sills rise two or three feet above the floor. Some walls are plastered; a few display paintings in red and white.

The pole-and-adobe roofs often sit so low that a person of average height today cannot stand completely upright in the room. Perhaps the Mesa Verdeans could. Judging from the bones found here, and from modern pueblo dwellers—who number the Mesa Verdeans among their forebears—we can visualize these

Climb through time takes father and son up a cliff that shelters Balcony House, the 13th-century home of Indians who labored up toeholds like these to tend mesa-top fields, then down again to eat, sleep, and worship in cliffside citadels of stone. Hundreds of ruins spanning seven centuries sprinkle Mesa Verde; the exact number is still unknown.

DAVID HISER

Indians as short and stocky, with bronze skins, straight black hair, prominent cheekbones, and somewhat slanted eyes.

Small storage rooms, often no more than bins, nestle in odd nooks and crannies. Once these were used to store corn, beans, and squash between harvests. Balcony House also has two kivas. These circular, subterranean chambers served as men's clubs and workshops as well as ritual centers; a small hatchway in the open courtyard above was the only visible indication that a compartment lay below.

Seven or eight centuries ago, Balcony House—like Cliff Palace and hundreds of other pueblos built on the mesa and under its overhangs—was a simple farming hamlet. Perhaps 35 to 40 people lived in Balcony House then. During the growing season men scrambled up and down toeholds cut in the cliff to tend crops on the great green mesa above. Craft work took up much of their remaining time: spinning and looming cotton, chipping arrowheads, crafting blankets by twining yucca cords wrapped in turkey feathers.

The women shaped pottery by hand; the potter's wheel was unknown. From plants and minerals they concocted paints. When firing was complete, only a heap of ashes could be seen, but from within those ashes came black-on-white pottery of superlative beauty—mugs, pitchers, ladles, canteens, jars, and bowls, gracefully shaped and artistically decorated.

The men produced cloth, weapons, tools, and the all-important ceremonial objects: sashes, prayer sticks, rattles, and the other trappings of ritual by which the life-giving rains could be assured. Each man could make any of these, but probably some preferred to specialize. Here lived a flint chipper, there a rope maker, across the court a weaver. Exchange of goods was by bartering, often by gambling. Knots of men could be seen betting on some game of chance, staking arrowheads against sandals, a blanket against a necklace. Beads were

Indians of Cliff Palace brace for winter, A.D. *1250. Workers mend a wall, hoist materials up a ceremonial tower, haul corn to overhead bins, cut squash in coils to dry on sticks. Hard times emptied this town of 250 people but left an impressive ruin (overleaf).*

PAINTING BY PETER BIANCHI. OVERLEAF: FARRELL GREHAN

In pithouses (below), then pueblos, workers refined their arts. In baskets, then pottery (opposite) made from coils of clay, they kept the staples of life—corn gruel, stew, water dipped from potholes. Now the vessels hold secrets for students (left) of a people who made the commonplace beautiful.
DAVID HISER

highly prized; an inch of them might buy a bow.

The sun, rising over the opposite canyon rim, awakened Balcony House. After a simple breakfast of corn bread, villagers went to their tasks. Women changed the juniper-bark diapers of their babies, bound the infants to their cradleboards, and hung them on the ends of roof poles to swing in the breeze. Long days with their heads strapped to the cradleboard flattened the backs of the infants' skulls; every cliff dweller bore the deformity for life.

The turkey had been domesticated, probably less for meat than for feathers used in blankets. In the morning the turkey flock was driven out of the cave to feed along the slopes. Children and dogs swarmed over the canyon, making life chancy for squirrels and chipmunks. When the sun grew too warm, the men left their fields

Visitors walk the walls of Sun Temple, stone enigma on Chapin Mesa. Its outer walls and nine of 24 rooms lack doors; cliff dwellers who built it—probably for rituals—entered from above. Free bus and mini-train take tourists to more wonders on Wetherill Mesa.

DAVID HISER

and dozed in the shade or worked at their crafts. With luck, the hunters might bring home a deer or even a mountain sheep.

At the elaborate evening meal, some version of corn bread baked on flat stone griddles was inevitable, with perhaps a thick stew, or some green corn, or a pot of green beans. Venison roasted over hot coals was a delicacy; a fat prairie dog or a grouse brought happy exclamations from the hungry diners.

Each family gathered in a tight little circle around its steaming pot. Fingers dipped in recklessly. It was a noisy meal—the better the food, the more finger-sucking and lip-smacking. After it was over, a deep, rumbling belch from each of the diners complimented the cook.

Near the end of the 13th century the gods turned their backs on these industrious people. For 24 years the crop-soaking downpours dwindled. Plants withered in the fields, springs dried up, game deserted the hunting grounds. Possibly nomads plagued the famine-weakened farmers. Turning from their homes at last, families drifted southeastward to better lands, where their descendants live in pueblos today. Soon every pueblo and cliff dwelling on Mesa Verde fell silent. Only the wail of the coyote and the mournful call of the owl echoed through the canyons.

Centuries passed. Stone fell from stone, adobe crumbled, roof beams gave way. Sand sifted in on the wind, and seeds blew in to take root in it. Some of what the Indians left behind was lost to time and the elements, but much was preserved, sealed in silt and sheltered under the mesa's beetling brows.

Other Indians gradually filtered into the area. Their tribal memories do not identify the builders whose empty citadels they found. And so the first Mesa Verdeans came to be called simply the Anasazi—the Ancient Ones.

More centuries passed, and finally the white man came on the scene. In 1874 a U. S. Geological Survey team discovered the first

Like Indians who built Long House, visitors puff up pole ladders to penthouses and granaries. Most queries bring answers, and some a grin, from rangers. Among those still unanswered: Why did Indians flee the mesas to crowd into cliff-edge caves?
DAVID HISER

cliff dwelling; 14 years later Wetherill and Mason spotted Cliff Palace, Spruce Tree House, and Square Tower House. Soon Mesa Verde's treasures began to disappear. Archeologists collected artifacts for museums in this country and abroad. And local people invaded the ruins, searching for pots.

Millions of visitors have poured through this popular park since it was established in 1906. Such numbers challenge the ingenuity of the staff in keeping the fragile ruins of Chapin Mesa from being trampled to dust. Fortunately there are other cliff houses—silent, remote, seldom visited over the years—on Wetherill Mesa, three miles to the west. And here opportunities for study and preservation are better.

In 1958 the National Park Service, with major grants from the National Geographic Society,, launched the Wetherill Mesa Archeological Project, one of the most thorough in the history of the United States. Teams of specialists are still excavating, restoring, and peering into prehistory through the compound lens of more than 30 different sciences.

Boring down to ancient underlying soils, they discovered evidence of severe water erosion, possibly aggravated by wind, that might have resulted in a disaster like the Midwest Dust Bowl of the 1930's. They also uncovered a pile of hardened clay patties that the cliff dwellers had prefabricated and stored, while the clay was soft, for later use as mortar in building the mud-and-stone walls.

Analyzing fecal matter some 700 years old, chemists found that these Indians consumed nearly anything that could be used as food, but

were gradually finding less and less to eat. Other experts analyzed the growth rings in ancient beams by means of a dendrograph, an instrument which measures otherwise imperceptible changes in a tree's diameter. Comparing the rings with a "calendar" of known growth patterns for good and bad growing years down through the centuries, they were able to fix dates ranging from A.D. 650 for several mesa-top ruins to 1280 for the latest timber found in Long House, the grandest of all Wetherill Mesa sites.

Long House truly deserves its name; it has 150 rooms and stretches 295 feet along its canyon wall. It has 21 kivas, plus one great kiva—a ratio of one kiva to seven rooms, well above that of most of the other cliff dwellings. This suggests that people from the smaller houses atop the mesa had crowded into the sheltered village; each group or clan probably required its own kiva. Ceremonies in these small chambers were private affairs, open only to family members and invited guests, and sometimes open only to men. Rites involving large groups or the entire village were conducted in the single great kiva.

Long House ranks second in size to the 200-room Cliff Palace—which may have had still more rooms before its upper stories collapsed. But until recently it was impossible even to estimate the number of rooms in Long House, so thoroughly had the early treasure seekers dismantled it. Spurred by the high prices offered for artifacts—Wetherill and his brothers sold one trove for $3,000—droves of "prospectors" shoveled, pried, and even blasted their way through ruin after ruin. A local banker grubstaked some of them in return for a percentage of their sales.

In the rubble of Long House, modern excavators found a dynamite fuse, a souvenir of men who overlooked the most priceless treasure of all—the ruins themselves. Today visitors tour the newly opened Long House and marvel that so much remains: multistory apartment units with walls built to conform to the cave's irregular ceiling, granaries tucked into ledges high overhead, deep gouges worn in solid rock by Indians sharpening crude stone tools.

A mile to the north, Mug House clings to the rim of Rock Canyon. It yielded some 430 mugs, pots, bowls, and jars—far more artifacts than were found in the much larger Long House.

From Far View Visitor Center, as many as 500 people a day can board free buses for the 40-minute ride to Wetherill Mesa; there a mini-train takes them to cliff's edge where they must descend by trail to the opened sites. Other areas remain closed to visitors as scientists probe for secrets from the forgotten past.

Here and there on the mesas of this 52,000-acre tableland, shed roofs and sprawling tarps protect the scientists' current digs. Though the most striking ruins are the great cliff dwellings, it is on the mesa tops above them that the experts read the story of Mesa Verde's earliest inhabitants.

Here the first arrivals began to sink roots in about the seventh century; for their skill in basketry we call them Basketmakers. They planted crops and lived in pit houses, simple but serviceable shelters of poles, interwoven sticks, and mud built over a shallow pit. In the 12th century the mesa was heavily populated; we find the ruins of stone and adobe pueblos, water reservoirs, granaries, and mysterious ceremonial "temples" dotting the tabletop. Then for some reason the people took to the caves—and after a century of ingenious home-building, they vanished.

And so the Mesa Verde story takes shape as clue joins clue. The scientists do far more than dig; they preserve, wherever possible, for visitors to see and enjoy at first hand, year round. Thousands make a visit to prehistory each year; some visit for a day, others bed down in Morfield Campground or, in warmer months, at Far View Lodge for a longer look at one of the great outdoor museums of the world.

Write Supt., Mesa Verde NP, Colo. 81330

JAMES P. BLAIR, NATIONAL GEOGRAPHIC PHOTOGRAPHER

The Golden West

Giant sequoias, largest of living things, stretch trunks—and belief.

Ross Bennett

Yosemite

NATIONAL PARK, CALIFORNIA

Ahwahnee, "deep, grassy valley," the Indians called it. "The greatest marvel of the continent," trumpeted journalist Horace Greeley. "The most beautiful place in the world," said Teddy Roosevelt. But it took lyrical John Muir to capture the essence of Yosemite Valley, a glacier-carved pocket seven miles long and a mile wide in California's Sierra Nevada. Setting out from San Francisco 150 miles to the west, the naturalist walked into the valley a century ago, lost himself in its embrace, and sang its raptures for 40 years:

"Every rock in its walls seems to glow with life. Some lean back in majestic repose; others, absolutely sheer . . . for thousands of feet, advance beyond their companions in thoughtful attitudes. . . . Awful in stern, immovable majesty, how softly these rocks are adorned . . . a thousand flowers leaning confidingly against their feet, bathed in floods of water. . . ."

Muir died in 1914, but if he were alive today would he grieve or rejoice over his beloved Yosemite? Seemingly cut off from the world, the valley is only a crease in greater Yosemite National Park's 790,000 acres of High Sierra splendor and lower level giant sequoia groves. Yet in recent decades the valley has been deluged with mounting tides of people. As the 1970's rolled around, I watched with some concern the annual visitation figures top two million. How well, I wondered, was Yosemite holding up under the impact of all those feet and the vehicles that brought them.

Driving in from the west on a summer weekday, my family and I coasted down beside the sparkling Merced River onto the valley road. It was strangely free of traffic. During our previous visit in the 1960's the road had crawled with vehicles inching along like a giant metal serpent ready to expire from its own noxious vapors. Now, except for a couple of cars, a

Yosemite Valley and the Merced River greet a misty dawn. Gently clothed in meadows, pines, firs, and oaks, the basin once felt the rasp of glaciers.

DEWITT JONES

truck camper, and a pair of wobbling bicyclists swiveling their heads up at the rocky titans, the valley seemed almost deserted.

We gave the cyclists a wide berth and zigzagged a bit ourselves, soaking up the magic of hanging glens tasseled by waterfalls. Ahead, Bridalveil Fall, 620 feet high, "clad in gauzy, sun-sifted spray, half falling, half floating," danced in the wind below the crags of Cathedral Rocks. Catch it right and you can watch the afternoon rainbow climb its misty column.

On the left loomed El Capitan, its 3,500-foot vertical granite wall a favorite of veteran rock-climbers. We craned for that first glimpse of 2,425-foot Yosemite Falls, of brooding Half Dome, of Glacier Point. Up there, high on the valley rim, we would later look out across Merced Canyon to Vernal and Nevada falls spilling down the Giant Stairway.

Burrowing deeper into the valley, we saw growing crowds of people but not much traffic. Where were all the cars? The question nagged as we rolled past family campgrounds and teeming Yosemite Village. When we pulled into rustic Yosemite Lodge I got my answer.

That's where all the cars were. In the parking lots and not out cruising the road. We soon saw why. Up to the lodge glided a three-unit minibus filled with people. Families with small children. Older couples festooned with cameras and binoculars. Kids in souvenir sweatshirts that commanded in big letters "Go Climb A Rock." And, weighted down with backpacks and guitars, tanned and shaggy youngsters—but no shaggier, really, than Muir himself.

Everyone spilled out, bumping shoulders and gear with a marvelous lack of hostility.

Lured from cars by a shuttle bus, motorists tour the valley in sight of Yosemite Falls, king of its many cascades. At their thunderous best in spring, nearly all dry up by summer's end. Nonpolluting pedalers on the one-way loop road wear vests for visibility.

DEAN CONGER, NATIONAL GEOGRAPHIC PHOTOGRAPHER

Fluted Vernal Fall rushes the Merced down a 317-foot step of the Giant Stairway to the valley floor. Hikers who reach it on the Mist Trail enjoy a refreshing spray. In the high country, swimmers find a Tuolumne River pool cools them quicker.

DEWITT JONES AND (BELOW) DICK ROWAN

Fascinated, we watched the bus swallow up a similar cargo and whisper away on propane gas toward Yosemite Village. There, visitors transfer to double-deck buses that make the short loop run to Happy Isles Trail Center, the stables, Indian Caves, and Mirror Lake.

"We call our buses the three F's—free, frequent, and fun," the superintendent explained one day as my two young daughters rode them around and around and around. "They reduce pollution and traffic jams, and they let dad enjoy a relaxed view of the valley. You noticed we made the valley road one-way? That discourages a lot of unnecessary driving."

On a summer weekend some 40,000 people invade what Muir deemed a mountain mansion of natural treasures. They spill into the meadows and woods, scale the cliffs up well-beaten paths, or, as my gangly son did, scramble to the brushy cliff benches for unexpected wildlife lessons. "I reached for this ledge," Nick breathlessly reported, "and almost shook hands with a rattlesnake!"

Wise visitors pick up a *Yosemite Guide,* the park newspaper. It lists programs designed to reach all ages, all tastes—ecology float trips on the Merced, dawn bird stalks, plant walks around Mirror Lake, night wildlife prowls, stargazing sessions on Glacier Point, Indian walks to learn the valley's human past.

In 1851 the Mariposa Battalion "discovered" the valley while rounding up Indians suspected of raiding mining communities on the Sierra slopes. Before that, Chief Tenaya and his tribe had Ahwahnee all to themselves. They numbered some 200 (one clan called themselves the Grizzlies, or Uzumati, hence Yosemite) and dressed the land in legends. One story about Half Dome told how the Great Spirit, angry at a love-sick chief for neglecting his people, rained devastation on the chief's throne atop the rock, splitting the dome asunder.

Half Dome's formation wasn't that simple for white men, and controversy raged. Geologist Josiah Whitney insisted the bottom fell out of the mountains, forming the valley and crumbling part of the dome. He scoffed at Muir's glacial theory, that rivers of ice flowing past the north side of the dome sliced it away. Today, scientists agree the scraping action was helped by exfoliation—surface rock cracking in onion-like layers as the granite expands. My wife, Vera, calls it geological dandruff.

The dandruff is not confined to Half Dome. One morning we drove from the 4,000-foot level

of the valley floor to the high country for a taste of wilderness. As we skirted lesser domes on the cross-park Tioga Road, we cast wary eyes at rugsize, foot-thick slabs of rock that seemed ready to slide down onto the highway.

Finally, at 8,600 feet, the "broad, velvet lawns" of Tuolumne Meadows spread before us. Off to one side bubbled Soda Springs. Pleasant-tasting waters charged with carbonic acid made the springs a favorite campsite in the old days. Around a fire there one night in 1889, Muir proposed to his influential companion, Robert Underwood Johnson of *Century Magazine,* the preservation of this high country as a national park. A year later Congress created the park and in 1906 included Yosemite Valley, which had been protected until then as a state park.

We sipped the bubbles at Soda Springs, took on provisions at the little Tuolumne store, and trooped down the dusty trail toward Glen Aulin. It's one of five High Sierra camps spaced a day's hike apart well beyond the reach of wheeled vehicles. For hikers who don't want to backpack, the camps provide a bed with sheets, in a dormitory tent, and food.

Our hike, however, would be a day trip, five miles in and five miles back before sundown—we hoped. Leaving flower-flecked Tuolumne Meadows behind, we wound from glade to glade through piney woods. So far we seemed to be the only hikers on the trail. Suddenly the path vanished on a vast granite field bare of vegetation. We stopped, searching for direction. Though the field was strewn with erratics—rocks left by retreating glaciers 10,000 years ago—it looked as trackless as a desert.

Hesitantly, we ventured forth. If we found our way across, would we be able to find our way back? Then we spotted the "ducks," small stacks of rocks obviously placed as trail markers, and forged ahead with lighter steps.

Two rest stops and a canteen of water farther along, we joined the Tuolumne River. Here it picked up speed on its journey to the Grand Canyon of the Tuolumne and eventual capture

Swing your partner in an old-fashioned hoedown at the visitor center—if your feet can take it after a day on the trails. Children held captive by marshmallows and Indian lore learn the ways of the Ahwahneechee, who stored acorns, their main staple, in chuck-ahs, *thatched caches on poles. Indians used bedrock mortar holes to grind nuts for meal.* Overleaf: *Downhill skiers get a lift in winter at Badger Pass on the Glacier Point road. Marked ski-touring trails also start here.*

DEAN CONGER, NATIONAL GEOGRAPHIC PHOTOGRAPHER. OVERLEAF: GALEN ROWELL

Indian paintbrush crimsons Tuolumne Meadows in Yosemite's high country, a place ideal for dozing with your boots off, talking to birds with your flute, or counting the ubiquitous Belding ground squirrel. More energetic visitors scale surrounding granite domes polished to glistening smoothness millenniums ago by 2,000-foot-deep glaciers. A two-hour ride from the valley via the Big Oak Flat and Tioga roads, the meadows launch hikers onto trails. At camps along a 60-mile loop, food and a bed await for a daily fee; summer finds the traffic heavy and camp reservations a must. Beyond main trails lie miles of lonely grandeur for the backpacker. Overnighters must have permits.

DEWITT JONES

by O'Shaughnessy Dam. Completed in 1925 to supply San Francisco with power and water, the dam flooded Hetch Hetchy Valley. The Sierra Club, led by Muir, fought for years to save this smaller version of Yosemite Valley, but to no avail. The loss still rankles members.

The last quarter-mile of trail to Glen Aulin High Sierra camp plunged tortuously down rocks worn smooth by a small glacier of humanity. Though we had met only a dozen hikers the whole trip, here on a wooded slope fit only for mountain goats we suddenly landed in a traffic jam. A mule train of five trail riders overtook us. Flattening our backs against a small cliff, we watched the mules tiptoe past, testing each foothold. A woman rider, clutching her saddle with both hands, smiled bravely in greeting and said, "I'd still rather ride."

Less sure-footed than the mules, we slid on down the trail and puffed into Glen Aulin. That's Gaelic for Happy Glen. We'll happily endorse the name, for the cluster of tents below a foaming cascade was a welcome sight. Backcountry use in Yosemite has skyrocketed recently—up to a quarter of a million overnight stays a year—and we knew that scores of iron-legged hikers were scattered over the area in search of solitude. Yet I couldn't help feeling a sense of isolation, and I asked the camp manager, a college student, if anyone ever got lost out here away from "civilization."

"There's a 13-year-old boy missing right now," he said. "Got separated from his party yesterday. Probably fell behind and took a wrong turn. But he was well equipped with camping gear. He'll most likely turn up along some trail." Sure

enough, the next day he walked out into the meadows. In the meantime, on our own trek back, I mended a couple of crippled ducks as we recrossed that field of granite.

"One must labor for beauty as for bread," wrote Muir. Indefatigably, recklessly, he probed every canyon, recorded every mist-borne rainbow on every waterfall—or so it seems from his detailed accounts.

At the foot of Yosemite Falls, we assumed with other pilgrims the standard valley posture—head back, hand shading the eyes. Somewhere up there one night long ago Muir edged along a narrow bench behind the falls to view the moon through the spray. The wind suddenly shifted and the full force of the water swept in and pounded him to his knees. Carefully he retreated from that brush with death, "better, not worse, for my hard midnight bath."

Half Dome's flaky visor juts into eternity 4,800 feet above Tenaya Canyon. The cleft monolith (top), as seen from Glacier Point, hides the 700-foot cable ladder up its far side. Overleaf: *Doing it the hard way, experts on the sheer face 400 feet from the top "climb clean," anchoring ropes with removable wedges instead of driving in rock-damaging pitons.*

OPPOSITE AND OVERLEAF: GALEN ROWELL. RIGHT: BOB RONEY.
TOP: DEAN CONGER, NATIONAL GEOGRAPHIC PHOTOGRAPHER

Memories golden as a sunrise at Tioga Pass fill the visitor who takes the time to explore Yosemite National Park's many mansions. Asked by a hurried traveler what he would do if he had only one day to see the park, a ranger replied, "I'd weep."

GALEN ROWELL

Down at the park road I set off through the pines in search of the spot where Muir, in 1869, had built a cabin. It took a while to find the memorial boulder in a tiny cathedral of trees. A bronze plaque recorded his words: "Climb the mountains and get their good tidings. Nature's peace will flow into you as sunshine flows into trees. The winds will blow their own freshness into you, and the storms their energy, while cares will drop off like autumn leaves."

Healing advice, that. Good for generations to come—even if all those generations come to Yosemite. For a reassuring thought struck me the next day when we stopped at the popular Wawona Tunnel turnout for one last backward look at the valley. Eager millions could smother Muir's mountain mansion, yet a century of visitors hadn't been able to humble the monuments he hymned. They still stood—immovable, majestic, their feet among the flowers.

YOSEMITE NATIONAL PARK

Area 1,189 square miles

Features: *Glacier-sculptured Sierra wilderness. Leaping waterfalls, sheer-walled Yosemite Valley, Grand Canyon of the Tuolumne. Three groves of giant sequoias; 295 bird and mammal species.*

Activities: *Visitor center, Yosemite Village; Happy Isles Nature Center. 251 miles of scenic roads, 783 miles of trails. High Sierra pack and hiking trips (wilderness permits required). Horses at valley, Wawona, Tuolumne Meadows. Fishing (Calif. license). Nature walks, campfire programs, junior rangers (ages 7-13). Pioneer History Center at Wawona. Rock climbing. In winter, ice skating at Curry Village; downhill and cross-country skiing at Badger Pass.*

Weather: *Summer days pleasant, nights cool. Valley elev. 4,000 ft.; Tuolumne Meadows 8,600 ft.*

How to get there: *From west, Calif. 140. South, Calif. 41. East, Calif. 120 (over Tioga Pass, 9,941 ft.; closed in winter). See insert map. Southern Pacific, Santa Fe Ry., United Airlines to Fresno or Merced, Calif.; TWA to Fresno; bus or rental car to park.*

Accommodations: *Hotels and lodges (two open all year), cabins, tents. High Sierra dormitory tents. Write Yosemite Park and Curry Co., at park. Camp and trailer grounds crowded June-Sept.*

Write Supt., Yosemite National Park, Calif. 95389

Drakes Beach strollers comb sands that may hold the secret of Francis Drake's visit in 1579.

Point Reyes

NATIONAL SEASHORE, CALIFORNIA

It rears out of the Pacific mist like some mysterious land apart. And in fact Point Reyes Peninsula, an easy drive north of San Francisco, is a geologic orphan. Adjoining the mainland along the San Andreas Fault, the peninsula has moved more than 300 miles northward over the last 80 million years. It advances in occasional leaps, like the one in 1906 when an earthquake jolted the land as much as 21 feet forward and devastated San Francisco.

The 100-square-mile national seashore, which covers most of the peninsula, preserves a wild, haunting beauty: forests of lichen-draped oaks and firs, grassy meadows, dizzy promontories, sandy beaches. Shorebirds dance with breakers below dunes whipped into ever-changing shapes by wind and water. Sea lions bark from surf-bashed rocks at the peninsula's apex, where a lighthouse (below) was built in 1870 to warn ships away from the foggy headland.

Inland, cows graze beside the Sir Francis Drake Highway, which runs from park headquarters near Olema to the apex. Centuries

DEWITT JONES

ago Coast Miwok Indians built villages on these rolling uplands, speared fish from the sea, hunted deer and gathered nuts in the forests. A peaceful people, they probably welcomed Drake in 1579, for some scholars say it was here, under high cliffs resembling those of Dover, that the explorer careened the *Golden Hind* for repairs and claimed "Nova Albion" for England. In 1603 the Spaniard Sebastian Vizcaino anchored near the promontory and gave it its royal name, La Punta de los Reyes.

Today's explorers, picnickers, and surf fishers can drive on public roads through a pastoral zone to five beaches: McClures, Point Reyes North and South (all facing the open sea), and Drakes Beach and Limantour on Drakes Bay, the only areas where surf is gentle enough for swimming. Summertime shuttle buses from headquarters make regular runs to the bay.

In the southern part of the preserve, hikers fan out from park headquarters on 100 miles of trails, including the Earthquake Trail along the San Andreas Fault. A popular hike follows the Bear Valley Trail 4½ miles to the sea, winding gently through forests fragrant with California bay and across flower-strewn Divide Meadow. (A bicycle can be ridden all the way.) Hikers seeking greater challenge scramble to the windy top of 1,407-foot Mount Wittenberg, highest point on the peninsula.

There are no drive-in campgrounds in the park; backpackers head for four hike-in camps. Reservations should be made.

From the coastal camps you can spend days exploring sand pockets, tide pools, and sea arches. The Coast Trail takes you to such treats as the Sea Tunnel, a tide-hewn passageway through the rocky cliff to a 100-foot-high chamber. Offshore, skin divers probe for abalone.

All the southern beaches flood at high tide, so plan your day accordingly. Carry a canteen and take charcoal or stove—no wood fires are allowed. It's a good idea to stay on the trails, unless you're immune to poison oak.

Write Supt., Point Reyes, Calif. 94956

Muir Woods

NATIONAL MONUMENT, CALIFORNIA

"Come to the woods, for here is rest," said John Muir, and what better place than this lovely haven just north of San Francisco—a 550-acre virgin stand of coast redwoods, *Sequoia sempervirens.* Like *Sequoiadendron giganteum,* it has rosy wood, but it is taller and slimmer than its massive cousin in the Sierra Nevada.

John Muir loved them both, as he did all wild things. He could not bear to see man wipe out in a day what nature took millenniums to produce. No doubt, he said at his soft-spoken, sarcastic best, the sequoias "would make good lumber after passing through a sawmill, as George Washington after passing through the hands of a French cook would have made good food." His writings crystallized public sentiment in favor of saving our natural heritage.

In 1905 Congressman William Kent purchased this valley of redwoods, saving it from the ax, and gave it to the nation. Nearly a million people a year now come to the monument, to walk quietly among the trees and to remember that our parkland riches are the legacy of men who fought hard for an ideal.

Write Supt., Mill Valley, Calif. 94941

DAVID MUENCH

Towering giants of Muir Woods dwarf delicate redwood sorrel (opposite).

Pinnacles

NATIONAL MONUMENT, CALIFORNIA

Approached on country roads through rolling hills, the pinnacles appear suddenly on the horizon, a jagged, out-of-place skyline that calls the traveler to stop and investigate.

A graphic lesson in geology awaits. These timeworn, 1,000-foot-high peaks were piled up by volcanic eruptions some 23 million years ago. Then the earth's crust shifted along the San Andreas Fault, tearing the volcanic rock in half. Ever since, the land west of the rift has inched northward, advancing a total of 195 miles, while land to the east stands fast. Someday the pinnacles may become separated from the mainland—in about six million years.

Visitors to the monument's 23 square miles find both gentle and rugged trails winding the slopes. A favorite is the Moses Spring Nature Trail, an easy stroll past lichen-splashed canyon walls, fern-filled grottoes, and rocky outcroppings eroded into weird and wonderful shapes. A prime example of Coast Range chaparral—rugged, water-saving shrubs—overhangs the path. The trail ends at a small reservoir, in spring an idyllic setting of bubbling brooks, masses of monkey flowers and shooting stars, and plenty of rocks to sit on for a pocket picnic. Those armed with a flashlight can return by way of the Bear Gulch Caves, a dark, narrow, boulder-canopied canyon.

Longer, higher, and more difficult trails lead to spectacular views of Pinnacle Rocks and Chalone Peaks. Here rock-climbers find a satisfying variety of challenges to their skills, and stealthy hikers may sight deer, foxes, or even a rare mountain lion. Golden eagles, falcons, and turkey vultures soar overhead, and bats dart through the evening skies.

The monument, open all year, provides campgrounds on both sides of the peaks. Campers heading for tent or trailer sites on the east side provision at nearby Hollister or King City; the western approach road via Soledad is too narrow for trailers. Bring your own fuel; the mantle of brush produces no wood to spare.
Write Supt., Paicines, Calif. 95043

Devils Postpile

NATIONAL MONUMENT, CALIFORNIA

Gold-hunting prospectors and restless pioneers were the first white men to make note of this 900-foot-long colonnade of basalt rising 200 feet out of the eastern California forest. To them, the sight was otherworldly; they called it Devils Postpile. Early naturalists wondered at its origin, and so do visitors today as they arrive at the 798-acre preserve from U. S. 395 along the base of the Sierra Nevada.

Geologists say a volcanic fissure spewed lava here perhaps 900,000 years ago. As the deep river of liquid rock cooled, it cracked, leaving splinters 2 feet thick and 40 to 60 feet high. The columns vary in shape—some have four sides, others as many as seven. Later, glaciers planed away the top of this freak formation and quarried out a vertical face which exposed the remaining posts. Sightseers mounting the easy trail remark that the surface looks like a huge mosaic or tile inlay.

Once part of Yosemite but now under supervision of Sequoia and Kings Canyon national parks, this monument 7,560 feet above the sea offers a surprising variety of activities. In summer you can picnic, fish in the Middle Fork of the San Joaquin River (license required if more than 16 years of age), hike along the John Muir Trail, even visit a soda spring that bubbles with naturally charged water, the makings for free soda pop.

From the Postpile, it's a two-mile hike to Rainbow Fall, where the 60-foot-wide river leaps to a green pool 140 feet below and at midday wears a rainbow. Tread carefully above the gorge and on the steep trail to the bottom. The reward is worth the effort: a grotto of pines and hemlocks, alders and willows, grasses and flowers. You can drive to within a mile and a quarter of the fall on the road to Reds Meadow lodge and store just outside the monument. Full services are offered there, and pack and saddle horses may be rented.

A campground near the ranger station inside the monument is open June 15 to October 15.
Write Supt., Three Rivers, Calif. 93271

Devils Postpile builds a talus slope of tumbled lava colu

DAV

Death Valley

NATIONAL MONUMENT, CALIFORNIA-NEVADA

Tomesha, the Panamint Indians called it: "Ground Afire." At the height of summer there is no better name for this sun-tortured trench between blistered ranges. But when a group of forty-niners blundered into it, they renamed it Death Valley.

Drive in from the east through Death Valley Junction to get an inkling of how those people felt. Short-cutting from Salt Lake City to the California goldfields, they had crossed a weary succession of deserts and hills. At last they came to a range, seemingly topped by a peak flying a banner of snow. Surely these must be the Sierras! They flung themselves at the bald mountains, wrenched their groaning wagons through the washes and gullies, then stared in numb despair at the trick nature had played.

Miles yet from the Sierras, they stood amid the Amargosa Range. Between them and the peak whose snow had lured them—11,049-foot Telescope Peak, high point of the Panamint Range—spread a desolate sink, four to 16 miles wide, mostly below sea level. Rather than turn back, the half-starved forty-niners decided to cross the salt-crusted, lava-smeared plain.

Thus the trap snapped on them.

Struggling to break out of this arid trough, the gold-seekers had little eye for scenic riches that half a million visitors enjoy each year. The monument extends 120 miles from south of Saratoga Springs, one of many water sources the forty-niners failed to find, to north of Ubehebe Crater, where an eruption shook the land early in the Christian era. At the Racetrack, a 3,708-foot-high dry lake southwest of the crater, visitors puzzle over stones that weigh as much as 39 pounds and move mysteriously across the clay floor, leaving visible trails. The most likely explanation: a combination of powerful winds and a moisture-slick surface.

Driving along the valley floor, you can spend

Mile-high Dantes View looks down on the inferno of Death Valley, 282 feet below sea level. In the west, Telescope Peak raises a snowy head.

DAVID HISER

Girl Scouts pick their way across Devils Golf Course, a vast sink of salt crystals left by an evaporated Ice Age lake. To the north, borax "haystacks" of the 20-mule-team era rest where Chinese laborers scraped the mineral into mounds for loading on wagons. You have to search for the palm-size banded gecko, one of 17 lizard species in the area. Look for it under rocks, but beware of lurking rattlers.

DAVID HISER

the night at Furnace Creek with its irrigated date palms, its inn and ranch, its tennis courts and swimming pool. Here the Jayhawkers, one of the emigrant parties, scrabbled for water. You may park beside the Devils Golf Course, a strange rubble of crystalline salt pinnacles and gravels stretching ten miles down the valley. This bed of an Ice Age lake blocked the Bennett-Arcane party of forty-niners when they sought escape to the south. The road skirts close under the Panamints where those desperate men and women clawed their way out of the valley, then looked back on it and cursed it with a lasting name—Death Valley.

It was a bitter name, and not entirely a just one, for there is life here. The kit fox, coyote, and bobcat pad across the desert at night. Rabbits and ground squirrels scurry through the mesquite. Pupfish, living fossils from the Ice Age, survive in saline creeks and pools. Some 600 kinds of plants thrive; burroweed

Brays rend the air as male wild burros battle for territory in the Panamint Range. Descendants of pack animals lost or abandoned by Spanish padres and grizzled prospectors, about 10,000 roam western lands. The burros threaten the native desert bighorn sheep by devouring vegetation and fouling water holes.

and creosote bush even sink roots among the sand dunes near Stove Pipe Wells.

Except in summer, when temperatures climb to a blistering 120°, Death Valley's climate smiles on man by day and treats him to technicolor sunsets as lowering rays play on mineral-stained hills. Nights are cool.

It took the ubiquitous prospector to discover that the place was livable. Legend has it that one of the forty-niners, searching for the gunsight accidentally knocked from his rifle, found a chunk of rich silver ore. His story brought miners with their burros; more than 1,500 feral descendants of those beasts now roam the monument. Though no one ever located the "Lost Gunsight Mine," other strikes were made. Boom towns sprouted, howled on Saturday nights, then withered away, leaving slag heaps of broken bottles.

In 1880 a destitute couple, trying to scrape a living from the desert, learned of borax's value in making pottery and what its deposits look like. Aaron Winters thought he might have seen some in the valley. With his wife, Rosie, he hurried to the place, carrying chemicals for a test. Kneeling, he poured alcohol and sulphuric acid on the white powder, then set it ablaze.

"She burns green, Rosie," he cried. "We're rich!" And for years, the 20-mule teams hauled tons of borax on the ten-day, 165-mile desert trek to the railhead at Mojave. About two miles north of Furnace Creek, crumbling adobe walls and the rusty hulks of boilers are all that remain of the Harmony Borax Works, where the mineral was refined and loaded onto wagons. Some of the originals can be seen at a museum at Furnace Creek Ranch—rear wheels stand seven feet high, and 16-foot-long beds each held 24,000 pounds of borax. A team pulled two wagons, plus a 1,200-gallon water wagon.

The mule trains rolled through heat and sandstorm, summer and winter, until richer discoveries in the mountains ended borax mining on the salt flats before the end of the century. Mining continues within the monument today, and huge trucks haul hundreds of thousands of tons of lump ore from an open pit near Dantes View.

Just inside the northern boundary of the monument, amid the desolation of Grapevine Canyon, Scottys Castle rises like a mirage, with crenelated towers, Spanish-tile roofs, latticed Moorish windows. In the baronial living hall, where water trickling down a wall helps cool the room, a huge wrought-iron chandelier hangs from a 50-foot-high ceiling. Oil paintings and tapestries cover walls and balcony railings.

Walter Scott, a former trick rider in Buffalo Bill's Wild West Show, hit the 1905 headlines when he emerged from Death Valley with padlocked sacks of gold. He scattered bills like confetti on Los Angeles streets, and hired a train for a record run to Chicago. For years he fostered the legend that a hidden gold mine kept his pockets jingling. Actually, a millionaire friend set up Scotty for laughs and built this fabulous home in the 1920's for $2,000,000. It shows off an opulence completely foreign to its surroundings. If those sun-struck forty-niners had seen it, they wouldn't have believed it.

DEATH VALLEY NATIONAL MONUMENT

Area 2,981 square miles.

Features: *Desert showplace in "North America's basement"; lowest point in hemisphere.*

Activities: *Visitor center at Furnace Creek; illustrated talks, guided walks, and auto trips. Roads lead to Dantes View, Panamint overlooks, sand dunes, borax works, Ubehebe Crater. Scottys Castle (admission fee). Trails up Mosaic Canyon and Telescope Peak. Horses at Furnace Creek. High country hikes.*

Season: *Most activities Oct. 15-May 1 (weather is pleasant). Roads open all year.*

How to get there: *Highways through monument intersect U.S. 95, 91, 395. By air to Las Vegas, Nev., where cars can be rented. Airstrips in monument for private planes.*

Accommodations: *Oct.-May: Furnace Creek Inn and Ranch, Stove Pipe Wells Hotel; limited services in summer. All year: camp and trailer grounds.*

For information write Supt., Death Valley, Calif. 92328

IRA S. LERNER

Joshua Tree

NATIONAL MONUMENT, CALIFORNIA

Grotesque, outstretched arms, seeming to point to a promised land, reminded westward-trekking Mormons of Joshua at prayer—hence the name Joshua tree. Ranging up to 40 feet high, this overgrown member of the lily family lives—who knows?—perhaps 500 years. It produces no telltale rings of age.

In southern California, where the Colorado and Mojave deserts meet at the Little San Bernardino Mountains, 872 square miles have been set aside to protect this shaggy plant. From monument headquarters at Twentynine Palms on State Route 62, the road runs south toward U. S. 60, following a gently rising plateau. Cholla cacti and scarlet-tipped ocotillos give way to Mojave yuccas; Joshua trees take hold around 3,000 feet. Swing west for Jumbo Rocks and a geology auto tour. Then drive on to Salton View at 5,185 feet, where the land suddenly tumbles away to reveal distant Salton Sea, 232 feet below sea level. Plan to camp. Maybe you'll be lucky enough to spot nocturnal wildlife—coyotes, kangaroo rats, ground squirrels, desert bighorn sheep. Take water, firewood (dead wood is protected), and warm clothes—even summer nights are nippy.

Write Supt., Twentynine Palms, Calif. 92277

DAVID MUENCH

Joshua trees, silhouetted by a sunset, brighten the desert with blossoms in March and April.

Anacapa Island's chain of peaks sweeps five miles through the Pacific.

ROBERT B. EVANS

Channel Islands

NATIONAL MONUMENT, CALIFORNIA

Pounding surf, sweeping winds, and rugged terrain belie a fragile ecosystem on the Santa Barbara Channel Islands, peaks of coastal mountains that slipped into the sea a million years ago. Such endangered species as the brown pelican and the torrey pine find haven here, along with the unique Channel Island fox.

Established as a refuge for marine animals and nesting seabirds, the monument embraces two of the islands, Anacapa and Santa Barbara. Human visitors find amenities nonexistent: no food, water, fuel, or services. Yet rich rewards await those who brave the channel chop in a charter boat from Ventura. Western gulls scream around the cliffs. Elephant seals and California sea lions bark from cove and beach. Tide pools, sea caves, and water-carved rock formations invite exploration. Trails lead to high meadows spectacular in midwinter with the golden blossoms of giant coreopsis.

Anacapa, itself a 700-acre island chain, lies ten miles from shore. Sheer volcanic cliffs and rocky beaches make it almost inaccessible, but landings can be made at Frenchy's Cove, which has a picnic area, and on East Island, where camping is permitted near the Coast Guard lighthouse. Rangers stay on Anacapa year round. Primitive camping is allowed also on 650-acre Santa Barbara Island, 40 miles to the south and 40 miles from the coast.

For information write Supt., 1699 Anchors Way Drive, Ventura, Calif. 93030

Once-rare elephant seal is making a comeback.

John M. Kauffmann

Sequoia Kings Canyon

NATIONAL PARKS, CALIFORNIA

The highway writhed and coiled up the Sierra Nevada ramparts. Behind, drenched in June sunshine, lay California's San Joaquin Valley; ahead beckoned the hazy, tumbled ridges of Sequoia National Park. Up this canyon of the brawling Kaweah River, Indians a century ago led a rancher along dim trails to see an incredible wonder—the giant sequoia trees, largest of living things. Now more than a million visitors a year drive these heights.

I rounded a bend and caught my breath. Before me stood the Four Guardsmen, immense sequoias flanking the roadway like pillars of a city gate. Cinnamon-red trunks rose massively amid the green. I parked and walked over to a group of trees. An auto passed; its driver said, grinning, "You look like a midget!"

He was right. In the Giant Forest we are all Gullivers in a Brobdingnagian world. I found the Sentinel Tree watching over hundreds of other Gullivers gazing skyward. "Relax, youngsters," the old tree seemed to say. "Your lives are short enough. Enjoy them!"

I joined a stream of human ants circling the General Sherman, most massive and one of the oldest living things, surpassed in age only by bristlecone pines. I wondered how many tons of tree towered here, high as the Capitol dome in Washington, D. C. Some say 2,000—enough wood to build 40 five-room houses. The 272-foot trunk is nearly 37 feet in diameter.

"I feel so . . . infinitesimal," murmured a young woman as she looked upward.

"I feel like a youngster," replied a white-haired grandmother with a twinkle in her eye.

Egypt was conquering an empire when the Sherman sprouted some 3,000 years ago. The tree was a thriving adult in the Golden Age of Greece. And on a winter's night when a great star blazed over Bethlehem, this tree stood straight and tall, more than 1,000 years old.

The *Sequoia* genus, born in the Mesozoic era more than 100 million years ago, once thrived throughout the Northern Hemisphere. The Ice Age wiped out most of it. *Sequoiadendron giganteum,* a Sierra Nevada native, survived in high basins sheltered from glaciers. The more widespread *Sequoia sempervirens,* or coast redwood, remained only along the mild shores of California and southern Oregon. In the mid-1940's *Metasequoia glyptostroboides,* the "dawn redwood," hitherto known only in fossil form, was found still growing in China.

Next to the Giant Forest, Grant Grove in Kings Canyon is the best known and most accessible of the two parks' numerous sequoia stands. The General Grant Tree, second in size to the General Sherman, is thought by many to be even more impressive and has been designated a national shrine by Congress in honor of this country's war dead.

Late that afternoon I raised my tent where the long light of sunset would filter through the pine boughs of Lodgepole Campground. No sooner had I unpacked than the welcoming committee

Noble sequoias loom like pillars of a cathedral, their crowns mantled in the mists of Giant Forest. The President, soaring 230 feet, presides over Senate and House groves along the Congress Trail.

DAVID MUENCH

arrived: inquisitive robin, bumptious chipmunk, and truculent jay, panhandlers all. The jay hopped onto my table, scolding for food.

At suppertime the forest filled with fragrant wood smoke, children's laughter, faint notes of a guitar. Families gathered, each united in primeval comfort around its evening fire. Birds began to sing, flute answering tiny flute in trilling antiphony—elfin music sung to giants.

Crash! I recognized what rangers call the "Trash Can Symphony." Bears were busy at the receptacles in search of tidbits. A mother bear and cub shuffled by. I knew they wouldn't harm me if I didn't molest or feed them, so I settled back against a tree to read by lantern light.

During the night I was awakened by the sound of galloping paws, of a great body passing overhead, and of tearing canvas. I gazed up at the stars. I had pitched my tent in Bear Alley, and bruin, frightened away from a midnight snack, had taken his usual escape route. Next day I moved what remained of the tent to a safer site.

A coyote chorus was my dawn alarm clock, and a delegation of deer trotted by to see that I was making the most of the morning.

"Climb the mountains and get their good tidings!" Alta Peak, rising northeast of the Giant Forest, seemed to echo John Muir's exhortation. A friend and I shouldered packs one day and plunged into red-fir forests. Above timberline we panted onto Alta's snow-splotched summit to gaze upon an endless world of mountains. From north to south the Great Western Divide sawed the sky. One summit far beyond must be 14,495-foot Mount Whitney, high point of the Sierra Nevada—the Snowy Range.

Since most of the snowfall melts away in summer, Muir, I thought, had a better name: The Range of Light. Dawn turns its peaks into

The westering sun silhouettes a ragged troupe of Sierra peaks, as seen from Moro Rock (opposite) in Sequoia National Park. "It is a sight well worth the climb up 456 dizzying steps from Giant Forest," notes the author, formerly a ranger here.
DEWITT JONES

pinnacles of pearl. The midday sun shimmers across the pale rocks with blinding intensity. The light mellows as afternoon wanes, and at sunset the cliffs blaze with alpenglow.

Sequoia and Kings Canyon national parks are so large one can hike or ride for days in the span of a single watershed. More than 900 miles of backcountry trails lure nearly 40,000 visitors each summer. But some trails and campsites have become so popular that their use has had to be curtailed. Several campgrounds have been eliminated and the number of hikers and riders permitted on trails through Taboose, Sawmill, Baxter, and other passes is limited to what fragile environments can bear.

Soon my friend and I were off to the mountains again, this time with ranger acquaintances on a three-day, 40-mile hike deep into Kings Canyon National Park. Our first objective was the Tableland, the vast plateau that divides the Kaweah and Kings River watersheds. On this 11,000-foot-high desert of granite, men feel as insignificant as insects—and perhaps a bit closer to God because of it.

A dragon-headed crag scowled down at us as we toiled up bench after bench, mile after mile, past pools of snow water. Let no one say that the Tableland is flat. Convinced that each domed horizon was our last, we reached it only to find another crest ahead. Our hopes came true with a suddenness that made us gulp. Before us, a glacier-dredged canyon yawned so deep that the stream watering its meadows seemed a silver thread in a ribbon of green.

Here stretched our route, we thought, and sat down with tired relief. But the rangers seemed puzzled. They consulted map and compass. "Wrong canyon," they announced.

We had veered too far north, but a short walk eastward put us back on course. Another canyon opened, and below us a tarn gleamed with the blue-green color of a tourmaline. We clambered down into Deadman Canyon, named for a sheepherder who fell ill and died there in 1875. Six miles beyond, we reached our destination—Roaring River ranger station at Scaffold Meadow. Although the names Deadman Canyon and Scaffold Meadow have given rise to tales of murder and frontier justice, the scaffold refers to nothing more than an old food cache built high to foil marauding animals.

The more I ventured, the more I longed to push deeper into the Sierra fastness. For, as John Muir wrote, "There is a love of wild nature in everybody, an ancient mother love showing itself whether recognized or no...."

On a subsequent trip into the heart of Kings Canyon country, a ranger friend and I began at Florence Lake a few miles northwest of the park. Here our pack mules sighed stoically at our pile of duffel, and my companion's horse made friends with the mountain-wise mare I had rented for the trip. We would not see a road again during our five-day, 90-mile journey.

Beyond Blaney Meadows we swung onto the John Muir Trail. The most famous in the Sierra, it begins in Yosemite and follows the mountain chain south for more than 200 miles. We were welcomed to the Evolution Basin country inside the park by a thundering waterfall and a shout from another ranger who had ridden down to meet us. We spent the night with him and his family, in a tiny cabin 14 miles from a road, swapping tales of adventure.

In the morning our horses' hoofs crunched through hoarfrost along the trail to Evolution Lake, named for Darwin's famous doctrine. But evolution has a sound and sense to it that could apply to all High Sierra country. Heaved up eons ago, scoured and plucked and polished in the geologic yesterday of glacial times, it is primeval country as yet unprepared for man. Glacial remnants still cling to mountainsides,

Born on the flanks of 13,000-foot mountains, South Fork of the Kings River cuts a foaming swath through Kings Canyon National Park. Awesome peaks and chasms of the twin parks lie within an easy day's drive of San Francisco or Los Angeles.

DAVID MUENCH

vegetation struggles for survival, while snow clouds and a chill breeze remind us that at 10,000 feet summer is a fleeting thing.

No comparable wilderness matches this High Sierra district of the twin parks for visitor use, for it is a convenient wilderness, close to one of the nation's largest and fastest growing population centers, Los Angeles.

During our trip, we encountered scores of outdoorsmen and women. Some families included campers so young they were carried papoose-fashion; one pig-tailed six-year-old strode down the trail carrying her own hefty little packsack. There were Scouts, too, and rock-climbers and fishermen. At Wanda Lake an angler showed me a catch of golden trout, the most sublime of fish, the Sierra's own native glory. Long ago the waters must have trapped the reflections of a sunset and transformed them into living things.

We paused at a stone shelter on the bleak, 12,000-foot summit of Muir Pass. Snow flurries spat on us, and we descended into Le Conte Canyon. What stupendous, incredible country! Hour after hour our horses picked their way down rocks and snow, slipping, hopping, into the abyss. Wind ruffled the sapphire surface of Helen Lake. Clouds scudded over Black Giant. And we plunged downward again.

Next day we started for Dusy Basin and Bishop Pass. We had hoped to mount the pass, to stand astride California's rooftree, but another storm sent us from the heights to the shelter of Grouse Meadows. We now headed down the Middle Fork of the Kings River toward Simpson Meadow. Far below us the river boiled among the rocks. Above the canyon rim we glimpsed the jagged Devils Crags.

Although frequented by fishermen, Simpson Meadow is not now traveled as much as the higher regions along the Muir Trail. But in old times? A ranger we met here showed us potholes in the bedrock where Indian women had ground their meal. Crude stone pestles were still in place and flakes of black, glass-like obsidian lay scattered nearby.

Only 23 miles of trail now lay between us and the roadhead at Copper Creek, six miles east of Cedar Grove in Kings Canyon. But what a 23 miles! All morning the trail climbed a mountain's shoulders. To our right we caught sight of the park's most poetically named body of water—the Lake of the Fallen Moon.

Atop Granite Pass, we first saw the Kings Canyon panorama of peaks and gorges, and beyond the granite basin we started down. It took all afternoon—5,000 feet, down, down, down into the South Fork canyon. In places the abyss plunges nearly 8,000 feet from mountaintop to riverbed. So measured, Kings Canyon ranks among the deepest in North America.

At last, specks of color below told us we had reached the road-end parking area. Both of us knew ours was a trip we'd never forget.

SEQUOIA and KINGS CANYON NATIONAL PARKS

Areas 604 and 719 square miles

Features: *Spectacular High Sierra setting for world's most massive trees, state's deepest canyons and some of its highest mountains.*

Activities: *Visitor centers at Lodgepole, Grant Grove. Scenic roads into both parks. Hiking, riding trails. Wilderness camping, fishing. Guided tours, nature walks, campfire programs; snowshoe walks and ski touring in winter.*

Season: *Open all year. Most activities June-Sept.*

Weather: *Nearly rainless days, cool nights in summer. Elevation at Giant Forest 6,400 ft.*

How to get there: *Calif. 180 or 198 from U. S. 99. See insert map. Air service and buses to Fresno or Visalia, Calif., bus or rental car to park in summer. Trails to high country from Owens Valley, east of Sierra Nevada, on U. S. 6 and 395.*

Accommodations: *Lodge, cabins; tent chalet on High Sierra Trail. Camp Kaweah all year. Write Sequoia and Kings Canyon Hospitality Service at park. Campgrounds, trailer sites.*

Services: *Coffee shops, supplies, gas. Garage, religious services in summer. Ski gear rental.*

Park regulations: *Calif. fishing license. Permit required for backcountry travel.*

For information write Supt., Three Rivers, Calif. 93271

DAVID HISER

The Pacific Northwest

Ferns and moss upholster a dank world in an Olympic rain forest.

Verla Lee Smith

Olympic

NATIONAL PARK, WASHINGTON

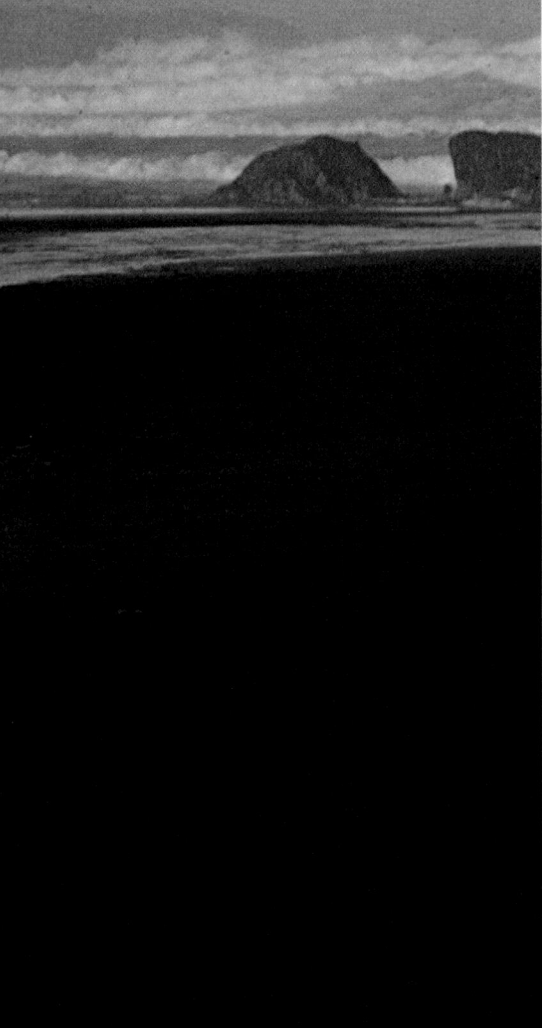

The stream was the Soleduck, and it had no bridge. On the far bank the trail pointed uphill and vanished in snowdrifts. With the steepest two miles of the day's eight yet to go, wet boots didn't appeal, so jeans rolled and boots in hand, I waded in barefoot.

Blame the current, icy water, slick bottom, my tender feet—whatever. In midstream I fell, emerging soaked to the waist—boots, jacket, and my only pair of pants. A wipeout.

It was July first, summer in the valleys, spring in the evergreen forests flanking ridges and peaks at the core of Olympic National Park. As for the high country, I had been warned. First at the Soleduck ranger station: "There's still snow on the High Divide. In Seven Lakes Basin you may need an ice ax." Next, from a trio turning back to trailhead, "Don't go." They had got lost and spent a night without shelter. Carrying tent and sleeping bag, and assured by the ranger that trails were well marked, I hiked on.

Up to that bridgeless stream—delightful. From road's end the trail delved into shade of fir and hemlock, played footlog leapfrog across brooks burbling cold and sparkling into the Soleduck. Sawing deeper shade, it climbs by switchbacks, looking down on trees jackstrawed over the river chasm. At five miles, I set down the pack for rest and a snack, wandered into a cirque carpeted white with marsh marigolds, accented at streamside with purple shooting stars—and lingered an hour. After that it didn't matter that the pack grew heavy, the trail steep, and a tyro backpacker weary from the weight. I was hooked.

The dunking was a minor mishap unless it meant a premature end to a planned five days of discovering these sublime wilds. Shivering in a wet nylon bikini, I wrung the Soleduck from my jeans and thought salvage. Dry wool socks and sweater helped. The swim suit, not much

Lovelier than fantasy, a sea stack some 50 yards off Olympic's shore looms in the looking glass of a tranquil pool stranded at extreme low tide.

FARRELL GREHAN

Slice of low-tide life: Starfish and sea anemone belie delicate looks. A hungry anemone ingests most anything—even stones. Starfish pry open mollusks. Any arm serves as head, and lost limbs grow anew.
FARRELL GREHAN

for warmth, did spare decency. Wet jeans draped over the pack, I plowed on.

The trail up through Soleduck Park to High Divide may be well marked—when the snow melts. But tracks of two men coming down from Seven Lakes Basin were the only visible path much of the way. The summer ranger had come in by helicopter only two days before, and his spare gear had helped them weather a 25° night. "At Heart Lake you'll see marks in the snow where I fell and sledded on my pack," one offered. I saw the marks after three hours and some of the hardest work ever done in the name of pleasure, lugging a 35-pound pack up a steep slope three feet deep in slushy snow. Try it.

The tiny knoll sticking out of the snow beside Heart Lake was more than beautiful, so much effort was invested. Quickly hanging my food from high limbs and wet clothes from low, I pitched the tent, and collapsed. Unspeakably content, I lay in a warm sleeping bag unwinding in the long daylight. At about nine, a deer mouse, exquisitely shadowed, moved along the base of the tent, front to back. Heart Lake bedcheck.

Three worlds—central mountains, rain forested valleys, detached ocean shore—unite in Olympic's 900,000 acres. Though 95 percent of the park is roadless, motorists can sample each type of environment via U. S. 101 which girdles the peninsula. Spur roads lead to the green realm of the Hoh Rain Forest on the park's west side; to the realm of surf, sea stack, and tide pool at Rialto, LaPush, or Kalaloch on the Pacific strand; to the lofty realm at Hurricane Ridge where you can stand with one foot in snow and the other in flowers and—weather willing—view both the encircling waters and peaks at the heart of this almost-island. "Rain forests are beautiful in rain or sun, but pick a clear day for Hurricane Ridge," a friend had advised me.

Arriving from Seattle on an overcast day, I heeded the advice and headed instead for Deer Park Campground and nearby Blue Mountain.

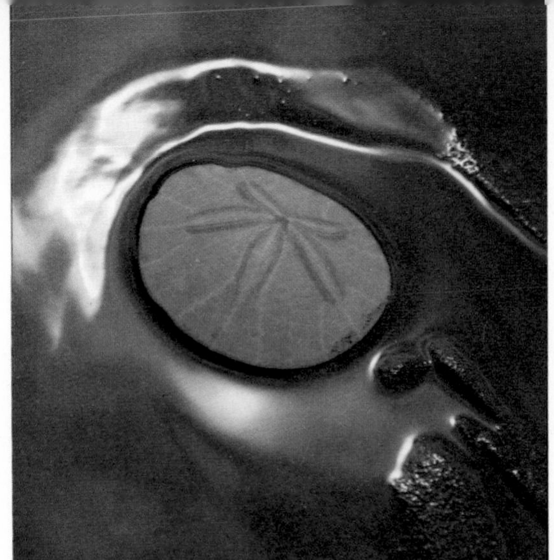

A shimmer of wet sand frames a sand dollar shell.

Black tegula live in turban-shaped shells.

Anemone's pretty "petals" can inflict a paralyzing sting.

Mile-high vantage, the High Divide Trail teeters between the jeweled splendors of Seven Lakes Basin and snow-capped peaks of Olympus and Bailey ranges. Some eight miles from trailhead a hiker (opposite) refreshes body and sole with a scenery break on Bogachiel Peak, daubed from September's palette.

ED COOPER. OPPOSITE: DAVID HISER

Along the winding dirt road, fog swirled up from the valley at the pace of the station wagon. Chances of a view from Blue Mountain seemed slim but, prepared to wait, I picnicked in moist and gauzy privacy at 6,007 feet. Before dark the curtains rolled back and Blue became a magic mountain floating in mauve and indigo. Sunset shimmered on the Strait of Juan de Fuca where dark dots of ships from the Orient pull for the harbor at Ediz Hook. On Blue's topmost crag a flower that had not heard of gravity leaned from its cranny out into space as if flowers, too, crave the sight of beauty. Clouds came. Clouds went. And over the barren shale the horned larks perched on their respective rocks and sang to the setting sun.

At dawn on Blue Mountain eight deer browsed leisurely downslope. A cheeky chipmunk upstaged a stellar cast of alpine blooms: mats of white phlox, lacy parasols of yellow lomatium, dainty bells of pink plume. As I edged toward a cliff-hung anemone, a plump bird strolled onto her balcony and, startled, gave me a fanning of propwash as she flew.

For a week I probed Olympic's north side by road: up the Elwha valley to a camp near torrential Boulder Creek; to Lake Crescent, the park's largest, where families fished by campfires, mallards ghosted the shallows, and trucks hauling logs from outside the park roared by the shore from dawn to last light.

At midweek came the awaited sun-glistened

day that brought out the superlatives—and appreciative crowds—on Hurricane Ridge. Panoramas stretching to the Canada shore, flower-bedecked meadows where deer feed, a day-use lodge, and accessibility mark the park's most-visited mountain.

Fewer wheels roil the dust of a byway winding from the Ridge road to Obstruction Point, also noted for mountain vistas. Clouds shaped the mood of a softly timeless afternoon I spent on its high shale ridge. Clouds were the view, churning, rolling like puppies in the grass. A solar eclipse duly came and went, moon-shadow unseen, eclipsed by Olympic clouds.

Lush tangerine light filtered into the tent. The snow-free sliver of Heart Lake caught the sun like a pop fly as it topped High Divide. Here in the roadless inner reaches of the park, pre-season solitude reigned. From the forested Soleduck valley to the mile-high ridge above, footprints and my camp were the only human intrusions on a pristine mountainscape.

Rested, dried out, and well fed, I buckled the pack over my red nylon jacket, ready to set out over the snow to the Divide. Something fluttered at my chest. A rufous hummingbird, "glittering fragment of the rainbow," a thousand-mile migrant, darted at my jacket. It hovered, then back-winged to fly on. No nectar in nylon.

High Divide splits its waters between Hoh and Soleduck rivers—and knits stupendous views. Ranks of mountains south of the Hoh were on dress parade that day, white epaulets gleaming. Mount Olympus, hub of the park, yearly garners 200 inches of moisture, mostly snow, to nourish ten square miles of glaciers.

For a heady two miles atop the snowy Divide, views got better; perhaps exhilaration is cumulative. Shaded ice-white Seven Lakes Basin on my right; heather and lilies and the sunny Hoh valley on my left. The more I looked at the green valley veined by the Hoh some 4,000 feet below, the more I was tempted.

It wasn't wise, not knowing the terrain. But

near Bogachiel Peak where the trail ahead led uphill into snow, snow, snow I took the primrose path, an elk walk threading flowerbeds with golden-furred marmots policing their beats, down a hill directly toward the Hoh valley.

A day later I was trapped in a ravine full of stream with waterfalls above and below and soft vertical walls on each side that I couldn't climb. About halfway to the valley the vegetation had become too thick to penetrate with the bulky pack on my back. I had been trying to work my way down a stream; along the top of its ravine, slide alders and evergreens tangled like parade crowds vying for curbspace. A branch I was hanging onto gave way and in I went. In the ensuing hours I dragged the pack partway up the 20-foot bank and slid back down so many times the denim on my seat wore out. It seemed time to try to get help.

From a tiny ledge above the lower waterfall, I couldn't quite see the trail along the Hoh far below, but hundreds walk it each year on their way to climb Mount Olympus. Using a metal cup as a mirror, I dot-dashed cupfuls of sun toward the visible stretch of river bottom. Between SOS's I waved the red jacket, persisting until the sun sank. It would have been a nice touch if even a hummingbird had responded.

How to rest in this hostel? The best—only—prospect was a flat rock jutting three feet from the bank, just above the lower falls. I had food and unlimited water. Most of the wood was in the stream. Searching for tinder, cones and twigs, I looked at the ravine walls from a new angle. Taking a long slant to the top without the heavy pack, I just might make it. Carrying only food, matches, map, flashlight, wallet, keys—I took a long breath. And made it.

With darkness near and my shelter left behind, I had to get back to the Divide and the

High browsers, nanny and kid pick wallflowers and mountain greenery. Some goats, shy no longer, now greet park visitors who puff up the steep ridges; a hiker's sweaty palm makes a handy salt lick.

FARRELL GREHAN

Pine sap (Indian pipe)

trail without delay or blunder. The hill was steep enough coming down; climbing, I met flowers growing at my nose level. Time telescoped. I recognized a clump of bushes. But then I looked back. Fog was racing me, wispy at first, then a virtual cocoon. Landmarks now useless, I groped upward unable to see clearly at arm's length. Then out of the isolating haze a whistle —I was back in marmotland. Less timid than furry natives I had seen a day ago, this one stood fast by its den as I approached; it may be that in deep fog no one molests a fellow creature. We looked at each other. "Marmot, show me the way to the trail," I said softly.

A strange thing happened. The marmot turned and dived not into its den but uphill into the fog. I followed. Another whistle. Homing on its sound, I came to the trail. There sat my guide—with a marmot friend. I had no answer, only a question. Perhaps this is what marmots always do on a foggy night on Bogachiel Peak.

No quibbling this time about the snow. I followed the tracks that served as trail a mile or so until, by flashlight, I reached Hoh Lake. Some kind young backpackers from Oregon made room in the shelter and lent me spare clothes as cover. It rained that night. The thought of a certain flat rock in a rain-washed ravine made the cold, hard wooden bunk feel pretty good.

Western pasqueflower

FARRELL GREHAN

Avalanche lily

Mertens cassiope

Indian paintbrush

DAVID HISER

's on the High Divide frame sun-crowned Mount Olympus, rising to 7,965 feet beyond the cloud-sheathed Hoh River.

Green alcoves glorify the luxuriant forests nurtured by 150 inches of rain along the Hoh, Queets, and Quinault rivers. Maples thrive under a sun-pierced umbrella of ancient Sitka spruce and western hemlock; ferns and mosses mantle humus, and moldering logs nurse seedlings in a continuum of new life for old.

Fifteen miles from Hoh Lake to roadhead at Hoh Visitor Center proved a Fourth of July picnic. A whisper-soft trail zigzagged the ferny, flowery big woods. No snow. Downhill all the way. A fine drizzle only enhanced the spell of Hoh rain forest. Ten miles in a luminous greenhouse ages old left me not tired but replete. Road in sight, I walked both nature trails.

Over the cliff at Kalaloch Campground, lines of cloud interlaid with streaks of sky hang like tenement wash on a promising Monday. Wind irons Pacific waves into little white wrinkles. On the beach, past drift logs and shingle a fly-in of gulls peck listlessly at the sand, then caucus, uncertain where to go for kicks. Nearby a lone blue heron stands head back, splayed against the waves, one stilt-leg flexed. For long minutes he holds his street-corner stance, eye-fishing. A quarter pivot, repeat vigil. Then—no luck here—flapoff.

A day for beachcombing and sand castles, for pondering tracks at the scalloped rim of freshwater streams come home to the sea, for tuning in to the slap, slap of surf on rocky islets—creation music. A day for visiting rangers.

Enthusiasm for the beauty and variety of the Olympic setting, for the special peace of spirit to be sought in its sublime wildness, keyed the talk of park personnel I met. But there is a prosaic side to their working day. Waiting for Bill Ferraro, area ranger at Kalaloch, to finish a task, I read the bulletin board, listing routine and special fix-it chores for staff members. Notes to the senior ranger that day included:

- Remove initials from big cedar. Use chisel.
- Putty in profanity on Trail #3 sign and stain.
- Place barrier post in A-34 to keep vehicles from driving off pavement into trees.

About the first item—it wasn't just *a* big cedar but *the* biggest western red cedar, one of seven tree species that grow to record size in the park. Near Kalaloch, I visited the patriarch cedar. How many centuries it must have taken to grow an awesome 21 feet across! This magnificent giant, far gone in senility and other natural ills of trees, doesn't need people carving initials a foot high. Sorry, MK, your misplaced ego gets the ranger's chisel treatment.

"Not vicious so much as thoughtless," had been Bill Ferraro's comment. "Some problems we face relate to overcrowding. Sometimes it's just people out of their own environment and not knowing what to do, or not thinking.

"Two girls went on one of the beach trails and wandered up a creek. They had been in the Outward Bound program but all they remembered was, when lost, sit and wait. They sat two days and were in sad shape when searchers found them, but one girl spoke up, 'I knew I was all right because in Outward Bound I survived three days without food.' One of the men said, 'I'm a day early,' and turned to go.

"Apparently it hadn't occurred to the girls to go back down the creek they came up. All creeks end at the ocean."

OLYMPIC NATIONAL PARK

Area 1,400 square miles

Features: *Wilderness park embracing snow-capped peaks, ocean beaches, rain forests. Olympic elk.*

Activities: *Visitor centers at Port Angeles, Lake Crescent, and Hoh Rain Forest. U. S. 101 nearly circles park; spur roads to key areas. 600 miles of trails. Nature walks, campfire programs. Trout, salmon fishing. Climbing. Hurricane Ridge—wild-flower display best in mid-July; weekend skiing Dec.-Mar.*

Season: *Park open all year. Best weather summer and early fall. Deep snow at high elev. Nov.-July.*

How to get there: *U. S. 101. See insert map. Also ferry across Puget Sound; toll bridge over Hood Canal. To Port Angeles by air or bus from Seattle, by ferry from Victoria, B.C., Canada.*

Accommodations: *Lodges, inns, cabins. Campgrounds high and low; some take trailers. For services outside the park write Olympic Peninsula Travel Assn., Seattle Ferry Terminal, Seattle 98104.*

Park regulations: *Permit required for fires, overnight trail trips or beach hikes. Only stoves allowed on some trails. No fishing license needed except for steelhead and salmon.*

For information write Supt., Port Angeles, Wash. 98362

DAVID HISER

Nathaniel T. Kenney

North Cascades

NATIONAL PARK, WASHINGTON

If there is wilder country than North Cascades National Park, then I have missed it in a lifetime spent poking into the wild and woolly places of the Lower Forty-Eight. Here, along the Canadian border, is a land so raw, so sternly hewn that even Indians and trappers kept to the valleys. Many of its peaks—scabrous needles of ice-wracked rock—to this day remain unnamed, unclimbed.

The Cascade Range, a chain of volcanic peaks that starts in California as an extension of the Sierra Nevada, curves northward for 700 miles through Oregon and Washington, and ends at the Fraser River in British Columbia. Moisture-laden winds from the Pacific Ocean copiously bathe the range's western slopes with fog and rain, or snow, while its eastern foothills taper gradually into semi-desert.

The park, established in 1968 in the range's northern section, consists of two units divided by an L-shaped national recreation area that encompasses Ross Lake and the valley of the Skagit River. Only one paved road, recently completed Route 20, traverses the region, providing access to the backcountry and to the recreation area's resorts and campgrounds.

Trapper Alexander Ross, the first white man to push into Cascades country, came here in 1814. He described forests "almost impervious with fallen as well as standing timber. A more difficult route to travel," he continued, "never fell to man's lot. My companions began to flag during the day."

So did mine. So did I. We were headed up the Park Creek bridle trail from Stehekin, a rugged ride in the park's South Unit that corkscrews up to where the vault of the sky begins. One horse wide, the trail fords foaming streams, clings to scree slopes, and crosses alpine meadows. Skirting living glaciers and majestic peaks

Sharp as cougar fangs, 8,000-foot pinnacles of the Picket Range spike a summer sky in the Cascades. Living glaciers fed by 50 feet of snow a year make these peaks among the world's toughest to climb.

JAMES P. BLAIR, NATIONAL GEOGRAPHIC PHOTOGRAPHER

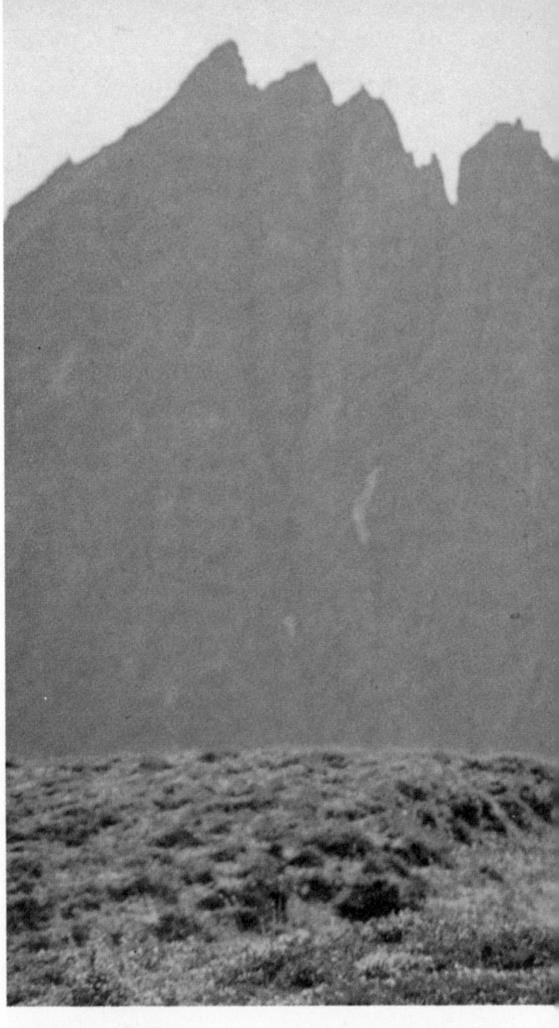

Oh for a horse! Students of the National Outdoor Leadership School endure the trudge-work of a high-altitude bivouac along the trail to Cascade Pass. Determining their whereabouts, they set up camp near an old Indian path across Sahale Arm.
DAVID HISER

crowned with everlasting snow, it tops out on Park Creek Pass 6,050 feet above sea level.

Below the crest, in a heather-clad bowl by a crystal stream, we pitched camp. While trout sizzled in the frying pan and the first stars winked on in a purpling sky, camp robbers—gray jays—screamed in the stunted, storm-tortured trees at timberline. A water ouzel sang its evensong from a lichened boulder. A bush moved—and became a bear combing the brushy slope for blueberries. In the night, black-tailed deer drifted nearby to greet our horses.

My next favorite trail starts outside the park's North Unit and winds near the Pickets, sharpest peaks in the Cascades. Named for their fancied resemblance to a picket fence, they rank with the most challenging mountains for climbers.

I wonder whether Alexander Ross met hornets. We did. They nest beneath rocks, likely as not in the middle of a trail. You can imagine what happens when a horse or pack mule steps on a hornets' nest!

Suffering from saddle-and-hornet-bestowed aches and pains, we gained Whatcom Pass and feasted our eyes on the Pickets. To the south rose Mount Challenger, and on its flank, Challenger Glacier, glory of these mountains. Easy Peak frowned down from the west; I wondered what humorist gave it the name!

White avalanche and yellow glacier lilies closely followed the snow receding up the slopes near our campsite. Blooming heather shared the meadows with lupine, Indian paintbrush, and harebells. Wild phlox tinted the landscape with lavender and white.

Easier than a ride over Whatcom is a voyage to Canada by boat on Ross Lake, created by a 540-foot-high power dam across the Skagit River. You begin by driving to Diablo Lake, another man-made reservoir, then take a boat-and-bus shuttle to Ross.

At Wayne Dameron's resort, built on huge rafts, I rented a fast outboard. After a delightful two-hour run I was in Canadian waters. But when

Through fragrant forest and high mountain passes, North Cascades Highway winds above Diablo Lake in Ross Lake National Recreation Area. Park rules ban trailers from true wilds but welcome them in beauty spots like Colonial Creek Campground (right), handy to the cross-state motor road.

DAVID HISER

I started back, it rained and I was soon soaked. Seeing a plume of smoke at the mouth of Little Beaver Creek, I landed and found a campfire, a bubbling coffeepot, and a wilderness wanderer snoring under a shelter. I poured myself a hot cup, as one has a right to do in the wild lands, and finished my trip without ever waking my unknown benefactor.

Once I visited Colonial Glacier on the flank of a mountain by the same name. Although small, the glacier is heavily crevassed and steep. Terror clouds my memory of this ice river. I could hear and feel its movement down the valley it has carved through the centuries. It crackled like a ragged rifle volley, it roared like summer thunder, and when it trembled, my knees followed suit.

I do remember unexpected patches of color on the glacier's glistening breast. Blue streaks were narrow crevasses of fearful depth. An opening in a wall of ice led into an azure cave. Crimson algae splotched last winter's snow.

In the North Cascades you can expect spring-like temperatures all through the summer. Winter's first breath comes by October. In the spring, when I toured the South Unit by floatplane with veteran bush pilot Ernie Gibson, I saw that winter had lingered into May.

"No guarantee today," said Ernie, as we took off from Lake Chelan, south of the park, in flurries of sleet and snow. "In a floatplane you don't

Anglers' paradise: Thunder Creek arm of Diablo Lake, milky green from glacial runoff, serves up outdoor solace and fighting trout. In Lake Chelan National Recreation Area south of the park, fishermen try for codlike burbot and nonmigratory salmon, called kokanee, in waters 1,400 feet deep.

try to fly over 9,000-foot mountains. You detour through the passes—and if clouds close in behind you, you can only spend the day sitting it out on some lake, waiting."

As we climbed north and west up Stehekin Valley, so too climbed the peaks among which we threaded. At 8,000 feet by our altimeter their summits still rose above us—Sentinel and Spider on our left, Buckner, Booker, and hoary Sahale, with its gigantic glacial apron, looming ahead over the aircraft's nose.

We passed above Trapper Lake, a favorite haunt of fishermen in which dwell some of the biggest Cascades trout. But now its waters were clogged with chunks of drifting ice.

On the way home, we flew over a snowfield pocked with huge round tracks.

"Snowshoes," Ernie said. "A ranger must be measuring snow depths so they'll know how much runoff to expect at Lake Chelan when the thaw comes in late summer."

Lake Chelan. At its head, in another recreation area abutting the park, lies the tiny, isolated community of Stehekin. Most of the 870,000 people who each year visit the park see only the country accessible from the new North Cascades Highway, but a visit to out-of-the-way Stehekin is worth the effort. Rendezvous for trappers and prospectors of the past, it has more flavor of the old mountain West than any place I know. The passing years have not greatly changed Stehekin's way of life. No road, no telephone line links it to the outside world. But you can reach it by hiking or horseback, by floatplane, or by ferryboat from Chelan.

Once there, you'll find twenty miles of road leading nowhere in particular. You can hire an elderly "landlocked" car or take the Park Service's shuttle bus for a memorable woodsy trip. You'll see waterfalls, a clear pristine river, and, almost surely, wildlife. Deer. Mountain goats. I've seen five bears in one day, and once a moose, a stray down from Canada.

Above all, meet some of the thirty or forty local people. There is Ray Courtney, whose beautiful log home does not have electricity because, to him, it represents civilization. There is Harry Buckner, whose forebears homesteaded a place the Park Service is now turning into a living museum.

These and others of Stehekin are good friends of wilderness preservation. They helped save their land from loggers and miners. Their reward—and yours too—is pure air, unpolluted water, and the chance to savor the wildness of a land where perhaps no human has ever stood.

NORTH CASCADES NATIONAL PARK ROSS LAKE and LAKE CHELAN NATIONAL RECREATION AREAS

Areas 789; 167; and 96 square miles

Features: *Magnificent "American Alps"—massive and rugged peaks; 300 glaciers; alpine lakes, waterfalls. Park halved by Ross Lake reservoir in Skagit River valley and bounded on the south by fjord-like Lake Chelan in idyllic Stehekin Valley. See insert map.*

Activities: *Sightsee by car via North Cascades Highway (State Route 20) through Ross Lake NRA, by scheduled boat service on Diablo and Chelan Lakes, or by chartered plane. Backcountry hiking and horseback riding on 345 miles of trails. Superb challenges for experienced climbers. Camp in developed or primitive campgrounds. Excellent trout fishing in lakes and streams. Boating. Hunting allowed in NRAs.*

Season: *April to mid-October at lower elevations; mid-June to mid-September in higher regions. Western side of Cascade Range often rainy and cool; eastern side drier and warmer.*

How to get there: *State Route 20 from Burlington or Winthrop to Ross Lake NRA. Or U.S. 97 to Chelan; thence by boat or plane to Stehekin. Access to northwest hiking trails via State Route 542 from Bellingham.*

Accommodations and services: *Limited rooms, meals, and services in small communities within both NRAs. Full services at Marblemount, Chelan. Two developed campgrounds available at Ross Lake NRA; primitive hike-in and boat-in campgrounds in both NRAs and in South Unit of park. Horses, guides available in nearby communities.*

Park regulations: *State license required for hunting and fishing. Climbers and backcountry campers must register with park ranger.*

For information regarding park and recreation units, write Supt. at Sedro Woolley, Wash. 98284

DAVID HISER

Merle Severy

Mount Rainier

NATIONAL PARK, WASHINGTON

The great mountain played coy with us as we approached it over Chinook Pass from Yakima on the east. We caught only tantalizing glimpses through clouds clambering over its shoulders of rock and ice. We wound through forests of cedar and hemlock, past glacial moraines and waterfalls. Fallen timber streaked slopes where avalanches had thundered down. Arriving amid the swirling mists at Sunrise, 6,400 feet high on a northeastern spur, we found families of little firs huddling together, like jagged islands in a foggy sea.

"Guess we won't see Rainier today," said my wife, Patricia, as she spread lunch. Ground squirrels and chipmunks came to greet us. Jays flew in to share our picnic.

Then the fog parted and Rainier filled the sudden blue sky. Blinding sun danced on fresh snow. Enormous glaciers seemed poised over our heads. Here, close up, we beheld the "round snowy mountain" seen from afar by Capt. George Vancouver of the British Royal Navy as he explored Puget Sound in 1792. He named the peak for his friend Rear Adm. Peter Rainier.

Indians called this dormant volcano *Tacoma,* The Mountain, and feared a demon who waited at the top to cast trespassers into a fiery lake. But white men pushed up its slopes, and in 1870 Hazard Stevens and P. B. Van Trump struggled to the summit. For 11 hours they clawed over rock and ice, only to stagger into a numbing gale on the crest. Lacking shelter, they faced a frigid death as darkness closed in. Then on the crater rim they found an ice cave formed by a steam jet. There they survived the night, "freezing on one side," Stevens wrote, "and in a hot steam-sulphur-bath on the other."

I pictured them hurrying down the mountain the following day—but mists billowed in, erasing the image. Behind the swirls loomed a mystic mountain in a surrealist painting. An eerie chill gripped us and we hastened on.

Next morning, outside our window in the National Park Inn at Longmire, the 14,410-foot giant stood majestically alone in a cloudless sky. Signs to "Paradise" beckoned us to a 5,400-foot-high valley on Rainier's south shoulder. There we roamed slopes ablaze with autumn reds and dotted with dark green spires.

We surveyed blue-green crevasses and seracs on Nisqually Glacier and heard the rumble of ice crashing into the milky stream that snakes below its debris-littered snout. In the crisp distance Mount Adams and Mount St. Helens poked snowy crowns above the saw-toothed Tatoosh Range. Loping through sun-splashed alpine meadows, we felt a million miles from anyone, in a lofty, timeless realm. "Reminds me of *Heidi,*" Patricia said.

Along Stevens Canyon Road, carved out of Rainier's broad southern flank, we hiked over granite ledges polished in gentle swells and troughs by ancient glaciers, and peered into a breathtaking chasm at glacial melt frothing 180

Icy cloak frayed by a summer in the sun, Rainier bares volcanic slopes above the evergreenery of Paradise Valley and Reflection Lake. The view rewards rock-climbers toiling toward 6,562-foot Pinnacle Peak, waist-high to the white-cowled titan.

DAVID HISER

Winter drift and spring eavesdrop make for a cool reception at mile-high Paradise Inn, focus for lodgers and daytrippers bused from Seattle. Waning pile is all that remains of a season's snowfall that measured 89 feet. In the beamed lobby itinerant minstrels and local talent lend welcoming warmth.
DAVID HISER

feet below. At day's end the wind died; no ripple blemished Rainier's image in Reflection Lake. The sun's failing rays climbed the icy summit as we returned to Paradise, the Nisqually valley flaming wall to wall. As we came down the mountain, the evening star rose above the silhouetted Tatoosh peaks. A coyote howled.

"Want to see how Paradise looks in winter?" the superintendent asked us that evening in his Longmire home. A color slide flashed on the basement screen. Just the chimneys of Paradise Inn showed above the snow. "The snow was 30 feet deep, with drifts of 40 and 50 feet." A recent winter saw 93½ feet of snowfall there—a world record.

Mount Rainier National Park's 378 square miles have something for everybody. Each summer a million and a half visitors, lured by the Cascades landmark so convenient to Seattle and Tacoma, delight in the alpine flowers that garland it to glacier's edge. Campgrounds and trout streams beckon outdoorsmen; 300 miles of trails probe the wilderness haunts of deer, bear, elk, bobcat, marmot, and mountain goat. The 90-mile Wonderland Trail circles Rainier. Take trail foods, warm sleeping bag, tent, and rain gear, and allow ten days—more if you stop to identify the park's hundred species of moss, or thousand species of fungi. Or go looking for ice worms.

I thought a naturalist friend was kidding when he told me about *them.* Actually, they look like dark threads, not even an inch long. They feed on algae that patch the snow red, and on wind-blown pollen.

From mid-June to Labor Day, Paradise Valley hums with activity, kids sliding down snowbanks, teen-agers strumming guitars, grandmothers "Wish-you-were-here"-ing. Mountaineers-for-a-week hail new friends, and bask in camaraderie in that grand old timbered lodge.

"This is the fifth summer I've come here—and I have yet to see the mountain!" a Portland teacher told me in front of the crackling fire in

a great stone fireplace. I, too, had picked a damp June day to revisit my favorite mountain. But Rainier's weather came as no surprise. I had already learned about it—airborne.

Clouds overhung Puget Sound when I took off from Seattle. Climbing above lush dairyland, the plane sliced through the murk and emerged into bright sunlight. Ahead gleamed a line of Cascade peaks, Rainier tallest among them—white cones floating on a fleecy carpet. Spectacular! More than that. They form one of the world's most striking climatic boundaries.

Parts of western Washington get the heaviest rainfall in the contiguous United States. Parts of eastern Washington are so dry jackrabbits must have to pack canteens. Minutes later I saw why. Clouds abruptly ended as we soared past the Cascades barrier. Gone was the moist green quilt of forest and grass. Instead, a stark land baked in the sun. Deflected upward and cooling, Pacific winds drop their moisture on the Cascades' western slopes.

Circling Rainier, we got a thrilling look into the crater. Born of fire perhaps a million years ago, the volcano seemingly slumbers under a white mantle—though geologists keep an uneasy watch on its rising temperature; melting could precipitate disastrous slides. I did not count all 26 or more of the glaciers that furrow Rainier's brow—more glaciers than on any other U. S. peak outside Alaska. I held my breath as ice and rock whizzed by. That's my way of climbing Rainier.

Yes, Rainier appeals to individual tastes. Summer's crowds were gone when Patricia and I first visited Paradise. We found peace on the autumnal slopes, before winter's breath changed the snowshoe hare and ptarmigan from brown to white, slowed the heartbeat of the hibernating golden-mantled ground squirrel from 300 to 2 or 3 beats per minute—and turned the slopes into a skier's playground. Perhaps Rainier's special appeal is to the climber, eager to fight to the top of one of the world's most glorious mountains.

DAVID HISER

Snow-climbing: Step by Step

Lesser peaks loom like islands in a sea of clouds and ice; above rises the alluring cone of Rainier—goal of several thousand each year. But early-bird climbers at 12,000 feet have eyes only for the rough névé—hard granulated snow—pitting their path to the top.

Stop that slide! Beginning climbers learn the art of self-arrest, a lifesaving maneuver on crevasse-cut glaciers where a stumble can swiftly accelerate into a deadly drop. Falling headfirst and prone (left), the climber pivots on the axhead to swing the feet downslope; backsliding (below), he rolls over to put force on the dug-in ax. With toes and ice ax

DAVID HISER

planted properly, the emergency brake is set. Roping up—a must at higher elevations—gives a fallen climber a lifeline to the strength and skills of companions. Novice mountaineers bring desire and good health to the slopes; Rainier guides provide rental gear, schooling, and safety-first savvy in two-day or five-day sessions climaxed by a summit climb.

From Rainier's lofty cap, rivers of ice stream down like arms of a starfish, moving, at most, 12 to 18 inches a day. Where the course or the angle of the valley slope changes, glaciers crack. Early in the climbing season, snow masks the crevasses; by late summer snow bridges, such as this one on Ingraham Glacier, soften. The welcome shortcut across the chasm may end 100 feet down. So a prudent lead man, his rope secured by a bowline knot, steps out warily while his mates on solid ice prepare to stop a fall.

From 10,000-foot Camp Muir, guided novices trek the popular Ingraham route to the summit in about five hours.

DAVID HISER

Take a giant step or make a small one; to save strength, try a tightrope. When the going gets tough, seasoned alpinists go "technical," deploying special skills and equipment. Ice ax chops steps on a steep pitch or a ledge for an ice piton; high jumper clears a six-foot-wide gulf, ax at the ready lest he stumble. At a wide crevasse a suspension traverse avoids a tiring group detour. One man hikes around to anchor cable; then packs and climbers swing across on slings. Here Lou Whittaker, head of the Rainier guide service, tests a rig before students venture into the thin air. "If a girl will volunteer," he says, "we send her first. Then the guys feel they have to do it."

Some routes to the top test the ablest of mountaineers. Unguided climbers must register with rangers for a check of equipment and fitness. But even Sunday visitors may blunder into disaster when a sudden snowfall leaves them lost on cold slopes, dressed for a midsummer stroll.

KEITH GUNNAR

At 13,000 feet, near the ridge called Disappointment Cleaver, the climbers paused. Guides saw storm in the air, the trail ahead slashed by crevasses, the summit beyond safe reach. Turning back, they plod through "suncups" scalloped in the snow by sunrays—defeated this day, but alive to try another time.

DAVID HISER

Walter Meayers Edwards

Crater Lake

NATIONAL PARK, OREGON

DAVID HISER

Pale buff, powdery pumice swirled around our feet, filtering into our shoes. For a quarter of a mile we had toiled uphill, clambering over fallen trees, slipping on banks of snow that lingered into summer. My wife, Mary, a few steps ahead, brushed between the branches of two hemlocks and disappeared. Scrambling on, I found her gazing out over the edge of a cliff. Before us stretched Crater Lake—an enchanting vision of another world. It was a full minute before Mary broke the silence.

"That blue," she said. "Can you believe it?" Varicolored rocks and stately evergreens enhance the effect of the lake, just as a jeweler's setting points up the brilliance of a gem.

At first this Oregon lake did not seem large. Then we began to comprehend its size. The tiny island called Phantom Ship, near the caldera walls below, was as high as Niagara Falls. What looked like two water bugs were 42-foot launches floating on a lake with an abyss of 1,932 feet, the deepest in the United States, seventh deepest in the world. The boats put out from Cleetwood Cove on the opposite rim—more than five miles away, though it seemed a third as far.

I reflected on those terrible days some 6,500 years ago when Mount Mazama erupted with a titanic roar. Fiery magma poured out, forming avalanches. Then the 12,000-foot peak collapsed. It was a spectacle man must have witnessed. Mount Mazama pumice has been found on Indian cultural remains in Oregon caves, and Klamath Indian legends tell of war between two gods, Llao on Mazama and his rival on Mount Shasta 100 miles south. Explosions and smoke from burning forests darkened the sky as the mountains flamed. At the height of battle, Llao's throne tumbled down.

We entered the 250-square-mile park from the south, driving through the 2½-mile panhandle added to the park's basic rectangle to

Wraparound lens gathers a 20-square-mile lake into a sapphire fishbowl. Wizard Island lifts its peaked cap 760 feet above the snow- and rain-filled basin.

preserve a magnificent ponderosa pine grove along Annie Creek. It was early July, and road crews were just clearing the last of winter's snow from Rim Drive. Most tours of that breathtaking 33-mile circuit begin at Rim Village on the southwest side of the lake. With its lodge, campground, cafeteria, gift shop, exhibit building, and Sinnott Memorial Overlook, it is the busiest part of the park.

Walking along the rim one day, we came to the spot where John Hillman discovered Crater Lake on June 12, 1853. In a scrapbook at park headquarters, I read the reminiscences of prospector Hillman. He and his companions were riding up a long, sloping mountain looking for a rumored lost mine. "Not until my mule stopped within a few feet of the rim of Crater Lake did I look down, and if I had been riding a blind mule I firmly believe I would have ridden over the ledge to death."

North of Discovery Point stands Hillman Peak, 8,156 feet above sea level and highest point on the rim. A saddle between Hillman Peak and The Watchman, a neighboring peak, offers one of Rim Drive's best views of Wizard Island, a volcano within a volcano.

We visited the island and climbed the cone. In and around the 100-yard-wide crater grow a few stunted pines. When we returned to the island's shore, I resisted the temptation to swim in the chill waters—about 55° F. in summer. Later, we cruised around the lake, exploring the caldera walls. We seemed alone in this incomparable setting. People on the rim were too small to be seen without binoculars, but sometimes, when the breeze died, their voices floated to us across the stillness.

I landed two rainbow trout. We could watch the fish, deep down, trail the spinners, then strike. The water is so clear that moss has been found 425 feet down. Moss needs sunlight, and the kind of moss found here lives no deeper than 120 feet in most lakes. No license is needed to fish in the lake or in park streams.

Back from the Wizard Island expedition, we wandered through Castle Crest Wildflower Garden near headquarters. Here flowers and shrubs and trees abound in glorious variety. The garden's beauty reaches its peak in August when hummingbirds dart among the monkey flowers and lupine. The blooming season is short; by mid-September snow begins to fall.

The south entrance road is kept open to Rim Village for day visitors in winter. Motorists should bring tire chains, shovel, tow rope, and enough gasoline for the return trip.

"It doesn't get really cold," said the maintenance foreman. "It's seldom down to zero. But you should see the snow. More than 50 feet falls in a year and some years we've had more than 70. Snow gets 20 feet deep up on the rim, and the drifts nearly cover the lodge." He paused, then added in homage to this magnificent marvel, "But the lake sure is beautiful in the snow."
Write Supt., Crater Lake, Ore. 97604

Re-created Mazama clears its throat. Eruptions left a void; the crust collapsed to form a caldera that now cups Crater Lake. Erosion of pumice between fumaroles—gas vents—shaped these fantastic spires.

ED COOPER. PAINTING BY PAUL ROCKWOOD

Tunnels trace the flow of hot lava through cooler crust.

Lava Beds

NATIONAL MONUMENT, CALIFORNIA

"Watch for low ceilings. Lava's the most unforgiving stuff you'll ever run into." Too late. A resounding *klunk* proves the ranger's point—on a plastic "bump cap," luckily, not on your head. Treading warily by lanternlight over ropy pahoehoe and clinkery aa lavas, you probe the cool recesses of Golden Dome Cave, one of 300 in this relaxed, low-key, do-it-yourself park near Tulelake, California. Tubes in the lava labyrinth run up to 85 feet in diameter, up to 1½ miles in length; 19 are open to the public, others to experienced spelunkers.

No cave has a twin. Names hint at myriad hues and textures, contours and contents: Hopkins Chocolate, whose brownish walls resemble icing dribbled on a cake; Catacombs, full of tomblike crannies; Blue Grotto; Valentine (left). Skull and Bighorn yielded skulls of California bighorn sheep, which once wandered the 72 square miles of woods-fringed desert now included in Lava Beds National Monument. The bighorns died out here decades ago. In 1971 eight ewes and two rams were reintroduced in an 1,100-acre enclosure. Two years later the herd had doubled. Bighorns seemed on the way to a California comeback.

Outside the cool caves, purple sage scents the air in late June; blooms tint the sun-seared landscape. An orange blizzard of painted lady butterflies divides as cars ease by.

The road follows the ancient shoreline of Tule Lake to the contorted terrain of Captain Jack's Stronghold. In 1872 a band of Modoc Indians who earlier had fled a reservation in Oregon were pursued by the U. S. Army. Captain Jack led the Modocs into the lava beds. Outnumbered 15 to one, his ill-armed warriors held off the Army for five months. Then, cut off from water, the Indians gave up. "Out here on a moonlit night you can see 'Modocs' with no trouble at all," a park naturalist says.

A 40-unit campground stays open all year. Many visitors prefer spring and fall, when millions of migrating birds enliven the scene.

Write Supt., Box 867, Tulelake, Calif. 96134

RAY ATKESON

Oregon Caves

NATIONAL MONUMENT, OREGON

A lucky man, Elijah Davidson. He was out hunting one August day in 1874 when his dog took off after a bear and disappeared, barking and growling, into a dark hole in the Siskiyou Mountains. Davidson followed, discovering what must be one of nature's most elegant bear dens: a weird underworld of winding passageways and decorated chambers.

Formations resembling chandeliers, columns, cascades, and ghostly robes—shaped by the relentless drip and seep of water bearing dissolved limestone—embellish cool, silent rooms. Among the thousands who followed Davidson into Oregon Caves was poet Joaquin Miller, who sang the praises of "The Marble Halls of Oregon." Washable clothing and rubber-soled shoes are a good idea when taking the nearly mile-long tour, for the electrically lighted cavern is damp. The uphill walk is strenuous.

A nature trail and ten miles of hiking trails thread the 480 forested acres of the monument, reached by U. S. 199 and State 46. Cabins, lodge, and restaurant open in summer. Nearest campgrounds are in Siskiyou National Forest. *Write Supt., Box 128, Klamath Falls, Ore. 97601*

Stalactites grace a subterranean palace.

Lassen Volcanic

NATIONAL PARK, CALIFORNIA

Snow on the roof doesn't mean there's no fire in Lassen's furnace. Though steam vents hiss and mud pots bubble down in Bumpass Hell, the trail to the renowned thermal area is paved with snow late into June.

Wagon trains heading for Sacramento goldfields found 10,457-foot Lassen Peak a welcome landmark. An old volcano, extinct as its sister peaks in the Cascades, settlers judged.

In 1865 a backwoods hunter named Bumpass reported sulphur vapors and boiling mud pots near the mountain. They say he led a newspaper reporter to the display, warned him to watch his step, then himself broke through the crust and dunked a leg in bubbling mud. The thermal basin is today called Bumpass Hell.

In May 1914 Lassen awoke, belching ash and cinders in more than 150 explosions. Tongues of lava lapped from the crater and seared the mountain flank. Snowmelt sent a torrent of mud and 20-ton boulders plunging five miles into the valleys. A mighty, low-angle blast mowed down trees on Raker Peak three miles distant.

Lassen's eruptions died away in 1921. Out of the devastation emerged a wild and beautiful national park. Cones, crags, boulder fields, and seething thermal areas recall the violent past. But blue lakes and forest trails make this a hiker's and camper's park. A self-guided motor tour leads to lava flows and wild-flower meadows; a 2½-mile summit trail gives hikers a view of Lassen's lava-plugged throat.

Danger of avalanches from highly unstable Chaos Crags in the northwest corner of the park closed a campground and visitor facilities at Manzanita Lake, downslope from the Crags. But other campgrounds and a lodge are open.

Timber-free slopes and long winters attract skiers. Cross-country routes radiate from the ski chalet near the southwest entrance.

Named for Peter Lassen, an early California emigrant guide, the old volcano that settlers saw is still a landmark for tourists on State Routes 89, 36, and 44. Not extinct, it's a sleeper. *Write Supt., Mineral, Calif. 96063*

Nature provides steam heat in a Lassen winter sports area.

JAMES P. BLAIR, NATIONAL GEOGRAPHIC PHOTOGRAPHER. OPPOSITE: RAY ATKESON

Verla Lee Smith

Redwood

NATIONAL PARK, CALIFORNIA

One day in 1967 some 50 conservationists from all over the nation gathered at timber holdings near Crescent City, California. A thousand-year-old redwood tree was to be felled. A fever of controversy raged: While pros and cons of a long-sought Redwood National Park were debated, the great trees that once spanned 500 miles of Pacific Coast were being cut into board feet at an alarming rate.

Lucille Vinyard recalls that day. She lives in redwood country and with other conservationists keeps an eye on the nation's legacy of tall trees and their fragile environment.

"There was the drama of the two burly loggers standing on the pedestals. They'd cut straight in, then they'd cut in at an angle. The whine of the saw and all the yelling rang through the woods. Everyone was standing there with cameras cocked, waiting, expecting the big T-I-M-B-E-R! A tree a thousand years growing took just sixty minutes to cut down. And I think," she added quietly, "that when those cameras clicked there were a lot of wet eyes. Because the tree groaned before it hit the dust."

On an autumn day in 1968 some of those same conservationists attended a more auspicious gathering. In a grove of stately trees never to feel the slash of a saw, Mrs. Lyndon Johnson dedicated the nascent Redwood National Park "to the happiness of the people."

The 58,000-acre sanctuary includes within its boundaries three state redwood parks, connecting lands, parcels of beach, and a unit along Redwood Creek containing the tallest trees known (see insert map).

Driving U. S. 199 from Grants Pass, Oregon, my son Roy and I entered Redwood Park's northern gateway along the Smith River, one of the California streams famed among fishermen for salmon and tackle-busting steelhead trout.

"Not like trees, they are like spirits. The glens in which they grow . . . like . . . haunts of the centaurs," wrote poet John Masefield of the coast redwoods, native to a 500-mile ribbon of foggy Pacific Coast.

DICK DURRANCE II, NATIONAL GEOGRAPHIC PHOTOGRAPHER

Pholiota

Bird's nest

Angel hair

On warm, clear days picnickers, swimmers, and sun-baskers dot the banks and sandbars. Smith River and the state park bear the name of Jedediah Smith, fur trader and scout who led pioneers through the area in 1828. Most of the park today remains rugged enough to challenge the trailblazer.

Along unpaved Howland Hill Road, a few steps from your car will get you forest primeval. In palpable stillness the great trees reign. Ferns grow shoulder high. Cloverlike sorrel rugs the humpy-holey ground where shallow-rooted behemoths lived out their allotted centuries and fell. Fungi shaggy and geometric, garish and ghostly white, flourish on the remains. To see one redwood tree in its entirety is not easy; to appreciate the heights to which they tower, pick one fallen monarch and walk its length. In the unkempt magnificence of redwood forest the way nature does it, that was the longest walk I took without a trail.

A bit tamer and more "parklike," Stout Memorial Grove holds the biggest tree known in Jedediah Smith Park: Stout Tree, 20 feet thick, 340 feet tall, a short, easy walk from the parking area. Benches enable you to sit and look up at its sky-stabbing crown without falling over backward, but neck strain is chronic among visiting Jacks in this land of giants.

Campsites for tent or small trailer in the three state parks may be reserved in advance by writing the California Department of Parks and Recreation, Box 2390, Sacramento 95811. In summer many motels and private campgrounds along heavily-traveled U. S. 101 may fill early in the day.

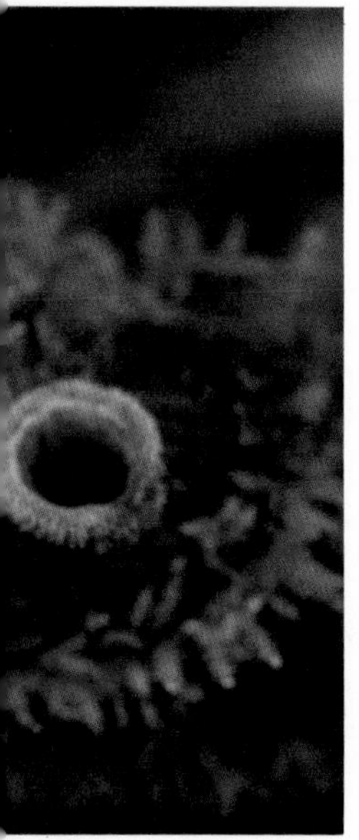

Scarlet waxy cap

DICK DURRANCE II, NATIONAL GEOGRAPHIC PHOTOGRAPHER. ABOVE RIGHT: TOM MYERS

Gold is still a gleam in the eyes of kids playing prospector near the site of a seaside gold rush of the 1850's. Others succumb to the lure of green treasure—along fern-draped 50-foot walls of Fern Canyon where Home Creek slashes its way to the sea, or (opposite) amid spiring trees of Jedediah Smith State Park, northern anchor of the national park.

DICK DURRANCE II, NATIONAL GEOGRAPHIC PHOTOGRAPHER

Drury Center in Crescent City, the national park headquarters, doubles as visitor information, exhibit, and program center until more facilities are developed. Pick up a *Visitor Guide,* containing maps, cues on current attractions, and tips on trails and scenic drives.

The Center was named for Newton B. Drury, past Director of the National Park Service and long a force in the Save-the-Redwoods League. Since 1918 the League has fought decimation of a natural legacy by scouting out prime redwood groves and raising funds to buy them as public parks. Scores of groves along Redwood Highway—U.S. 101—bear names of donors.

Travelers who have only one day to spend in redwood country often drive 101 north or south, stopping at scenic pullouts, taking short walks on marked trails in the woods or to the beach.

TALL
TREES
TRAIL

DICK DURRANCE II, NATIONAL GEOGRAPHIC PHOTOGRAPHER

Elk splash in a marsh at Gold Bluffs Beach, where redwoods overlook the sea.

At Mill Creek Campground in Del Norte Park we had a gargantuan stump for a back fence, a gurgling spring for music, rhododendrons in bloom by the picnic table, and juicy salmonberries as free dessert. Add a cold dip in Mill Creek and a hot shower... and some people think camping is rough. Reservations a must!

Irresistible as its name, Last Chance Trail high above the sea treads picturesque old Highway 101, now gone back to nature. Just beyond a detour named Damnation Creek Trail—a 900-foot drop in two miles—Last Chance breaks into the open for salt air, foggy ocean vistas, and, close by the old roadbed, spider webs and daisies jeweled with the morning breath of the sea. With time only to sample, we hoped for another chance at Last Chance.

Elk feed beside Prairie Creek, paralleling 101 for several miles. Ten of 21 trails that etch the creek's namesake state park fan out from an information and camping center. One of special interest, Revelation Trail, runs a brief .2 of a mile along a guide rope to "touchable" exhibits with signs in Braille.

Gold Bluffs, a few miles west, earned its name from a flurry of prospecting here in the 1850's, but the seaside cliffs have a golden hue unrelated to the elusive metal. Wild flowers take the sun on vertical faces; where the bluffs drop gradually, redwoods nod to the sea.

Jouncing north on the primitive beach road, we parked and walked up Fern Canyon, emerald with five-finger ferns from creek level to the top of 50-foot walls. After an easy, entrancing, but sometimes muddy walk, you may retrace your steps, continue on the James Irvine Trail to park headquarters, or climb to higher ground and loop back to the beach on a path overlooking the canyon and its silvery stream.

Heading back on the shore road, we passed cows and calves of the Gold Bluffs elk herd feeding among the tules. Driving on at snail's pace, Roy spotted a rack of antlers moving out of the brush. Another. One by one, five bulls emerged, one so superb he had to be boss elk. It is unwise to approach the animals on foot.

Anglers along the shore often share the surf with pelicans and sea lions. Whales may cruise by. There are good spots for clamming at low tide, lagoons and bays to swim in, tide pools to lure the biology buff. Considerate beachgoers try not to disturb helpless intertidal creatures; a rock upturned could expose tiny organisms to killing rays of the sun.

We drove slowly up Davison Road, edged by land logged in the 1960's. Over the stumps and feathery fringes that may be giants 500 years from now, a Pacific sunset shimmered, intensifying the aura of Gold Bluffs Beach.

Inside a bend of rushing Redwood Creek stands the tallest living thing yet found by man: a coast redwood measured at 367.8 feet by Dr. Paul Zahl of the National Geographic Society. An 8½-mile walk up the creek corridor also takes in the second, third, and sixth in height. Camping is permitted on sandbars. Bald Hill Road, which predates the park, gives access to Tall Trees Trail and to the park dedication site, Lady Bird Johnson Grove.

We park visitors shared the road with trucks hauling huge cylinders of newly cut redwood trees from adjoining forest to a nearby mill. After a quiet stroll to the dedication site, we drove on beyond the park and from an almost-bald hill looked down toward the tallest—and perhaps most endangered—trees in the park, in the half-mile-wide Redwood Creek corridor. On the adjacent steep slope a large block of privately-owned timber, intact when the park was created, was rapidly being cut. To keep valuable trees from shattering, bulldozers furrowed the soil, piling it to cushion the fall, thus creating an erosion hazard for trees downslope, including those "safe" in the park.

Conservationists like Mrs. Vinyard point out that the trees are on borrowed time until their watershed is protected. Should these titans crash, surely there would be a mighty groan.

Write Supt., Crescent City, Calif. 95531

DAVID ALAN HARVEY

The East

Nature whispers in the East, as gently as a butterfly visiting a dogwood.

Seymour L. Fishbein

Everglades

NATIONAL PARK, FLORIDA

The night dies slowly. Homestead sleeps. The migrant labor camps sleep. Entrance signs glow in the headlights, then fade. Onward I drone, along the park's single artery, past the unseen slash pines, across the channel called Taylor Slough, the broad "river of grass," the dwarf cypress forest, the mangrove edge where sweet and salt water meet.

It is hard to stay awake—though, in truth, I have dozed at midday along this 38-mile road. Beyond Taylor Slough and the Anhinga Trail, with its stunning show of snakebirds and alligators, there is little to tempt the motorist's eye in this strange, subtropic sanctuary where the piney highlands soar seven feet, where the sawgrass prairie sweeps to the horizon like an endless hayfield, where the most vital statistic on a winter day is likely to be the drying rate of the sloughs and marshes.

Abandon the road, a ranger had told me. Everglades National Park brims with life. Search out the right place; be there at the right time. Try Coot Bay Pond a half hour before dawn.

A few miles from road's end and the sprawling visitor complex at Flamingo, the sign comes into view, and I alight, shivering off the stiffness.

Around the pond, black and silent, a maze of mangroves throbs with a jungle-like din—clicking and cawing and nattering. Dawn begins to bleach the horizon behind me; I can make out the shapes of the noisemakers, but not their identities. They're no mystery, however, to Tom Teutsch and John MacRae, environmental health workers from Maryland, who have just parked and joined me. They have bird guides, field glasses, and—most important—a day's headstart in bird-watching here.

"Those dark ones are green herons.... The white splotches? Egrets.... That gray, stupid-looking one floundering around, an immature

New-style sightseers make the scene, wading wilds the Seminole called "pa-hay-okee—grassy waters." To 19th-century Americans the sun-washed sawgrass glades looked boundless—seemingly, "everglades."

DAVID HISER

Lore of the Glades: Hikers wallow past bald cypresses, deciduous conifers that turn "bald" in winter. Tiny organisms of periphyton, mainly algae, begin food webs, nourishing mosquito larvae, salamanders, tadpoles. Tender parts of sawgrass can feed humans.

DAVID HISER

black-crowned night heron." A flight of red-breasted mergansers arrives; they rise a bit as they break their glide, then plop in with a froth of side spray. By contrast, a great blue heron sails gently down, lowers spindly legs for a soft landing, and freezes into watchfulness, a most patient fisherman. A spotted sandpiper gleans the shore beside us, flicking its teetertail. But where are its spots? Bless the bird guides; in winter, we read, the bird's white breast is spotless.

Rush-hour traffic picks up. A strung-out flock of white ibises passes overhead, long needle bills warping downward at the tips. Then a roseate spoonbill, glamor bird, its name a perfect description. And a wood stork, its dark, knobby "flinthead" thrust flat out—worry bird, whose population trend in the park looks like a stock-market graph in the early '30's.

To watch this parade is sheer delight. In two days John MacRae and Tom Teutsch have checked off 55 species—30 they had never seen before. "The funny thing is," John smiled, "that with all of this, Florida made the mockingbird its state bird. That really throws me."

There's more. At the far end of the pond, maybe 300 yards distant, a tall dead tree gradually defines itself against the lightening sky. Then the sun balloons up out of Florida Bay behind us. Flat rays miss the pond, miss the mangroves, but kindle the treetop. There, poking up from a bowl of sticks, two snowy heads glisten in the sunlight. Bald eagles nesting!

Coot Bay Pond. A half hour after dawn.

"It's dead."

"No, it's plastic."

"Well, if it hasn't moved when we come back down the trail, we'll know it's not alive."

The young alligator slumped on a rock may not move, for there is something about a bright day and 80° F. that fills the beast with languor. But it is alive and well, as is the whole Anhinga Trail. Park officials take care to keep it so; in one recent year of shriveling drought, the slough was refreshed from wells pumping at the rate of 2,500 gallons a minute.

Golden moment captures a doe and fawn browsing the Shark Valley marshes at day's end. Like other land mammals of this spongy realm, the smallish white-tailed deer of the Everglades has learned to thrive in an aquatic environment. Tree islands offer breeding sites and a refuge from high water.

DAVID HISER

Set near the main entrance on the east, the Anhinga Trail lures endless throngs—daytrippers spicing a Miami vacation with natural wonders, families highballing down from the north for a precious winter week in the sun, nomadic retired couples gentling through their twilight years in bulky campers.

The alligator, even the motionless dozer, is a star. A few steps beyond beckons another attraction—an anhinga trolling for brunch at periscope depth. Only its skewer beak, head, and serpentine neck break the surface. You'll rarely see a snakebird flying up out of the water. Nature seems to have shortchanged the species on oil supplies for coating its plumage. So our trail now is strewn with water-soaked snakebirds, wings spread-eagled to the sun, tails angled furiously against a breeze that whips the pond lily platters off the slough's surface.

The path becomes a boardwalk leading out over sawgrass, pickerelweed, buttonbush, coco-plum. At the end of January we are months from the rainy season, either way; the brush is snap dry. Topsy-turvy world: In the north we look to spring for the stirrings of bird and bud, leaf and bug, all in phase in a great upwelling of life and renewal. Here the land has that tired, tranquil, late-summer look; yet the birds are approaching the height of the nesting season. By the calendar it is midwinter.

Where the boardwalk spans a pool, a battery of camera buffs, some with lenses the size of small cannon, have trained on a dark little copse. What's up? Purple gallinule, they whisper.

"Kevin, commere! There's a moving alligator." There must be a hundred Kevins on the trail; the boardwalk thunders with running feet. Heads crane over the side; there it goes, gliding in the shadows under the planking, perhaps eight feet long. "He's enormous," says a wide-eyed girl beside me. "He looks like he just finished eating somebody." The alligator will eat any meat it can get hold of—bird, fish, turtle. Human? Hardly ever. Here it concentrates mostly on garfish. And mostly at night.

Shark Valley tower looks down on the watery domain of the alligator, whose shining armor hints of ages when the archosaurians—ruling reptiles—held sway. Giant jaws crack a hard case to make a meal of turtle. Tower tour highlights a two-hour, 14-mile tram ride.

DAVID HISER. LOWER RIGHT: FREDERICK KENT TRUSLOW

Come back then, alone or on a scheduled night prowl. The moonflower vine will be in bloom. You can breathe its fragrance, and see the big white trumpets opened wide. A morning glory that glories in the night.

If you hold your flashlight just so (at eye level by your temple, as the naturalist will demonstrate) myriad pairs of eyes will gleam back at you. The red ones belong to alligators, yellow to frogs. You can hear the reptiles crashing about, and as the lights scissor the slough a lucky probe may cut through the submarine gloom to pick out a gator chomping on a gar.

"Walking the Anhinga Trail is like flying over the Grand Canyon at 10,000 feet." Strange thought, from the chief naturalist of Everglades National Park. George L. Robinson, Jr., smiled as he voiced it. He well knows the importance of the nature trails. But he is a child of the western wonderlands, and he also knows the difference between looking up at a mountain and climbing it, between touring a park and delving its mysteries.

"We have no grand scenes here," he says, "no Tetons, no Old Faithfuls. Our superlatives are miniatures." All the more reason, he felt, for people to wade out into the Glades, to explore the flowing water and the sweep of sedge, the complexities of a tree island. "Out of it comes a richer understanding of the park, informed concern—perhaps even a rediscovery of the sense of wonder we knew in childhood."

Thus evolved the Slough Slog or Swamp Tromp, scheduled several times a week in the winter season. Setting out from the Royal Palm visitor center, parties slosh through sawgrass flats to explore what Jean Craighead George in her *Everglades Wildguide* calls "the most incredible ecosystem of all the worlds within the world of the park"—a gator hole. The reptile scoops muck and plant life from a sink in the limestone floor. When the surrounding land dries, the gator's oasis offers sustenance to fish, frogs, snails, birds, and, to be sure, a living

smorgasbord for the landlord. From the Shark Valley entrance, hard by the Indian craft shops and villages along the Tamiami Trail, hikers may wade out to a tree island where Indians used to live, perhaps meeting the shy Everglades deer that still live there.

Northeast of Flamingo, another tromp lets you taste the difference in ecosystems—the south-flowing fresh water that sustains the sawgrass, and the salt water sluicing in from Florida Bay, upon which the stilt-legged red mangroves thrive. Here one day I joined a party led by Naturalist Jim Hart. Clad in sneakers and old slacks, we circled out around a tree island thick with cocoplum and poisonwood—a tree related to poison ivy and about as irritating.

Jim, his blazing red hair and handlebars a beacon on the flat prairie, held a sawgrass tasting seminar. We each plucked up a blade—carefully, for the fine teeth along the edge of this sedge can rip through skin like a hacksaw—and chewed the tender white base.

"It's edible," said Jim. "What's it taste like?"

"Kinda bland," noted David Hiser.

"Mild and tender," said Miss Gudrun Boethger of New York City.

"Typical sawgrass," cracked Cliff Tepper, of Schenectady, New York, a physician who had come down from a Miami convention to indulge his passion for birds and wild flowers.

Beguiled by a naturalist-charmer, kids and snakes relax at a Flamingo get-together. The indigo and the boldly checked corn snakes are harmless. The park's 63 kinds of "herptiles"—reptiles and amphibians—include four poisonous species: the cottonmouth, coral snake, and two rattlers, the pygmy and eastern diamondback.

DAVID HISER

Tenter and vehicle camper go their separate ways at Flamingo's drive-in and walk-in campsites. The walkers win a bayfront view livened with music of laughing gulls and windmilling palms. A nearby marina launches sport fishermen into Florida Bay for a bout with snook, redfish, snapper, or sea trout.
DAVID HISER

We came to a concrete bridge over an abandoned canal and gazed down into a scummy slackwater occupied by a small alligator and some bass; the banks were fringed by cabbage palms well whitened with bird droppings. Soon we were bushwhacking, calf-high in water and foot-sucking mud, hip-high in sawgrass, the cutting edges rasping against our trousers. A pause brought no relief; we sank deeper in the muck.

As we moved onto firmer ground, Jim halted to examine a flower blinking up from a stand of short scrub. "That's a grass pink," he pointed. Cliff bent low for a long moment. "That's an orchid," he said, with little doubt in his tone. Jim's luxuriant mustachio seemed to glow a bit more fiercely, but he didn't argue.

When I got back to the motel at Flamingo and showered off the muck, I broke out a park plant guide. Both men were right; our disputed flower was one of the park's terrestrial orchids, called a grass pink (genus *Calopogon*).

Scores of orchid species adorn the parkland, though many are epiphytes, or air plants, finding living room in the lush tropical hardwood hammocks by fastening on to the limbs of trees and living on air-borne nutrients.

A hammock shows us how minute variations in terrain can make a world of difference in the Everglades. A bump of land, as little as a foot above the watery Glades and undisturbed by fire, in time evolves into a jungle island that may include live oaks, mahoganies, royal palms, and gumbo-limbos—whose coppery, flaking bark looks like a sunburned nose peeling. Caribbeans made a medicinal salve of the gumbo-limbo's resin; its light wood was used for net floats and merry-go-round horses.

In the hammocks too grow lianas, ferns, mosses, and the weird strangler fig which begins as an air plant, sends roots down to the soil, and gradually clamps a death grip on the host tree. You can see the difference between the open, sunny Taylor Slough through which the Anhinga Trail winds and the dark jumble of nearby Royal Palm Hammock cut by the Gumbo-Limbo Trail.

In wintertime you'll have to imagine the gorgeous orchid show of spring and summer, but if the floral display is less exciting, so is the winter-thinned gantlet of mosquitoes.

The yearling wood stork puttered around the Royal Palm visitor area with the cool of a barnyard chicken; neither clicking cameras nor outstretched hands distracted the young flinthead. Park animals, of course, can be real friendly; the resident alligators at Long Pine Campground have been known to trundle up out of their pond to join the evening campfire programs. An alligator hide brushing against your legs in the dark adds a little something to a slide show.

There was a point to that tame stork, however, and as we crowded around it, a ranger told me its story. Its parents, along with some 1,200 other storks, had gathered in the park rookeries, had mated, and had brooded the eggs. Then, as they nursed the young, the adults abandoned the nests, leaving their offspring to starve. Some 30 nestlings were removed and raised by hand-feeding—a messy business of gathering fish, cutting them up, dodging the finicky eaters that spat unwanted pieces back.

The effort had saved some individuals—but did little for the species. It may be too late to save the wood stork in Everglades National Park. Nesting failure has become the rule, a successful year the exception. In 1933 one park rookery held some 50,000 storks. In 1965 the entire park population numbered 5,200; in 1972, about 1,500. If the pattern continues, wrote research biologist John C. Ogden, "the southern Everglades stork will cease to function as a viable population by the early 1980's."

Worse, the stork's breeding cycle is so closely attuned to the natural rhythm of the wetlands that scientists regard it as a "barometer species"—its fate provides a clue to the ecological stability of the remaining Everglades.

Until a century ago the river of grass, nourished by an average annual rainfall of 60 inches, flowed unhindered 120 miles from Lake Okeechobee to Florida Bay and the Gulf of Mexico. To the west, runoff from Big Cypress Swamp joined the lazy river that trickled southward on a slope of about three inches to the mile.

The Everglades system was not a delicate watchworks movement. It could absorb the shock of hurricane and frost, natural fire, drought, and flood, and resume its intricate processes, according to laws which men still have not fathomed. It had been evolving for 5,000 years, a wondrous blending of temperate and subtropic life unmatched in our land.

Now farms and urban sprawl and the canals and levees they require have permanently disrupted the flow; fire and drought take a hideous toll. In recent years conservationists have scored notable gains as they fought to preserve the wilderness remnants in Big Cypress and the park. But the Everglades stork kept failing. It is hard to put Humpty Dumpty together again.

Just how hard is shown in a study conducted by John Ogden and U. S. Geological Survey scientists. For years the park thirsted as its lifeblood from the north was diverted. Then water managers agreed to provide a minimum annual flow to the park. But instead of flowing down on a broad front as in nature, water deliveries funnel through the Tamiami Trail gates into the Shark Valley Slough. Parts of the park at times get too much water; the number and kinds of fishes in the system may be changing.

As the rainy season ends in November and the park begins drying, the flintheads return from their wanderings and move into the rookeries. In their fishing strategies, wading birds basically divide into lookers (herons and egrets) and gropers (storks and spoonbills). Thus, as the stork probes the shallows with its bill, its feeding efficiency is linked directly to the density of prey fishes—mollies, killifish, small bass, and bluegills.

If fish stocks are normal and the park dries at the optimum rate—about .183 centimeters per day at the Shark *(continued on page 346)*

FREDERICK KENT TRUSLOW

Winged Stars on a Watery Stage

Only remnants endure of the spectacular flocks that lured Audubon to the steamy keys, yet enough of wonder and grace to make the spirit fly: some 310 species, 75 nesting in the park, including the national bird.

Breakfast at Mrazek Pond: As the river of grass dries each fall, waders feast on fishes left in ponds like this—and early-bird visitors feast their eyes on common and snowy egrets, white pelicans, wood storks, and roseate spoonbills (also at left, flaunting the brilliant red of adult plumage).

FREDERICK KENT TRUSLOW

An odd couple, limpkin and anhinga hunt swamp and slough in distinctive ways. Wading with the limp that inspired its name, the limpkin pincers its favored prey, a Pomacea, *or apple snail. If the snail keeps its trapdoor shut, the snailer twists and pries with its bill until the muscle is cut. Swamp folk heard the limpkin's haunting night wail and dubbed it the "crying bird."*

The anhinga swims for its prey. Spearing a fish, the anhinga tosses it up and catches it headfirst; fins angled back won't snag when the diner swallows. After a plunge the bird clambers ashore and spreads silver-spotted wings to dry. Many call it snakebird, for its slender, overlong neck, or water turkey, for its buff-tipped tail, fan-shaped in flight.

DAVID HISER. OPPOSITE: FREDERICK KENT TRUSLOW

Tranquil repast: A week-old barred owlet accepts a fillet of rat in a smooth beak-to-beak transfer. Seconds? Plenty in the furry bundle on the ground.

A transition zone between temperate and tropic climes, the Everglades mingles the life of both: pine and oak, mangrove and gumbo-limbo; thriving raccoon and dwindling manatee; barred owl, blue jay, mockingbird, and pileated woodpecker, and mangrove cuckoo, white-crowned pigeon, and magnificent frigatebird—the winged "man-o'war" of tropic skies.

FREDERICK KENT TRUSLOW

Ordeal by fire preserves the piney woods. Thick pine bark resists flames that check encroaching hardwoods; color-coded sensor takes temperatures. Everglades was the first national park to attempt the restoration of natural communities with controlled burning.
DAVID HISER

Valley checkpoint—fish are concentrating in shrinking pools as the burdens of bird breeding intensify; parents can gather food as the nestlings grow bigger and hungrier.

If, however, unseasonable rains or deliveries from the north keep water levels high, the birds may delay nesting for months. The next rainy season may begin with young still in the nests; fish stocks thin out and the adults, overwhelmed by the workload, quit trying. In 1974 a drought seems to have helped; 1,500 young storks were bred, the best record in seven years.

Research indicates a need for more sensitively timed water deliveries, yet no one is sure it will work. Man's tinkering may have doomed any chance to recover the primeval rhythm.

There is another, brighter side to the story in the 300,000-acre expanse of Florida Bay, where nature simmers a rich bouillabaisse for man and bird, fish and reptile. It harbors most of the few hundred wild crocodiles left in the United States. On its mangrove-fenced keys breed bald eagles, ospreys, spoonbills, common and snowy egrets, cormorants, great white and Louisiana herons, and brown pelicans.

Park Biologist William B. Robertson, Jr., has kept an eye on them for more than 20 years.

"They're in good shape," he told me one day. "Spoonbills were down to about 250 when the park was established in 1947. Now they're up to 2,500." Great white herons, he went on, had been recovering under park protection until Hurricane Donna in 1960 destroyed all but a few hundred; now they too number about 2,500.

For John Ogden's research the osprey, or fish hawk, played the same role in Florida Bay as the wood stork did in the interior. Elsewhere the fish hawk suffered serious setbacks from man's encroachment and pollution. In Florida Bay the news is good.

For years Ogden has gathered data from 55 osprey nests. "We've checked eggshell thickness and found it in the normal range," he said as we boated out to Frank Key for his bi-weekly survey. "We've checked the contents of eggs

FREDERICK KENT TRUSLOW. OPPOSITE: DAVID HISER

What ails the wood stork? Food shortages frustrate nesters, threaten the species. Surveys of sites like Madeira Rookery (below) record the grim pattern. Wings in the air belong to "tourist birds"—white pelicans that nest up north and winter in Florida.

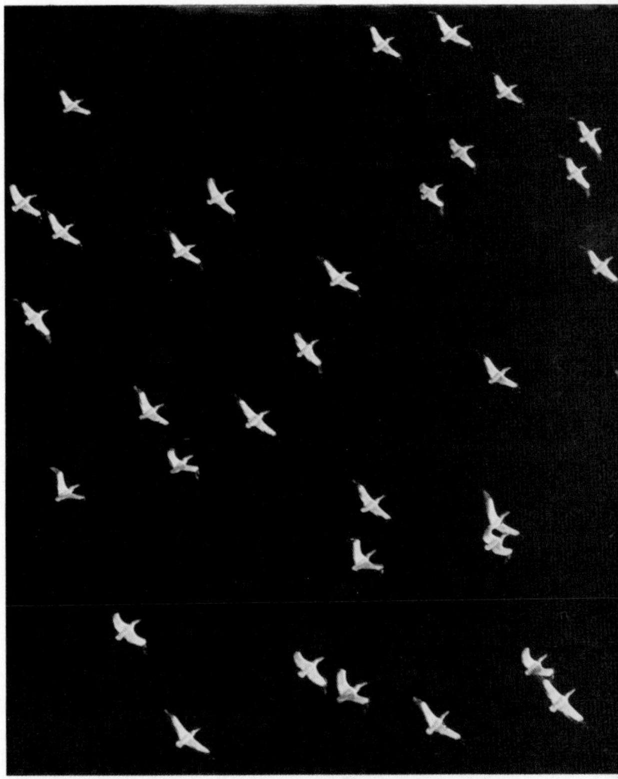

for pesticide and metal traces—everything was low, less than five parts per million. Only about half the breeders are successful, but half is enough to maintain a stable population."

Man treads warily on these inner keys and their precious nurseries. Visitors can cruise well offshore in their own or chartered vessels. Sunset cruises in tour boats offer unforgettable views of homebound flocks. But the bird keys themselves are off limits.

As we neared Frank Key, Ogden slipped overboard and shinnied up a red mangrove to a stick nest lined with turtle grass from the bay bed. "Two eggs, probably just laid," he called out; an assistant jotted it down. We tied up and threaded the island's interior prairie of salt-tolerant plants—sea blite, purslane, glasswort, and saltwort. As Ogden peered into another nest, the father arrived clutching a mullet in a claw and circled screaming while the mother swung as

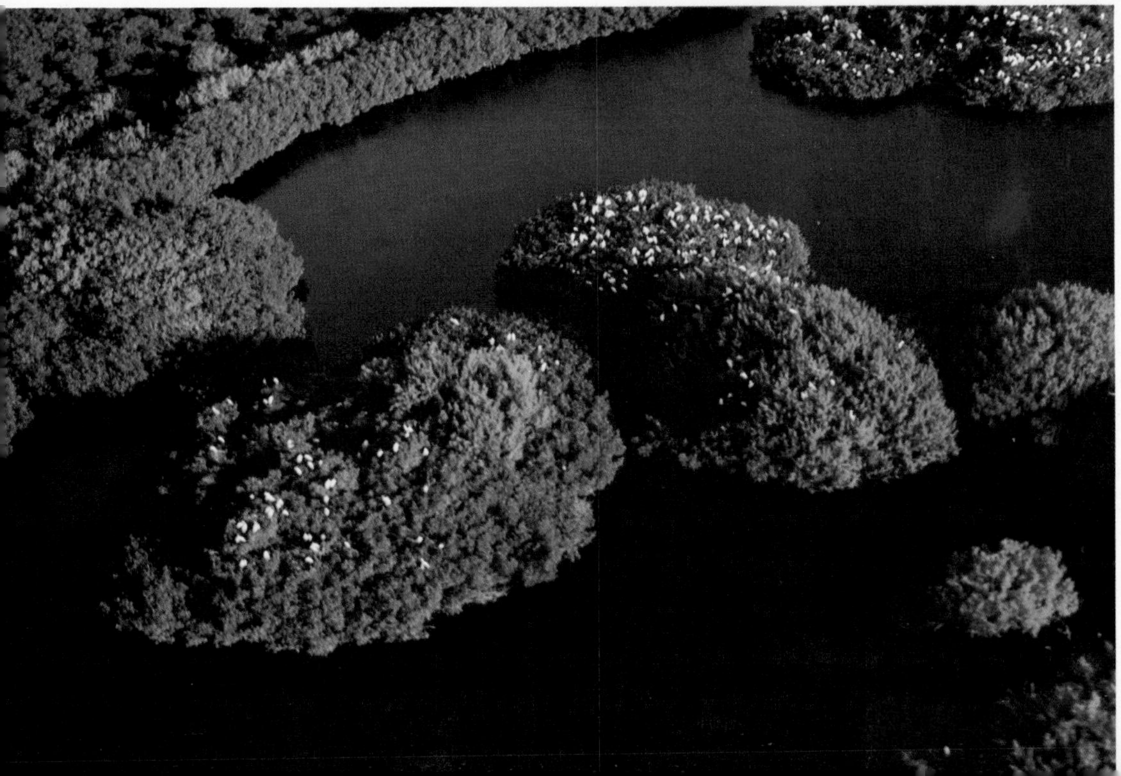

A robust fledgling tongue-lashes an intruder during a check of Florida Bay osprey nests. Biologist John Ogden studies nestlings and the eggs they broke out of; shell thickness of .50 millimeter is well in the normal range. While osprey numbers fell as much as 14 percent a year in other eastern and northern states, Ogden found them holding steady here.

DAVID HISER

if on a pendulum—swooping in low over the intruder, pulling up, tumbling back into a return dive. Ogden gently examined their five-week-old daughter and hurried down.

We skirted a tangle of thorny saffron-plum and blackbead alive with cormorants, pelicans, and common egrets. At the edges hovered crows, looking for unattended nests to raid. "I've seen an osprey kill a crow flying low over an osprey nest, but pelicans and egrets don't seem to defend theirs," Ogden said.

In the distance I spied an osprey diving on a cruising bald eagle, sheering off as the bigger bird feinted with its head. Recalling the classic picture of a fish hawk yielding its catch to an attacking eagle, I cheered the osprey on.

"We think the eagles out here may be helping themselves to birds from the rookeries," Ogden said. "We found bones of young spoonbills in one eagle nest. I thought of asking the Office of Endangered Species which one of these species we should save."

With a balky motor and the tricky maneuvering required to tie on to a towboat in the shallows, we were a long time getting back to Flamingo. Bay boaters tend to spend much time out of their boats. Low tide exposes vast mud banks; sun and calm opaque the water, making it impossible to "read." Once I saw a charter boat take a shortcut over low water by planing the keel at full throttle, the propeller churning mud. The bay bottom, a vital link in a unique food chain, deserves better.

A few days around the baking parking lots of Flamingo builds a craving for the backcountry water trails. Most famous is the Wilderness Waterway, winding 99 miles from Flamingo through breeze-swept bays and dark, narrow channels to the park's northwestern gateway at Everglades City. A powerboat can roar through the marked course in six hours—though that would scarcely do justice to what Bill Robertson has called "perhaps the largest and best developed mangrove forest on earth."

Tracery of mangroves, root and branch, frames paddlers on Bear Lake Trail and campers at the North River chickee, named for the open-sided, thatch-roofed dwellings of Florida Indians. More than a score of primitive campsites offer haven in the backcountry.
DAVID HISER

A canoe makes for a more leisurely exploration —seven days, at least, to do it all.

You can enrich and extend your voyage—by detouring into Hells Bay, say, and learning why it's called that ("Hell to get into, and hell to get out of"), or by spending extra nights at primitive campsites. On Onion Key in Lostmans River, Indians once lived; in the booming 1920's, developers were based there. The boom burst; a hurricane—so often the killer of dreams on Florida's tip—delivered the final blow. At "The Coming Miami of the Gulf" you will find tables, grills, and a pit toilet.

On the Chatham River you can camp at the Watson Place site, where Ed Watson raised sugar cane and a reputation for murder. Neighbors gunned him down in 1910. Charlton W. Tebeau recounts such lore in his *Man in the Everglades*—a good companion for the trip.

My companion was backcountry ranger Fred Whitehead, a skillful paddler and a man of awesome serendipity—he was the only one I'd met who had seen one of the few Florida panthers left in the park. We'd have two days; Fred quickly dismissed a venture into the mangrove wilderness. "We'd spend hours pulling through mangroves in those channels," he said. "For a two-day trip the Bear Lake canoe trail is the best around." It stretches 12 miles, mainly along the old Homestead Canal, westward to Cape Sable, the southernmost tip of the United States mainland. The logistics are uncomplicated—priority items consisting of fresh water, insect repellent, sunburn lotion, a small tent with screening, a variety of snacks.

Along our trail grew red mangroves, with their familiar arcing roots, and black mangroves, with their breathing roots, called pneumatophores, sticking up like asparagus spears. Tannic acid from the trees stained the water red.

Land's end: Florida Bay strews shells at Cape Sable, then pounds them to the fineness of sand. Angel wings crown a trove that includes arks, mactras, and carditas. The park bans shelling, discourages swimming in waters often murky, pulled by strong tides, and ranged by five kinds of sharks and the southern stingray.

Once Fred spotted a manchineel, the legendary "poison apple" that Spanish explorers dubbed *"el arbol de la muerte*—the tree of death." Some scientists have called it the most poisonous tree in the hemisphere; others believe it is no worse than poison ivy. No one recommends eating the crabapple-like fruit.

At times the canal was aboil with fish; every stroke triggered the explosive sounding of a garfish, or the quiet flip of a tarpon. Where Mud Lake and Bear Lake opened out to either side, glorious vistas spread before us.

Shoals of white pelicans blotted out a distant shore. Pintails and blue-winged teal rattled up from the waters, their swift, blurred wingbeats in sharp contrast to the stately flapping of the waders. A file of feeding storks looked up as we passed close by, and flew off. They seemed to rise laboriously, heavy heads hanging low, then lifting as the birds gathered speed. Sometimes we could hear only the fanning of wings as a flock swept away, hidden from view by a tangle of trees. We swung south down East Cape Canal and soon were out of slack water and into Florida Bay, broadside to the breakers, jouncing every foot of our last mile.

A grand sweep of shore curved away to the west—clean and light and beautiful. Only a few tents dotted the expanse—no crowding here. Mounds of seashells edged the tide wash.

Inland lay a prairie of wave-heaped marl. Hurricanes had battered it. Man had tried to alter it. The Army had built forts here. Men had raised cattle and coconuts. Inevitably, the 1920's spawned a Cape Sable Development Company with talk of a whole new city here.

But when I looked back from the beach all I could see was prairie, covered with spartina grass, palm, agave, yucca, Jamaica dogwood, and mangrove. All I could hear was wind and wave, soughing and crashing, soughing and crashing.... I slept soundly that night.

EVERGLADES NATIONAL PARK

Area 2,188 square miles.

Features: *Largest subtropical wilderness in U. S. Teems with wildlife; fascinating plant and animal ecology. Marshy prairies, mangrove, cypress swamps, tree islands, tidal rivers, lakes, shell beaches.*

Activities: *Visitor centers at park entrance, Royal Palm Station, Flamingo. Campfire programs, guided swamp hikes, night prowls in winter season. Cassettes and players available at entrance to relate the park story along a 38-mile drive. Gumbo Limbo Trail: tropical hardwoods, air plants. Anhinga Trail: alligators, birds. Pa-Hay-Okee Overlook: "River of Grass," untracked swath of sawgrass, bald cypress. Mahogany Hammock: largest mahogany trees in continental U. S. Mangrove Trail: boardwalk through mangrove jungle. Shark Valley: two-hour tram ride through sawgrass wilds, fine for spotting alligators, aquatic birds, deer; observation tower at midpoint. Wilderness Waterway: 99-mile marked trail through Ten Thousand Islands and mangrove coast (see insert map) for canoes, powerboats; primitive campsites en route. Snook, tarpon, marlin fishing offshore; boating tours at Everglades City and Flamingo. Canoe trail to Cape Sable beaches. Short hiking trails. Excellent biking on level park road.*

Season: *Open all year. Most birds nest in winter; temperature usually 60-80°, little rain, waters may become rough for boating. Summers hot, humid, buggy; brief, heavy showers; waters calmer.*

What to bring: *Cottons, visor cap, light jacket, insect repellent, sunglasses, binoculars, telephoto lens. For swamp walks, extra sneakers, socks, trousers.*

How to get there: *I-95; U. S. 1, 41; Fla. 27. Air, rail to Miami (40 miles); car rentals at Miami, Homestead. By cruiser on inland waterways.*

Accommodations: *In park: motel at Flamingo; campgrounds at Long Pine Key, Flamingo (one section for tenters only). Motels in Miami, Homestead, Everglades City area.*

Services: *Restaurant, stores, gas, marina, charter boats, and houseboat, canoe, skiff rentals at Flamingo. Hospital, churches in Homestead.*

Park regulations: *Backcountry camping by permit; campfires only in designated areas; file float plans for wilderness boating. No molesting of alligators or other wildlife. Boaters must practice rules of water safety; charts of park waters available at Flamingo. Florida fishing license in fresh water.*

For further information write Supt., Box 279, Homestead, Fla. 33030

DAVID HISER

Gordon Young

Great Smoky Mountains

NATIONAL PARK, NORTH CAROLINA-TENNESSEE

Which is the most visited national park in the United States? Yellowstone? Yosemite? Grand Canyon? Guess again . . . and look eastward. Great Smoky Mountains National Park, straddling the Tennessee-North Carolina border, welcomes eight million visitors a year—more than twice the number at any other park. That means as many as 60,000 people on a single summer day! Some are just passing through; U. S. 441 between Knoxville and Asheville bisects the park. But most are seeking at least a brief escape to a less crowded world of forests and hills and streams.

Can anyone find solitude in a place so heavily visited? The answer is yes. I once strolled a Smokies trail in peak season and in half a day encountered not a soul.

For one thing, the park is large—by eastern standards. Only 226 miles of paved roads traverse a domain that encompasses some 800 square miles of mountainous terrain.

Then, too, the vegetation is overwhelming, even along the transmountain highway. Driving our camper through the park early one morning, my family and I were impressed with the tangle of oak, pine, hemlock, yellow poplar, rhododendron, and mountain laurel growing along the road. How could nature cram the steep hills with so much greenery, we wondered. The close-packed leaves exude hydrocarbons and water vapor, which in turn produce the filmy "smoke" that gives the mountains their name.

And we had been forewarned about crowds: To find a campsite and to avoid horrendous traffic jams, come early in the day, preferably in midweek. We did, and were rewarded with a pleasingly uncrowded feeling. For only a small fraction of the visiting throngs use the park's camping facilities. Most stay in motels outside the park and drive in on day trips.

Hikers lured by the Great Smokies' hazy heights scramble across Cliff Top on the rocky brow of Mount Le Conte, one of 22 summits topping 6,000 feet. Shadowed West Point rears its head nearby.

MARTIN ROGERS

Many attractions can be seen without leaving your car—on drive-in nature trails, no less! One of these traces an 11-mile loop around Cades Cove, past split-rail fences and sturdy log buildings that pioneer settlers would recognize. We visited a blacksmith shop, saw corn being ground into meal in a water-powered grist mill, and watched honeybees swarm around a hive called a "bee gum."

Motor nature trails have their place here in the Smokies, but those who switch from car to foot will see much more. Yet less than five percent of the visitors take advantage of the park's 700 miles of hiking trails, nature walks that offer

RIGHT: THOMAS NEBBIA. UPPER AND OPPOSITE: JAMES L. AMOS, NATIONAL GEOGRAPHIC PHOTOGRAPHER

Spiral ramp leads visitors to a lookout tower atop 6,642-foot Clingmans Dome, highest of the park's peaks. Some hike up the mountain, others drive. Their reward? A sweeping view of fir-clad slopes. Nearby winds the Appalachian Trail. Youngsters take part in an evening campfire program, as park naturalists cover topics that range from fish and flowers to bears and pioneer settlers.

abundant opportunity to see at close range the park's great wealth of plant and animal life.

"Geologists class these mountains among the oldest on earth," the park's chief naturalist told me. "They were already old when the Ice Age came. The glaciers stopped north of here, and northern plants shifted southward, mingling with local species. Walk up Mount Le Conte, and you'll find trees on the upper slopes similar to those of southeastern Canada."

I had heard of Mount Le Conte. Motorists see it only from a distance, for no road winds up its green slopes. Perched on the summit is a concessioner-operated lodge, supplied by pack-train, that accommodates 50 overnighters. To reach it, guests must walk up or ride horseback.

Leaving my wife and son to visit friends, I started up the mountain from Newfound Gap. For the next six hours I was alone with the mountain. I saw no other hikers. But as I strolled the eight-mile trail, juncos fluttered down to *tsk tsk* at me, and a black-throated blue warbler flashed through the trees, showing off his white vest, black bib, and blue coat.

For the first three miles I walked a section of the Appalachian Trail, which stretches 70 miles across the park. Then I turned off on another trail—a narrow one ironically called The Boulevard. Tough going. Spruce and fir gradually appeared among the rhododendron and mountain laurel. The naturalist was right. I'd climbed all the way to "Canada."

BRUCE DALE AND (OPPOSITE) JAMES L. AMOS, NATIONAL GEOGRAPHIC PHOTOGRAPHERS

Home to the hiker, a trailside shelter nestles amid forest greenery on the Smokies' crest. Campgrounds and some 95 backcountry campsites also dot the park. Snug retreat for non-campers, Le Conte Lodge (below) and its rustic cabins open in April and must be reserved. These lodgers snack before hiking down.

A cheerful welcome awaited me at the lodge. We 40 guests had varied backgrounds, yet most of us had climbed the 6,593-foot mountain on foot, so we were a fraternity. New friendships made the day fly. In the evening we all strolled out to watch a descending sun set the clouds aflame. Then into the lodge, to the warmth of roaring fireplaces—though it was midsummer in the valley below.

At Smokemont Campground the next day my son Michael greeted me with fish stories about the big ones that got away. There really are good-size trout in these fisherman-lined streams. Park authorities keep the waters productive by allowing only children 12 or under to fish near the campgrounds. In other "fish-for-fun" sections of the streams, anglers must free any trout less than 16 inches long.

We climbed another mountain a few days later—this time the easy way. The three of us drove up Clingmans Dome to its high-perched parking lot, then walked the paved, half-mile trail to the summit. At the top, the trail continues skyward, spiraling up the ramp of an observation tower. A dozen people shared our view, one of them in a wheelchair. The easy, asphalt trail suddenly took on new meaning: How else could handicapped visitors enjoy this beauty?

Our platform rose above the park's tallest peak. We seemed to be adrift on a stormy sea. Wherever I looked, mountains rose in great green billows, motionless waves given movement by the shadows of passing clouds.

Next day we moved to Elkmont Campground in the park's northern section. Our tenting neighbors all seemed to have bear stories to tell—like the one about the ranger who caught a motorist trying to push a bear into the front seat of his car. The man wanted to photograph it there—next to his wife! And the tale about the camper who smeared cold cream on her face before retiring. She woke up, the story went, to find a bear in her tent licking off the cream.

Interesting but imaginative yarns, my wife and I assured each other as we walked to our campsite. Still, we stole nervous glances at bear-shaped shadows that seemed to prowl just beyond our lantern's circle of light. There

Cades Cove, green-carpeted valley in the western reaches of the park, preserves a slice of pioneer America. In the Methodist churchyard rest many who settled here in the 1800's. A one-way road loops past restored cabins, barns, and a grist mill from frontier days. Farmers still tend their fields.

are bears here, of course, about 300 of them, and once I met one raiding a trash can, so it is always wise to keep food beyond their reach.

One excursion took us to the eastern end of the park, along corkscrew roads to the rolling pastureland of Cataloochee, an idyllic valley surrounded by peaks and ridges. It seemed like Shangri-La. We took a 15-minute reconnaissance drive and saw two deer, a wild turkey, a fox—but not one other visitor.

Later I talked with the superintendent about the park's future. "We'll do what we can to handle the growing numbers of campers," he said. "But more and more people will have to camp outside the park and drive in for the day.

"We allow wilderness camping in most of the park, but backcountry fire permits are required. And we get quite a few winter campers, too—most of them skiers who come here with heated camping rigs and spend their days on the slopes near Gatlinburg."

The superintendent explained that meeting the needs of campers and other visitors must be balanced against preserving the park's wilderness character and its history.

"Part of our job," he continued, "is to define the limits beyond which there will be no more development. And when we reach those limits—well, that's it."

Suddenly it was September, and school bells would be ringing. Our stay was at an end. On Labor Day weekend a torrent of cars poured out of the park, our camper among them.

I went back again that winter—back to an uncrowded park. It was a much more open park, now that most of the leaves had gone. The mountains were still magnificent from the tower on Clingmans Dome, though now they were white instead of green.

Once more I returned. This time in May, to visit friends who live just outside the park: Jim Gray—advertising executive turned mountain artist—his wife Fran, and their three children.

I sat with Jim one evening on the veranda of his hillside home and watched a distant thunderstorm flicker its way across the mountains. As it moved, lush green slopes turned to shadowed blues and violets.

Jim sighed. "Before I came here, I'd always thought of a mountain as something that just sat there being a mountain. But look at that movement—those changing lights!"

The storm moved on then, and a heavenly theater curtain opened to reveal the Smokies in infinite detail. For a few minutes they would be free of their veil of mist.

Six-year-old Matthew Gray joined us briefly, then rushed back into the house to spread the momentous tidings.

"Hey, everybody come here quick and see! Daddy's mountains are out!"

GREAT SMOKY MOUNTAINS NATIONAL PARK

Area 800 square miles.

Features: *Roof of eastern America astride Tenn.-N.C. border, cloaked in verdant forest. Some 1,400 varieties of trees, shrubs, herbs; 50 fur bearers; 200 birds; rainbow, brook, and brown trout.*

Activities: *Pioneer Museum at Oconaluftee Visitor Center. Gristmill, log houses, drive-through barn at Cades Cove. 226 miles of roads; one-way, slow-traffic wilderness motor trail near Gatlinburg; Clingmans Dome Highway rises to 6,311 ft. Some 700 miles of horse and foot trails (70 miles of Maine-to-Georgia Appalachian Trail in park with trailside shelters). Fishing in 700 miles of streams; state license required. Wilderness camping. Illustrated talks May-Oct.*

Season: *Park open all year. Lowlands warm in summer, mild in winter; summits always cooler. Autumn has least fog and rain.*

How to get there: *U.S. 441 between Knoxville, Tenn., and Asheville, N.C., crosses park. See insert map. Air and bus via the two cities; Smoky Mountain Tours in summer. Rail to Asheville.*

Accommodations: *Seven camp and trailer grounds. Le Conte Lodge, reached only by foot or horseback, open Apr.-Oct.; write Le Conte Lodge, Gatlinburg, Tenn. 37738. Hotels, motels in nearby towns.*

Park regulations: *Do not feed or approach bears. Camping, fires outside campgrounds by permit only.*

Write Supt., Gatlinburg, Tenn. 37738

BRUCE DALE, NATIONAL GEOGRAPHIC PHOTOGRAPHER

Blue Ridge Parkway

VIRGINIA-NORTH CAROLINA-GEORGIA

There are faster routes between the Great Smokies and Shenandoah National Park. But a leisurely drive along the 469-mile Blue Ridge Parkway is not a journey to a vacation; it is a vacation in itself.

Aside from the 45 mph speed limit, you may find this high road slower than you'd planned. Spectacular views of the southern Appalachian Mountains demand halts at overlooks. Nature trails, historical exhibits, visitor centers, and picnic areas call you to park the car for a while. Lodges and campgrounds suggest a layover to fish in a mountain stream.

No neon signs or billboards assault you. Instead, there are deer browsing at roadside, gleaming waterfalls and dark tunnels, fascinating rock formations with such names as Devils Courthouse and Wildcat Rocks, and ridge after ridge of rolling forested mountains.

Once our western frontier, these ancient hills still cradle the weathered log cabins and split-rail fences of mountain folk whose forefathers left the settled valleys to wrest a living from the highlands and secluded hollows.

At Mabry Mill, water powers a creaking wheel and a blacksmith's hammer clangs in the clear air. Short trails lead far back into history at restored canal locks along the James River and the Yankee Horse logging railroad near Wigwam Falls. At the Parkway Craft Center in Cone Memorial Park, weavers, woodcarvers, and basketmakers demonstrate the old-time arts, and the Craftsman's Trail shows you the natural materials they use.

Daniel Boone's Wilderness Road intersects the parkway in the south; the Appalachian Trail crosses and recrosses it in the north.

The parkway is open year round, though snow and ice may cause temporary closings.

Write Supt., Box 7606, Asheville, N.C. 28807

Rhododendron's late-spring blossoms refresh both man and beast along the Blue Ridge Parkway. Such scenes as mile-high Craggy Pinnacle (overleaf) lure tourists from cars to top-of-the-world romps.

DAVID ALAN HARVEY (ALSO OVERLEAF)

Shirley L. Scott

Shenandoah

NATIONAL PARK, VIRGINIA

Jeremys Run. Matthews Arm. Thornton Gap. Marys Rock. Lewis Mountain. Along the 105-mile Skyline Drive that bisects Shenandoah National Park, the old names recall the old times when settlers cleared homesteads, planted corn and tobacco, hunted squirrel and deer, bear and beaver, and harvested nuts and bark from plentiful chestnut trees.

Since establishment of the park in 1935, a gift to the nation from the people of Virginia, nature has reclaimed these ancient Blue Ridge Mountains. Hardwood forests again cover the slopes. Wildlife is abundant. Even cougar, nearly extinct in the East, are again seen here. Almost half the park's 193,500 acres now qualify for the National Wilderness Preservation System.

From the windy top of Hawksbill, at 4,050 feet the park's highest peak, to the deep woods and rugged terrain of wild, lonely Riprap Hollow (see insert map), Shenandoah annually welcomes 2½ million visitors. Most of them tour Skyline Drive, stopping at one or another of the 66 scenic overlooks to enjoy the new greenery of spring or the riotous colors of autumn. Resultant traffic jams have sparked planning for a future shuttle-bus system.

Picnic areas, wayside restaurants, and two visitor centers add to the pleasures of a one-day excursion. For longer stays, lodges and campgrounds are available—and often full. Write ARA Virginia Sky-Line, Box 727, Luray, Va. 22835, for lodge reservations.

More than 360 miles of trails entice both novice and veteran hikers to take a closer look at these gentle mountains. The popular Stony Man Nature Trail, a relatively easy 1½-mile round trip, leads to a sweeping view of Shenandoah Valley from the park's second highest peak. A walk in Nicholson Hollow

Sunrise greets a tree-sheltered campground in Shenandoah Park. Backpackers too are encouraged to seek solitude. Backcountry camping regulations require them to tent in isolated retreats of their choice. Group size and length of stay are limited.

DAVID ALAN HARVEY

Silvery waters of Dark Hollow Falls tumble toward a rendezvous with the Rose River. This 70-foot cascade, the closest one to Skyline Drive, may be reached by a steep half-mile trail from the road. Another visitor finds that happiness is a hammock at Big Meadows, one of four auto campgrounds.
DAVID ALAN HARVEY

brings you to crumbling stone walls and log cabins. Along the Swamp Nature Trail, poignant "ghost forests" of blight-killed chestnut trees remind you that the chestnut was once king of the Eastern forests. Whiteoak Canyon trails meander along rocky streams and wend past six waterfalls. Or you can tramp to Herbert Hoover's presidential fishing retreat close by the Rapidan River.

Seasoned hikers take on Big Devils Stairs or the boulder-strewn summit of Old Rag, or head for remote sections of the Appalachian Trail, which closely parallels Skyline Drive.

Backpackers find solitude in the park's innovative "camp-anywhere" system. Your tent must be out of sight of roads, trails, and other campers. Permits are required; open fires and glass containers are prohibited. All traces of your camp must be erased when you leave.

From bus or car, campground or trail, you can usually count on seeing some of the park's wildlife. White-tailed deer browse at the edge of the woods. Chipmunks enliven lodge grounds. Haughty skunks stroll the roadside. Bears and raccoons prowl campgrounds at night. Look up to see hawks circling the peaks. Look down at a walkingstick *(Diapheromera femorata)* as it lurches across your picnic blanket.

Virginia's mostly mild winters invite visits to the park in months when trails may be snowy. The lodge, campground, and a restaurant at Big Meadows are open all year, though roads may be temporarily closed by storms. A walk in the still winter woods adds yet another dimension to the beauty and pleasures of this park.

Write Supt., Luray, Va. 22835

David F. Robinson

Cape Hatteras

NATIONAL SEASHORE, NORTH CAROLINA

Hurl towering waves, whipped to a boil by frequent Atlantic gales, against a slim barrier of lonely islands. Add the ghosts of pirates and the hulks of hundreds of shipwrecks. Season with wheeling seabirds, scrappy game fish, dunes sculptured by the winds, shells and sunsets in rainbow hues. From these ingredients nature brews a magic tonic: Cape Hatteras.

There is little permanence here on the Outer Banks of North Carolina. Winds constantly rearrange the dunes; wave, tide, and storm reshape the shoreline. For decades men fought back with bulldozers, dredges, and trucks, laboring doggedly to put back the sands that nature swept away. In 1974 the effort was abandoned; the sea again reigns undisputed.

Seen on a map or from an airplane, the chain of islands—Bodie to the north, then Pea, Hatteras, and Ocracoke—blends into a thin golden ribbon pinned to the wrinkled Atlantic by the black-and-white spire of Cape Hatteras Lighthouse, loftiest in the country at 208 feet. From its base the ribbon trails northward to Cape Henry and southwestward to Cape Lookout. In the 70-mile portion between Whalebone Junction and Ocracoke Inlet, Cape Hatteras National Seashore preserves 45 square miles of one of the nation's stormiest coasts.

Offshore the sands of these barrier islands shelve away to form a shallow ledge reaching a dozen miles out to sea. Here on a windy day the great waves rear up like stags and ram each other to froth over the shoals. Off Hatteras Light the warm Gulf Stream meets colder Atlantic currents, adding strength to surf and undertow.

Hurricanes in the summer and fall sometimes lash great breakers right over the narrow wisp of land and into Pamlico Sound; a tamer blow can still erase an inlet or cut an island in two. Called the "Graveyard of the Atlantic," this

Surf's up but sun's down; surfers head home amid flags of sea oats. Long Atlantic swells bring out boards at Hatteras even in chilly spring and fall. The lure of sea and sand brings visitors year round.

GEORGE F. MOBLEY, NATIONAL GEOGRAPHIC PHOTOGRAPHER

Winds that rule the Cape belly a blanket and enliven a game of double catch. Fences help pin down blowing sands. At nearby Kitty Hawk in 1903 the Wrights rode these winds on the first powered flights. A monument (below) crowns a hill where they practiced gliding; a visitor center re-creates their shops and frail craft.

region has claimed 700 ships in 400 years. Sir Richard Grenville's flagship *Tiger* opened the grim roster in 1585 when she ran aground in Ocracoke Inlet; as late as 1969 the seagoing tug *Marjorie McAllister* vanished off Cape Lookout. A ghost fleet lies forever anchored in the sea: schooners and steamers, fishing boats and battlewagons, submarines and the vessels they torpedoed in two wars.

On the last day of 1862 a steamer towed a strange craft down the Outer Banks. It was the *Monitor,* the first Federal ironclad in the Civil War, a turreted gunboat sailors called a "cheesebox on a raft." In March, thousands had seen her pit her two guns against the *Merrimack's* ten in a standoff near Hampton Roads, Virginia; now she faced a Hatteras gale.

"The sea rolled high and pitched together in the peculiar manner only seen at Hatteras," her helmsman later recalled. Cut loose from her tow, she sank with 16 of her crewmen. For more than 100 years she eluded searchers. In 1974 a team aided by the National Geographic Society located the rusted hulk—too weak to be raised, too historic to be forgotten.

Wrecks hold a special fascination here. Visitors puff to the top of Hatteras Light, more than a century old, to view this battleground of ship and sea and to peer at the lamps that still point warning fingers of light to helmsmen 20 miles at sea. In a visitor center that once housed lighthouse keepers, vacationists look over maps and relics and pick up a list of wrecks they can find along the beaches. Then off they go to let cameras and imaginations explore the haunted hulks. Now and then the fickle sands unveil a long-forgotten wreck or swallow up a familiar old relic, perhaps for a few months, perhaps forever. That's part of the fascination.

Turbulent tides of history have washed over these shores, too. On Roanoke Island in the 1580's England's first North American colony struggled for three years, then vanished. Historians still puzzle over the word "Croatoan"

EMORY KRISTOF AND (OPPOSITE) GEORGE F. MOBLEY, BOTH NATIONAL GEOGRAPHIC PHOTOGRAPHERS

found carved on a stockade post. Many visitors to the Cape take a short side trip to the restored bastion at Fort Raleigh National Historic Site. A summer pageant, "Lost Colony," dramatizes the enduring mystery.

Nearby stands the Wright Brothers National Memorial at Kill Devil Hills. Beside the grassy dune where Orville and Wilbur Wright launched themselves into the sea wind on flimsy gliders, visitors pace off the four short spans of the world's first man-carrying powered flights. Forever becalmed in a visitor center, full-size reproductions of glider and flying machine fascinate visitors accustomed to rockets and jetliners.

Great Blackbeard's ghost! The fearsome shade of swashbuckling pirate Edward Teach lurks in every hidden bay. He and his cutthroats often holed up on Ocracoke Island in the early 1700's. Before a fight the burly buccaneer would strap on daggers, a cutlass, and half a dozen pistols, then light wicks stuck under his hat. One look at this unearthly apparition—shaggy-chested, smoke-breathing, surely the Devil's kin—took the fight out of many a Royal Navy tar. A score of slashes and five pistol shots slew the legendary Blackbeard off Ocracoke in 1718—but who knows whether a storm may one day strew a beach with his booty?

Doubloons or no, the Cape's real treasures reward several million swimmers, anglers, campers, and bird watchers each year. They board the fleet of islands by causeways at the upper end or ferries at the lower. State Route 12 hops Hatteras Inlet by ferry to thread the chain from end to end. Motorists find supplies, lodgings, and friendly folk in villages strung like beads along the route.

Interpretative programs tell of the early Life-Saving Service whose valiant boatmen oared through surf and storm to rescue stricken sailors. "The rules say you gotta go," the maxim went, "not that you gotta come back." Rangers bring the old days to life with shipwreck tours, ghost stories, and "treasure hunts" for kids.

You can even learn to surf-cast. You furnish luck and tackle, and a ranger will show you how. Then slap your lure into the foam for bluefish, spot, whatever's running. The group demonstrations end with the summer—but then the best fishing begins as the scrappy striped bass start biting. Cold winds or no, anglers of every sort school in, all equals at the edge of the sand.

Mackerel, tuna, dolphin, sailfish, amberjack, and marlin are taken by sport boats offshore. But you don't need boat or tackle to "catch" a trophy. Keep your camera handy as you beachcomb and you may take home the unforgettable sight of porpoises frolicking so close inshore you can hear their blowholes snort.

Most visitors arrive in summer, holing up in motels near the park or in seven campgrounds within. Tenting on the sand takes a special love of sunshine and a tolerance for the heat it can generate in a tent. It takes long tent stakes, too, to stay put in soft sand against the tug of the ocean breeze. Only the hardiest campers brave winter's rigors.

Spring and fall bring bird watchers to see migrating birds by the thousand funnel through this leg of the Atlantic flyway. At Pea Island National Wildlife Refuge, birders who visit in winter can spot brant, whistling swans, and the greater snow goose that here reaches the southernmost limit of its range. Some 300 species of birds have been spotted at Cape Hatteras.

To every visitor, Cape Hatteras offers empty miles of clean, broad beach—and miles more as Cape Lookout to the southwest becomes a part of the national seashore system. On any strand of it you can ponder a bit of weathered wreckage, small change from the price paid by those who gambled with the sea and lost.
Write Supt., Box 457, Manteo, N.C. 27954

Scalloped beaches stretch away below Cape Hatteras Lighthouse. At the cape's distant elbow the dreaded Diamond Shoals jut seaward beneath a briny froth. Old roads scar the dunes—but none cleave the sea; each ship must find its way where countless others lie.

FREDERICK MYERS, VAN CLEVE PHOTOGRAPHY

David F. Robinson

Cape Cod

NATIONAL SEASHORE, MASSACHUSETTS

Scramble all terns! Up from the flat-topped dune they boiled, squadrons of little black-and-white forktails hanging on the wind, peeling off to buzz me at scalp level, screaming and chattering as they pulled up in tight wingovers and bore in for another run. One good tern deserved a medal; a limey blotch marked his hit on my hat.

Their skittering shadows dappled the dune, where speckly eggs waited in twos and threes on the bare sand among swaying flags of grass. We had to work fast; in minutes the sun would bake each egg in the oven of its own shell.

District Ranger Frank Montford and I fenced the dune with poles and string, then retreated down Jeremy Point until the last pilot landed back aboard the flat-top. In a wider arc we ringed the dune with signs warning the curious away. Then we left Great Island to the terns, jouncing away in a four-wheel-drive jeep on tires fat as doughnuts.

Frank and I had spent a June afternoon on a trail through Great Island, latest of five major areas in Cape Cod National Seashore to be opened to the public. We had stood on bluffs high above tawny beaches and felt the whoosh of winds deflected upward, then stepped back a few paces into the hush and lull of piney woods. We had staked off a rookery of perhaps 800 common and roseate terns. And we hadn't glimpsed another human all afternoon.

At New England's southeast corner, Massachusetts flexes a golden arm. Along Route 6's busy artery a lifeblood of tourists flows east toward the elbow, north up the forearm—though it's called "down-Cape"—and west to the beckoning hand at Provincetown. Green woods and blue ponds drape the arm like a tattered sleeve, but around the edges and in great patches within, the sands lie bare to the sun.

Thigh-high in a salty meringue, a youngster frolics at Nauset Beach. Here on Cape Cod's seaward side the Labrador Current can keep bathers shivering into July. Cape Cod Bay offers a warmer, calmer dip.

JAMES P. BLAIR, NATIONAL GEOGRAPHIC PHOTOGRAPHER

While landlubbers rear a castle that soon must fall to siege by wind and sea, young salts seize a breeze for an offshore run. English sea dogs plied these waters centuries ago, fetching Cape Cod sassafras for medicines. Vacationists still go down to the sea in ships for hire at ports all along the Cape.

JAMES P. BLAIR, NATIONAL GEOGRAPHIC PHOTOGRAPHER

Some 28,000 acres of the forearm, including most of its Atlantic shoreline (the 40-mile-long Great Beach), is now a national seashore.

History lives with prehistory on this cape. Glaciers roughed it out, and the sea reshapes it daily. A boulder on Skiff Hill in Eastham bears grooves like giant claw marks where Nauset Indians whetted bone harpoons. Cape Cod may be the "Keel Cape" sighted by Thorvald the Viking in 1004. It was the *Mayflower's* first landfall, and nearly her last when she almost ran aground. It was the home of whaling ships and the grave of some 4,000 wrecks. And midway down the Great Beach, radio was born.

One morning I stood with dawn in my eye and the Atlantic at my ankles, alone on the strand where Guglielmo Marconi's wireless reached out across the sea in 1903. The stubs of two towers remain; two more and a sending station stood on land long since washed away.

Where, I wondered, are the five million people who visit this national seashore each year, who stream through visitor centers at Salt Pond and Province Lands, who pedal the bike trails, hike the nature trails, take to the beaches to swim, fish, get a tan, shed a care? Later I think I met them all at once—at Phil Schwind's shellfishing demonstration in Nauset Marsh.

"How do you show 360 people what a clam hook looks like?" he lamented after one unusually heavy turnout. But somehow Phil—who is not a ranger but the shellfish constable of Eastham—manages to rub off a little of his four decades' worth of know-how onto his listeners. And those families with licenses and luck slog into the ooze and come out with the limit of ten quarts a week of quahogs, steamers, razor clams, blue mussels, whatever.

Phil and his college-student helpers also demonstrate surf-casting. Their audiences need no licenses, just luck, to haul in striped bass, mackerel, pollock, and bluefish in the warmer months. From fall to spring the codfish run, sharing the bottom with the ungainly flounder.

The honor of namesake belongs to the codfish alone. In 1602, explorer Bartholomew Gosnold dubbed the Cape "Shole-hope." But then "wee tooke great store of Codfish, for which we . . . called it Cape Cod."

I took great store of delight from Shole-hope. At Marconi, I trod the boardwalk through a cedar swamp, dark and spooky as a delta bayou. Near Pilgrim Heights I roller-coastered on trails over hills of sand in a dune buggy. From an old sightseeing plane I looked down on Provincetown and promised myself a hike to Long Point Light on the Cape's fingertip.

When I got to the light I found it was an automatic; no keeper lives there. But I wasn't alone. On a battered ship's timber sat an old-timer who might have sailed in that ship when they both were young. He was chewing on—what? A size 19 sandal sole? He proffered me a chaw. Maybe it *was* a sole; to my taste, one dried fish is as gamey as the next. "You live in P-town?" I said through a mouthful.

Long silence; maybe he didn't hear. Finally, "Ayuh." He wasn't being cranky. Just Yankee.

We gazed across Provincetown Harbor. I thought of 1620 and the Pilgrims who anchored the *Mayflower* right over there, drew up their Compact, exulted in fresh water from what we now call Pilgrim Spring. He thought, I suppose, of fish, of toil and danger in tiny boats and fortune that could fill a net or drown a friend.

"Thanks for the fish," I called as he trudged to his skiff. A wave, a yank on his outboard, and he was gone. But though his town has filled with visitors and the myriad attractions some expect, his Cape—and yours and mine—keeps much of the flavor it had when Pilgrims trod its sand and harvested its seaborne gifts. The national seashore that keeps it so is a fitting echo of their pioneering conservation act; in 1670, with a continent before them, Plimoth Colony looked back to what is now Province Lands and set aside the area as a preserve.

Write Supt., South Wellfleet, Mass. 02663

On a ribbon of pavement six feet wide, cyclists wheel among the dunes. Some 15 miles of bike trails thread major park areas. By a lonely stretch of Nauset Beach a onetime Coast Guard outpost—now used as a summer home—seems to keep an eye on a sea that still brings storm and wealth and pleasure.

JAMES P. BLAIR, NATIONAL GEOGRAPHIC PHOTOGRAPHER

Edwards Park

Acadia

NATIONAL PARK, MAINE

At dawn an outbound lobster boat pants through a muffling fog, "so thick ye cud stick yer knife in it to mark the passage back." Gray waves boom and suck on kelp-slick rocks. A breeze clears the air, and the morning sun lights up panoramic vistas of dense forest, rocky summits, and the island-studded sea. Gulls scream above the lobstermen as they chug homeward in midafternoon. Finally, a gold and purple sunset turns pointed spruces black against the sky.

This is the coast of Maine.

And this is the essence of Acadia, mostly on Mount Desert Island, where mountains tumble to the Atlantic to end in battered cliffs, where breakers claw into coves and inlets, where you can fish with one hand and sample blueberries from a wind-stunted bush with the other.

Superlatives adorn this national park, oldest east of the Mississippi and first to be donated to the U. S. Government for use by the people. Nowhere else along the East Coast does such high land overlook the ocean. The highest point, the pink granite summit of Cadillac Mountain, rises 1,530 feet above the waves. Somes Sound, cutting the island into the shape of a giant lobster claw, is the only true fjord on the U. S. Atlantic Coast.

Most sightseers stop at Hulls Cove Visitor Center, just inside the main park entrance, then drive the scenic 20-mile park Loop Road on the island's eastern side. Branches of this road provide access to the park's most spectacular sights. One turnoff is Ocean Drive, winding six miles within sight and sound of the crashing surf. A walk on Sand Beach, where the sand is mixed with pulverized shells and the green spines of sea urchins, may lead to a plunge in the icy waves; but dip a toe in first—the water temperature hovers around 50°. A shore path parallels the road from Sand Beach to Otter Cliffs, the rugged coastline's highest point.

Farther along the road, Cadillac Mountain rears above the clouds. In the late 1800's people hiked to the summit or rode in horse-drawn buckboards or a miniature cog railway. The modern road to the top is excellent, never exceeding a seven percent grade. But hiking up is still popular.

From Jordan Pond, a glacier-gouged lake, and other points on both sides of Somes Sound, Acadia's 120 miles of hiking trails meander through forests, climb mountains, and wander along the edge of the sea. A web of carriage paths, constructed in the 1900's by John D. Rockefeller, Jr., attract horseback riders, hikers, and, on a stretch around Eagle Lake, bicyclists.

The history of Mount Desert Island echoes the struggle between France and England for North America. Samuel de Champlain coasted its shores in 1604. "This island," he wrote later, "is very high, and cleft into seven or eight mountains.... I named it l'Isle des Monts-déserts [the Isle of Bare Mountains]."

Schooner Victory Chimes *threads the labyrinthine waters off Mount Desert Island, once a haven for fishermen and a playground for millionaires. Windjammer cruises from nearby ports offer visitors a chance to savor this picturesque coast.*

MANUEL LOPEZ

RICHARD FREAR, NATIONAL PARK SERVICE. OPPOSITE: ABRAM SCHOENFELD, PHOTO RESEARCHERS

Beacon for mariners in a realm of rock and fog, Bass Harbor Head Light has guided ships to safety since 1858. Thunder Hole (below), reached via the Loop Road, gets its name from explosions of air caught and compressed by pounding surf. Best time to visit the show: half-tide after a storm.

Crossing Frenchman Bay from Schoodic Peninsula the explorer saw smoke rising from an Indian encampment at Otter Creek. On a smooth sea at high tide he tried for a landing, but struck a ledge, tearing a hole in his boat. A bell buoy warns mariners today.

After Champlain's visit, Mount Desert Island bounced between French and English hands. Jesuits established a mission on it in 1613. Virginia colonists raided the island; Pilgrims from Plymouth, paying off the *Mayflower* expenses with Maine furs, used it as a base. Louis XIV gave the island as a fief to Sieur de la Mothe Cadillac, the French founder of Detroit. At the close of the French and Indian Wars, permanent settlers arrived from New England.

In 1820, when Maine became a state, Mount Desert Island was still remote and obscure. It was not until 1844 that artist Thomas Cole "discovered" the island's beauty and began to sing its praises. A growing stream of summer people turned the fishing village of Bar Harbor into one of the country's most fashionable resorts. By the 1900's huge mansions, each staffed by at least seven indoor servants yet invariably known as "cottages," looked down on gleaming yachts that crowded the anchorage. "With no income tax," wrote one historian, "a plethora of servants, and eggs twenty cents a dozen, joy could be unrestrained."

Through the generosity of such "cottagers," Acadia National Park was born. A square rod of

land, donated for public use in 1903, started it. Huge slices of private property followed. The park, formed in 1919, now includes 65 square miles, partly on Schoodic Peninsula on the mainland, and partly on Isle au Haut.

Thronging people seem to vanish from sight along Acadia's inland roads and trails. Yet carloads of sightseers, old-time summer residents tending their neat lawns, artists, yachtsmen, sun-tanned children—all are here. Among them are the down-Easters who fill gas tanks and grocery orders, and answer questions with sober courtesy. With a sense of relief, these year-rounders say goodbye to the "summer complaints" in September—yet with furtive pleasure welcome them back again next June. For the summer folk are part of Maine, part of Mount Desert, and certainly part of the park they conceived and brought to life.

ACADIA NATIONAL PARK

Area 65 square miles

Features: *Rock-bound coastal scenery, forests and lakes, offshore islands; Cadillac Mountain; Somes Sound, only true fjord on U. S. Atlantic Coast.*

Activities: *Hulls Cove Visitor Center. Sightseeing boats tour Frenchman Bay and offshore islands. Nature walks, self-guided tape tour; hiking, bicycling, horseback riding, fishing; swimming for the hardy only. Wild Gardens of Acadia; Abbe Museum of Stone Age Antiquities; Islesford Historical Museum on Little Cranberry Island. In winter, skiing, snowshoeing, and snowmobiling.*

Season: *Park open year round.*

Weather: *Temperature varies from below zero in winter to 80° (rarely above) in summer.*

How to get there: *Mount Desert Island via Maine 3 and Schoodic Peninsula via 186; air service to Bangor and Trenton; bus to Bar Harbor.*

Accommodations: *Two campgrounds, Black Woods and Seawall; private campgrounds outside park. Motels and hotels in Bar Harbor and coastal villages.*

Services: *Restaurant, gift shops, kennels.*

Park Regulations: *Fires in designated areas only. Freshwater fishing license required.*

Write Supt., Route 1, Box 1, Bar Harbor, Me. 04609

Acadia evensong: Trailing a veil of burnished gold, the setting sun hovers above Cadillac Mountain—five miles by water across Frenchman Bay, but fifty by land over a winding road. Here at Schoodic Point, a park outpost on the mainland, the cries of gulls and lapping of waves complete an idyllic tableau.
ROBERT E. GILKA, NATIONAL GEOGRAPHIC STAFF

Charles H. Sloan

Mammoth Cave

NATIONAL PARK, KENTUCKY

The ticket seller seems to peer at me with unusual intensity, though it may be that my imagination has been stirred by the tour folder's warning: "Participants must be in excellent physical condition." Come what may, I have just signed up for the Wild Cave Tour, a trek along one of several trails threading Mammoth Cave's underground wonderland 90 miles south of Louisville. I pick up kneepads, helmet, head lamp, and a bag lunch, and board the bus that will take our group to Carmichael Entrance, two miles from the visitor center.

For the next six hours we stoop, scramble, slither, and squirm through narrow passages and gray-walled rooms. In a dignified bow we walk interminably under low stone ceilings, then exult in the simple act of standing up straight. An opening that looks barely big enough to admit a basketball looms ahead. "Put your right arm through first," advises the guide. "Keep your left arm against your side, dig your chin into your left shoulder, and shove with your toes. Move by inches."

Strangers a few hours earlier, we dozen venturesome cave explorers urge each other on like longtime friends. We stop for lunch on the puddled floor of a pit some 260 feet underground. Our guide smiles. "Whatever you started out with is puree now." At the end of the tour, we blink back into sunlight with new respect for moles, miners, and spelunkers.

Charred remnants of reed torches found far from the Historic Entrance, a natural gateway, show that people have roamed the dark depths of Mammoth Cave for at least 2,500 years. Today visitors by the thousands stroll well-lit subterranean trails on a variety of tours into different parts of the cavern. All but the Historic and Lantern Tours require a bus ride from the visitor center to outlying cave entrances.

In a cavern beauty contest, Mammoth Cave wouldn't stand much of a chance. Its largest corridors have the eerie look of rooms in a decaying mansion. Size alone makes the cave remarkable. A close look, however, reveals fragile, flowerlike formations of gypsum that adorn passages and erupt into a thick ceiling garden in the Snowball Dining Room. Here members of the Physically Handicapped Tour reach the cave via elevator from the surface.

In the Rotunda, an impressive chamber 142 feet wide, 139 feet long, and 40 feet high, history turns up underground. The Historic and Lantern Tours pass leaching vats where nitrate was extracted from cave dirt to make gunpowder during the War of 1812. Beyond the Rotunda the trail divides. The Historic Tour twists behind 2,000-ton Giant's Coffin, through Fat Man's Misery and 192-foot Mammoth Dome. Here (and at Frozen Niagara at the opposite end of the cave) lie massive flowstone formations, where mineral-laden water has left part of its burden to build cascading drapery.

The Lantern Tour goes on toward stone huts built in the 1840's for tuberculosis victims who

Captured in a multiple time exposure, a torch-tossing guide illuminates a vaulted dome in Mammoth Cave. The three-mile, three-hour Lantern Tour takes visitors off electrically-lit paths for a taste of early caving.

DAVID ALAN HARVEY

Like toothpaste oozing from a tube, cave crawlers master the Mole Hole, tightest squeeze on a five-mile scramble along cavern byways. A side corridor gives wider passage. Spunky spelunkers proved Mammoth and Flint Ridge caves connect—the world's longest known cave system. Explored tunnels total 165 miles.

tested a doctor's theory that the cave's 54-degree temperature and pure air might work a cure. The experiment failed, but the crude huts remain as reminders of the ill-fated sanitarium.

At peak visiting hours, the cave entrances may be jammed with people, but outside there is elbow room—80 square miles of field and woodland, with hiking trails and a campground (see insert map). Scenic boat cruises on the Green River are popular. In the park's sunny upstairs, visitors can see farmland turning back into wilderness—sassafras saplings mark the edge of forest slowly spreading over fields already tangled in dense growth.

But the big attraction, the cave, remains a haunting presence. Strolling the Cave Island Nature Trail one evening, I climb toward the cavern's Historic Entrance. Where cool cave air meets summer breezes, streamers of mist hover like ghostly fingers, gently beckoning surface dwellers to the stony wonders below.

Write Supt., Mammoth Cave, Ky. 42259

DAVID ALAN HARVEY

Carl F. Miller

Russell Cave

NATIONAL MONUMENT, ALABAMA

He was a hunter clad in animal skins, and he was desperately afraid. He ran, bending over to make himself smaller, for an enemy was close behind. Suddenly he felt a stabbing pain as a stone-tipped shaft plunged into his back. Somehow he managed to drag himself back to his dark cave home on an Alabama mountainside. There he died. His body, with the spearpoint still in his back, was laid in a shallow grave in the cave floor and covered with earth. This Stone Age American lived and died about 1000 B.C., yet he was a comparative latecomer to the great limestone cavern. For at least 6,000 years before his lifetime it had sheltered primitive man.

Russell Cave, named for Thomas Russell, an early settler at the site, gave up its secrets during three years of excavation sponsored by the National Geographic Society and the Smithsonian Institution. I was privileged to lead the expedition. To preserve the cave for scientific study, the Society purchased it and the surrounding 310-acre farm eight miles northwest of Bridgeport, made research grants to further the work, and in 1961 presented the site to the people of the United States.

A few inches below the present cave floor we found artifacts of Indians who lived here during early Colonial times. These people, of the culture labeled as Mississippian, date from about A.D. 1000 to 1650. Through the next four to five feet we read the floor-by-floor record of the Woodland peoples, residents from 500 B.C. to A.D. 1000. Bone needles and fishhooks, arrowheads and ornaments tell their mute story.

What was it like to live in Russell Cave in Woodland times? Morning sun pours into the mouth of the great cavern, 107 feet wide and 26 feet high, facing northeast. The men soon leave for the forest to hunt game with bows and arrows,

Through Russell Cave's gaping mouth, brawny Stone Age hunters dragged bear, deer, and raccoons to roast in shallow pits. Carbon tests of charcoal prove man's fires flickered here at least 9,000 years ago.

DAVID ALAN HARVEY

Ladder of time in an early exhibit keyed the floor levels to history. Most recent Indian remains, found a few inches deep, date from A.D. *1650. Untidy cavefolk tossed rubbish on the floor, then spread a layer of dirt, preserving a trove of yesterday's treasure and trash for workmen to uncover (right).*

stone-headed spears and axes. Berries and nuts are theirs for the taking.

The women squat at work under hide canopies which keep off dripping water. They roll moist clay into ropes, then coil and shape them into wide-mouthed jars, some holding five gallons. Other women scrape bear hides with stone knives or sew deerskin bags. Naked children frolic. As sunset nears, the men return to divide their kill. If the hunt has been good, no one will go hungry. Each family gathers around its fire to eat, laugh, and boast. The hubbub dies; only the glow of embers testifies that human beings are here, asleep.

Generations pass. Whenever the stench of refuse grows too great, women bring in baskets of earth and spread a new floor. In some eras, better housekeepers dig storage pits lined with limestone. We found many such pits packed with broken pottery, animal bones, and other litter of flesh-and-blood folk.

Four feet down, in the early Woodland period, we found the grave of a newborn baby. Nearby at the same level my wife, Ruth, came across the remains of an adult male. Very carefully we brushed the earth away.

Close beside the man's backbone lay a large quartz projectile point. The spear had been driven in from behind; it had struck a major nerve and must have left the legs paralyzed. Neither in these graves nor in a third at the nine-foot level was anything buried with the dead—no ornaments, weapons, or provisions for the journey to the hereafter. Perhaps possessions were too few, or were owned in common.

At the five-foot level we had entered the time of Archaic man, whose chief weapon was the spear and throwing stick, or atlatl. At six feet the soil changed to sticky clay, and we had to knead each handful like dough. Here we began finding artifacts of a type never before discovered in the southeastern United States: hinged fishhooks, unlike the single-piece hook of the Woodland peoples; and polished foreleg bones of large bears, cut cleanly and scraped out so that bear fat and a wick could be stuffed into the cavity. Cave man could carry this torch like a candle.

How did such tools, heretofore found nearer the Arctic, come to be used so far south? During the last Ice Age, 10,000 years ago and more, there was apparently a slow migration eastward across the continent. Later, Archaic peoples moving south, perhaps bringing tools of the Far North, met peoples of the West and South at the southern end of the Appalachians—the region around Russell Cave. No other site in the Southeast has yielded a layer-by-layer cross section of continuous human life over so long a period.

At the visitor center you can see tools and weapons, then view the excavation in the cave entrance. Rangers show how early man threw spears and chipped arrowheads. Visitors to Russell Cave truly enter a vanished world.

For information write Supt., Rt. 1, Box 175, Bridgeport, Ala. 35740

BROOKS HONEYCUTT
ABOVE: BATES LITTLEHALES, NATIONAL GEOGRAPHIC PHOTOGRAPHER

Harvey Arden

Buffalo National River

ARKANSAS

"Let go!" my companion shouted, voice verging on hysteria. "Let go of the branch!" I did. The kayak, which had pivoted stern first when I grabbed the jutting tree limb, started to roll over, righted itself, then spun loose, bow once more pointing downstream. We were flying free again—a miracle. My heart flip-flopped several times, but I had tasted my first draught of white water on the Buffalo National River, and I found it heady stuff.

My ride had begun a few minutes earlier at the Ponca bridge, a narrow concrete slab that spans the upper Buffalo and serves as a popular launch site for river trips in times of high water. I had parked to watch a group of canoeists put their craft in the water. One of them, a burly fellow with the voice and manner of a drill sergeant, had unloaded a blue and white double-cockpit kayak from his car roof. We got to talking, and when I saw that no one was accompanying him, I asked if I could sit in for a short ride. He agreed—reluctantly when I told him I'd never kayaked before.

"But don't paddle unless I give a yell," he warned. "You'll only foul things up."

No sooner had I squeezed myself into the forward cockpit than I began to have misgivings. The river, swollen and muddy from spring rains, churned ominously past the bridge. We pushed away from the bank. The current gripped us, surging and singing beneath the canvas-covered hull. Spume flew. Riverbanks raced by in a blur of browns and greens. I whooped as we boomed through a foaming chute, my knuckles death-grip white on the paddle.

We dipped and dodged between rocks. In the distance, limestone bluffs loomed above the turmoil, as stationary as pictures on a postcard. We rounded a bend, and suddenly

River of enchantment, the Buffalo rolls past gravel bar and meadowland 350 feet below in this view from the Goat Trail. The ledge walkway cuts across the face of 525-foot-high Big Bluff, tallest of the cliffs carved by the stream's winding waters.

WALTER MEAYERS EDWARDS

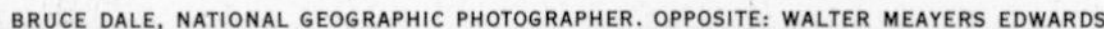
BRUCE DALE, NATIONAL GEOGRAPHIC PHOTOGRAPHER. OPPOSITE: WALTER MEAYERS EDWARDS

Ozark odyssey: A flotilla navigates a stretch of the Buffalo below Ponca. The river displays many moods—clear and calm (left) or, along its upper reaches, a white-water challenge from April to mid-June. Local outfitters provide rental craft.

I heard my partner's voice above the river's roar: "Paddle left! Paddle left!" We had swung wide on the turn and were headed for a tree dangling into the water.

I pulled furiously. The kayak jumped sideways, nearly clearing the obstacle, but then an errant branch whipped across my chest and I grabbed hold of it instinctively. A mistake. Instantly we spun out of control, stern downriver, and my partner began shouting to let go.

Moments after our brush with the tree, we found a quiet eddy and slid onto the bank.

"That's it," my companion announced with finality. "I'll take her alone from here. Better hike out while you still can."

Such was my white-water baptism on the Buffalo, a river of springtime thrills and year-round idyllic beauty that loops 148 miles through the Ozark hills of northern Arkansas. Its waters are not always so boisterous. Downstream, below Pruitt, the river is reasonably placid most of the time. During summer dry spells even its upper waters slow to a trickle between deep, bass-filled pools of emerald green overhung with trees and massive bluffs that curve to the sky. The stream winds past hollows swathed in ferns and hung with ribbon-like falls, past shoals and ledges, past gravel bars that offer nearly bug-free camping to those who come here to float, paddle, fish, or hike.

There would be other river trips for me, other ego-denting bouts with places like Gray Rock and Clabber Creek Shoals, but not today. Now I hiked back to my car to pursue another of my favorite pastimes here: exploring the old dirt roads that lace these hardwood-clad hills.

Driving down a precipitous rut of a road near Ponca, I jounced toward the river until confronted by a puddle big enough to swallow a car. I pulled over and walked on. Here, less than a mile from the river's tumult, all seemed strangely quiet. I passed a pioneer cabin, its chimney stones tumbled, its tenants obviously long gone. But near the door, defiantly abloom, grew a marvelously unkempt rambling rose.

Thanks to conservation groups throughout the state, the Buffalo will remain among the few free-flowing, relatively unspoiled streams left in the eastern half of the United States. Congress in 1972 passed a law to protect it as a national river—America's first. Eventually, Buffalo National River will encompass nearly 96,000 acres in a strip extending 132 miles between Ozark National Forest and the White River. For now, visitors should take care to respect lands still in private ownership.

The major visitor facility, at Buffalo Point, offers a modern campground, canoe launch area, and swimming beach. Private campgrounds are located outside the park. Plans for the future include hiking and horseback trails along riverbanks, and interpretative services to describe the area's history and prehistory.

"Amenities inside the park will be kept to a minimum," the superintendent told me. "We plan to keep the Buffalo as wild as we can."
Write Supt., Box 1173, Harrison, Ark. 72601

Voyageurs

NATIONAL PARK, MINNESOTA

Time has stilled the voyageurs' paddles and hushed the echo of their songs. But along the Canadian border, in the vast forests of northern Minnesota, the memory of these fur company canoeists lingers in one of the nation's newer national parks—Voyageurs.

This is the haunt of wolf and bear and moose, a realm of rocks, trees, and water where the call of the loon at twilight evokes the spirit of the wild. Authorized by Congress in 1971, the park eventually will stretch 40 miles from International Falls nearly to the Boundary Waters Canoe Area. At its center lies Kabetogama Peninsula, a 75,000-acre tongue of land jutting into large, island-studded lakes—part of a voyageur route to shuttle goods and furs between Montreal and the Canadian hinterland.

Loggers have scarred the region. But time will heal the wounds, and the towering pines the voyageurs knew may reclaim their ancient kingdom. *"Huzza! Huzza! pour le pays sauvage!* Hurrah! Hurrah! for the savage land!"

Write Supt., International Falls, Minn. 56649

Scudding sails grace a sunset at Voyageurs Park.

Apostle Islands

NATIONAL LAKESHORE, WISCONSIN

They ride like battleships at anchor, 22 low-slung islands capped with lush green forests and seemingly afloat upon the vastness of Lake Superior. Twenty of them—plus a 12-mile strip of coast along the tip of northern Wisconsin's Bayfield Peninsula—eventually will be developed as Apostle Islands National Lakeshore, a place of solitude for camper and beachcomber established in 1970.

Ice and waves have worked their wonders here, battering cliffs of ruddy sandstone into a goblin's dream of grottoes, chambers, pillars, and arches. Lore and legend hover like morning mist: tales of pirates, hermits, and buried treasure; accounts of gales and wrecks.

Getting to the islands can be tricky, even hazardous. Small boats risk squalls, shoals, and treacherous currents. Campsites on the islands are primitive—and often buggy. Summer excursion and charter services operate out of Bayfield, ten miles south of the lakeshore's mainland headquarters at Little Sand Bay.

Write Supt., Bayfield, Wisc. 54814

Sandstone steps rim a leeward shore on Devils Island in the Apostle group.

RICHARD FREAR, NATIONAL PARK SERVICE (ALSO OPPOSITE)

Isle Royale

NATIONAL PARK, MICHIGAN

This isolated wilderness park, famed as a habitat for wolf and moose, lies in the western reaches of Lake Superior, a score of miles from the mainland shore where Canada meets Minnesota. Outdoor devotees cruise among the archipelago's 200 rocky islets in powerboats, or spend chilly nights in sleeping bags beside wooded lakes teeming with pike and perch. Those who prefer more comfort stay in lodges at Windigo or Rock Harbor.

On Isle Royale everybody hikes; they must, for there are no cars or horses. But hiking is a joy. Trails springy with moss wind past beaver ponds and glades purpled with wild iris. Pits deep in blueberry thickets mark sites where Indians mined copper with stone hammers and fire about 4,000 years ago. More than 160 miles of trails—including those that run along Greenstone and Minong ridges—traverse the 210-square-mile main island and in places offer sweeping vistas of land and water.

French trappers, traveling by canoe, took possession of Isle Royale in 1671, naming it in honor of Louis XIV. Today, visitors reach the island by passenger ferry or floatplane, embarking at Houghton or Copper Harbor, Michigan, or at Grand Portage, Minnesota. Small craft can be ferried over or rented on the island. Lodging is available mid-June through Labor Day.
Write Supt., Houghton, Mich. 49931

CHARLES STEINHACKER

Ice Age glaciers shaped Isle Royale, leaving a fretwork of land adrift upon a field of blue.

Edward Lanouette

Pictured Rocks

NATIONAL LAKESHORE, MICHIGAN

From the water, massive bluffs bolt sheer into the sky . . . 100 . . . 150 . . . 200 feet. And waves mutter sullenly against the wall of rock as if to protest the sudden halt in their unbroken sweep across Lake Superior. Luckily the waves are gentle today. For the foot of the Pictured Rocks cliffs is no place to be when a booming norther stirs the water.

Stratified sandstone curving mile upon mile to distant headlands, a giant mural painted by lichens and seeping metallic oxides—such is the facade of part of Pictured Rocks National Lakeshore, a park stretching 40 miles between Munising and Grand Marais on the north shore of Michigan's Upper Peninsula.

"It was our constant amusement to look for shapes among the forms and colors on the cliffs," a visitor wrote a century ago. "One would discover . . . a group of horses . . . and another see a long procession of boys carrying fish. . . . Here were elephants grouped with serpents a hundred feet long. . . . There a city dimly pictured, with roofs, towers, and spires."

Indians revered these rocks. In them they saw shadows of the past, tribal histories inscribed by the Great Spirit, Gitchee Manitou.

There are more than painted forms here. Water and frost have carved stupendous features in the cliffs: Miner's Castle broods like a squat fortress, with doorways, loopholes, battlements; Grand Portal arches 200 feet above the water; and Chapel Rock displays wave-cut pillars reminiscent of ancient temple ruins.

Cataracts spill from precipices or cut deep gorges in the rock, forming secluded beaches among the crags. Bridalveil Falls begins a 150-foot tumble to the lake only to have powerful updrafts seize its waters and hurl them back over the lip of the cliff.

Eastward beyond the rocks curves Twelve-Mile Beach. Sand bluffs 30 feet high and forests

Twin turrets of Miner's Castle, a Pictured Rocks landmark, rise 90 feet above Lake Superior's waters. A wave-cut tunnel pierces the cliff base.

HOYT AVERY

of pine, hemlock, spruce, and fir hem this seldom-visited strand—Superior's longest. Scattered amid the trees along the bluff's edge are primitive campsites served by a gravel road. Beachcombers here poke among egg-shaped stones of every hue and size to find wave-polished agate, jasper, and carnelian.

Beyond Au Sable Point and its abandoned lighthouse, along the park's easternmost segment, can be seen one of nature's great spectacles: a steeply pitched wall of sand known as Grand Sable Bank. It rises from the lake to a height of nearly 300 feet. Behind it lie the Grand Sable Dunes, five square miles of drifting, forest-swallowing sand that reminded a French explorer of "the great and vast wildernesses of Turkey land." Paddling along these desolate shores in 1658, Pierre Esprit Radisson found "banckes of sand so high that one of our wildmen went upp for a curiositie; being there, did shew no more than a crow." It was a stretch "most dangerous" in a storm, he noted, "being no landing place...." A prophetic observation: Storms since have claimed more than 30 vessels along the banks.

Later visitors have more favorably regarded the region Ojibwa Indians knew as Gitchee Nagow—Great Sands. "Whosoever undergoes the labor and fatigue of ascending to the top," wrote a traveler in 1833, "is amply repaid by the diversity of scenery brought before the eye. There is something grand and majestick in the whole exhibited to it." Another, enthralled by the sight of polished pebbles strewn in the sand, compared the dunes to "the valley of diamonds in Arabian tales." And it was here, too, on the whispering, restless sands Longfellow called Nagow Wudjoo, that Hiawatha came with Minnehaha and old Nokomis; here Pau-Puk-Keewis whirled and danced beside the cold depths of Gitchee Gumee, the shining Big-Sea-Water.

Behind the Pictured Rocks shoreline lies 28,000 acres of forest—mostly second- and third-growth timber—interspersed with lakes, ponds, marshes, and streams. Bear, deer, beaver, bobcat and coyote, mink and muskrat dwell here and, because the lakeshore is classified as a recreation area, bear, deer, and wildfowl are hunted in season. And the fishing? Best in spring and fall.

Throughout the park's interior, picturesque waterfalls splash beneath canopied forests of maple, beech, and yellow birch. One of them, Munising Falls near the western entrance, drops 50 feet from an overhang into a bowl-like amphitheater; a natural walkway enables visitors to stroll behind the cascade without getting wet.

Spring wild flowers such as white trilliums and Dutchman's breeches carpet areas where the forest floor is free of underbrush. The road to Twelve-Mile Beach winds through a copse of white birch shimmering in the pallid green light that filters down from above.

On the Kingston Plain just outside the park, graying stumps of a forest felled by fire and ax a century ago rise like headstones amid acres of bending grass. Ice Age caves carved by Lake Superior's ancestral waters lie within hiking distance of Little Beaver Lake.

Graded roads and old logging trails provide access to most of the lakeshore. But many are not marked by signs, so maps and a compass are advisable. Campgrounds with limited facilities (fire grates, trash barrels, pit toilets) are available on a first-come basis. Primitive hike-in camping lures the adventurous to out-of-the-way nooks. Summer weather usually is pleasant, but cold storms sweep in from the lake unexpectedly. Hikers and campers should be prepared for the worst, including zero visibility, which can be dangerous near the cliffs.

Because of storms, most small boating takes place on inland lakes and ponds. Large cruise boats do make daily runs along the cliff in summer, but only if weather permits. Park headquarters is located in an old Coast Guard station near the Munising entrance.

Write Supt., Box 40, Munising, Mich. 49862

CLOCKWISE FROM CARIBOU: ENTHEOS; GORDON W. GAHAN AND JAMES L. STANFIELD, NATIONAL GEOGRAPHIC PHOTOGRAPHERS

Alaska, Hawaii, Virgin Islands

McKinley caribou; Haleakala silversword; Buck Island tropical fishes.

Aubrey Stephen Johnson

Mount McKinley

NATIONAL PARK, ALASKA

The tracks were fresh, deep-pressed in the silt of the Sanctuary River Valley, which intersects the park road some 20 miles from headquarters. The wolf had passed with purpose and directness, its toes spread wide in an all-out run. In ponderous contrast, the grizzly appeared to have poked into every bush, aimlessly interlacing its tracks.

Lost in a moment of reflection, I realized that my concept of "wilderness" had suddenly changed. The pattern of footprints before me had once been common in the wild places of the Lower Forty-Eight, but no longer. Never again could I think of such areas as true wildernesses, for they lack the combined presence of the grizzly and the wolf. Supreme indicators of wilderness quality, neither can exist without the earth's wild places, and it was a joy to share with them, however briefly, one of the last great expanses of unpeopled land.

All around the bear's huge, manlike tracks were signs of digging—the black soil stripped of that grizzly delicacy, the tuberous roots of the peavine. My wife, Marilyn, and I walked on upstream, talking loudly to avoid surprising the owner of those awesome paws. Smaller tracks told us that a yearling accompanied the adult, making us doubly careful. We knew that the grizzly's reputation as a "man-killer" was grossly overblown—but not entirely groundless.

"Steve, grizzlies!"

Marilyn's soft-voiced warning was drowned in the rushing torrent of the river; I went on, unaware. Then I sensed heavy running and knew instantly that we had found our first grizzly in Mount McKinley National Park.

As I turned, peering downstream for my wife, two piercing screams told me where to look. Marilyn was crouched against the edge of a

Roof of the continent, 20,320-foot Mount McKinley rises more than three miles above the lowlands to dominate its park. Snowmelt from its sprawling slopes waters the tundra that sustains the caribou. Indians called the mountain Denali, *the Great One.*

WILLIAM E. RUTH

steep, upward sloping bank, arms covering her head, her back toward a huge honey-colored grizzly approaching at a rolling run.

To me the bear seemed to be upon her when suddenly it pulled up, throwing sod and gravel frantically as it changed course. Marilyn's screams had evidently transformed an attack into headlong flight. As the sow ran by me and crashed through a willow thicket to rejoin her fleeing cub, she looked very tired. I heard her breath coming in ragged sobs, with the tongue and teeth plainly visible through the open jaws. I have never seen a more frightened animal.

Marilyn, untouched though the bear had passed only three feet from her, recalled her moment of terror: "I knew that any second I would feel the claws in my back. I was in complete panic, and squatted where I was."

Evidently the bear had been betrayed by its weak eyes into believing that something other than human was near, and available as prey. A strong wind had kept our scent from her, and the roaring stream muffled our sounds. In the course of several summers we had photographed many grizzlies, from Yellowstone to the shrouded forests of Admiralty Island, and had heard the sound of their running many times. Until this June day on the Sanctuary River, they had always run away from, never toward, us.

Next morning we hiked out of our base camp, upstream from Sanctuary Campground, to the single gravel road that bisects the park, and waited for the shuttle bus. The park began the service in 1972 to cope with the flood of visitors pouring in on the new Anchorage-Fairbanks Highway. Resisting demands for more and wider roads, determined to safeguard the wilderness, park officials opted for busing. During the busy summer, private car use is limited to campground access.

The free buses run from 6 a.m. to 10 p.m., making stops at all seven campgrounds. There's no hurrying along those winding 87 miles—and little formality. We could ride the same bus all day or take a short hike and flag down a returning bus. Or we could be "abandoned" for days or weeks for an extended backcountry trek. Often, we hopped the bus just to hear the latest wildlife news—who saw what, when, and where—so that we could know how best to spend our day. Our packs, bulging with cameras, food, and raingear, were always with us, making us as free as the animals we sought.

The drivers, young and enthusiastic, were excellent wildlife spotters. With 50 pairs of intent eyes behind them, they had to be. Unscheduled stops came frequently, with the sighting of a majestic golden eagle *below* the road level, a caribou on a snowbank, a mother moose nursing her calves, a family of willow ptarmigans taking a roadside dustbath.

Once, a band of Dall sheep, rice-white on the velvet green of the slopes, appeared tantalizingly close. A few of the more hardy passengers got out to hike up for a closer view. But I knew from past experience that any attempt to stalk these keen-eyed mountain sheep would be futile. Only by a very slow, direct approach, walking upright in full view, can you get near enough to see the Dall's yellow eyes and distinctive rectangular pupils staring back at you.

No one gets out at Sable Pass, heart of a wildlife protection zone where hiking is restricted. You may spot a grizzly anywhere in the park; at Sable Pass you're almost certain to.

TEE BALOG. LEFT: JOHN S. CRAWFORD. OPPOSITE: FRANK CRAIGHEAD

From spring to fall, bears find abundant food here—roots, grass, squirrels, marmots—as well as sunshine and snoozing room. Keeping hikers out keeps the bears near the road, for the enjoyment of all. When we rolled slowly into the area, laughter rumbled through the bus at the sight of a grizzly sprawled by an interpretive sign entitled "Grizzly Bear."

McKinley has often been called a hiker's park, though certainly not for the man-made amenities it offers. For the most part, trails exist only in the hiker's mind as he toils up broad river valleys, along gravelly ridges, through bog and brush. The streams must be dealt with on their own unique terms. At 7 a.m. you hop easily over a trickling rivulet. Returning 12 hours later you may find a thigh-deep river, though no rain has fallen. Belatedly you recall that glaciers form the source of rivers here, and each flows according to its rate of melt on any given day.

Through weeks of walking, Marilyn and I came to know something of the struggle of life in these wilds. We watched a caribou press its nose to the snow, shudder convulsively, and lurch away in a desperate effort to shake off nostril flies, which deposit larvae in the caribou's nose. In time the larvae move to the throat entrance and spend the winter there, tormenting the host until they reach full growth in spring and drop to the ground.

Crossing a meadow, we heard a raucous calling and looked up to see a pair of long-tailed jaegers, wind whistling through their gray, black, and white plumage, diving in on us from opposite directions. Apparently trying to bully us away from a hidden chick, they seemed bent on burying their curved beaks in our heads. Each time they swooped, I was determined not to duck—but I invariably did.

In a tundra walk near Eielson Visitor Center I was surprised to find similarities between the plants here and those of my native Arizona desert land. Both areas must make do with little moisture, and the plants consequently have extensive shallow root systems as well as waxy or leathery leaf surfaces to conserve water. Tundra plants, however, must also conserve and absorb heat. Hence, some have "hairy" stems and leaves that increase surface area. The moss campion grows in a dense mat. Many plants and trees lie close to the ground. A willow may grow as much as 15 feet horizontally, but only six inches in height.

We often found ourselves with more than enough opportunity to observe the habits of one of Alaska's most prevalent forms of wildlife—the mosquito. McKinley reputedly harbors about 30 species of *Culex;* whatever the number, we can offer lengthy testimonials to their tenacity. We often used windy vantage points to avoid them, and actually observed them coming upwind toward us, using each twig and grass stem as a brace against the wind. If they couldn't fly, they walked!

The planned addition of more than three million acres to the park promises more walking room for all of us—caribou, grizzly, mountain sheep, and man. For the wolves, the added

For the wild bunch McKinley offers sanctuary, not a hideout. Visitors easily spot golden eagles riding the currents. Red foxes hunt brushland along the park road. Canada lynx (center), an exception, is hard to see in timbered haunts; its numbers vary with those of its main prey, the snowshoe rabbit.

VELMA HARRIS

At 8:30 one August morning Charlie and Velma Harris of Mariposa, California, spotted this bull caribou where the park road crosses the East Fork of the Toklat River. Wolves had gashed its flanks. Maybe the wolves would come back; the Harrises decided to stay. Friends from Denver, Colorado, and Billings, Montana, came along the road and joined them. Bus tourists stopped to ask questions, then moved on.

At 5:30 p.m. a sow grizzly and two cubs came up the river. Velma Harris began to shake; she didn't know if she could stand to watch what was coming. But she did. Head down, the bull stood off several charges; then the sow got in behind the antlers and worked around to the neck. The cubs sat on the river bank and bawled. For six days the Harrises watched the bears feed on the kill, nurse, and play. On the seventh they were gone; the river had washed the kill away. There wasn't much left.

Social climbers, Dall sheep keep a wary eye out for upward-striving strangers. Humans are tolerated in this rarefied domain—if they come openly, without trying to hide. Photographer Peterson saw these handsome rams from the park road and went visiting—a 19-hour hike up and down tortuous ridges.

lands would be an especial boon, offering them ecologically intact hunting grounds entirely within the park, and thereby reducing their exposure to trapper and poacher.

Summer in McKinley is a fleeting thing, magnificent in its changing moods. The sun in June overwhelms the park. June 21 is a day that has no end. The sun sets in a northerly direction around 11:30; twilight lingers for 2½ hours, then lifts in a northern sunrise. The camera never rests.

Above the summer green of the rolling low country lies the true color of the park—in the snow that never melts, the ice that never thaws. The Alaska Range stretches 100 miles along the park's southern boundary. Above the lesser peaks, the ghostly bulk of Mount McKinley seems to float on clouds, intimidating us with its vastness. Yet a summer day rarely passes without a climbing party toiling up its slopes.

Though hundreds have known the glory of its summit since Archdeacon Hudson Stuck and his party attained the South Peak, or true summit, in 1913, a McKinley expedition remains a daunting challenge for even the veteran mountaineer. Altitude, knifing cold, and hidden crevasses can make the climb as hazardous as any on earth. Climbers must submit biographies detailing their experience along with medical certificates. Each party must set up a base station in two-way radio contact with both the climbers and a monitoring facility.

Most of us, then, will know the radiance of McKinley only at a distance. The park road comes no closer to the summit than 27 miles. The mountain first comes into view nine miles from the entrance; from Mile 60 onward the views are splendid, weather permitting. Sadly, in summer the weather permits them only about 40 percent of the time. McKinley's majesty may be shrouded in clouds for days on end.

From the top of that windswept mountain the Indians called the Great One, to the tundra nearly 18,000 feet below, true wilderness is everywhere apparent. Frozen peak, tundra, grizzlies, wolves, even mosquitoes—all are part of McKinley, as essential to its character as air is to breathing. The park offers countless discoveries, though it may hide much of its mystery and beauty from those who rush through its vastness. It rewards exploration in leisure and tells us that speed of travel compresses not only time, but awareness as well.

MOUNT McKINLEY NATIONAL PARK

Area 3,030 square miles

Features: *Immense wilderness areas of towering mountains, alpine glaciers, rolling lowlands cut by rivers. Grizzly bears, caribou, Dall sheep, wolves, moose roam its tundra.*

Activities: *Short-range family hiking or long-range backpacking. 87-mile scenic road from Riley Creek entrance to Wonder Lake carries scheduled shuttle buses; hike to Muldrow Glacier from Eielson Visitor Center (Mile 65); canoe and fish in Wonder Lake, no license required. Wildlife bus and air tours. Nature walks, slide talks, sled-dog demonstrations, campfire programs. Park open all year for snowshoe hikes, ski touring, sled-dog trips. Mountain climbing for experienced climbers only.*

Season: *June-Aug. cool, wet, windy; temp. 40-80°.*

What to bring: *Raingear, light coat, insect repellent, head net, binoculars, telephoto lens for wildlife photography. Campers need camp stove and fuel (firewood is unavailable), and waterproof shelter.*

How to get there: *From Anchorage or Fairbanks on Alaska 3; by rail, or scheduled or chartered flights. From Paxon on Denali Highway, open only in summer.*

Accommodations: *Late spring to early autumn—hotel at park entrance; campsites along road.*

Services: *Food, gasoline, automobile services, camper supplies at park entrance only.*

Park regulations: *Firearms prohibited; pet dogs and trail vehicles not permitted in backcountry. Some campsite use by reservation; backcountry camping by permit. Carry no spiced or smoked food, candy, scented soaps or lotions. Pack out all refuse. Warn animals of your presence by making noise as you hike. Register with superintendent to mountain climb or travel on glaciers.*

For further information write Supt., Box 9, Mount McKinley National Park, Alaska 99755

WILLIS PETERSON

Glacier Bay

NATIONAL MONUMENT, ALASKA

Naturalist John Muir believed that the Creator taught His children with every sublime expression of nature. Glacier Bay was one of Muir's greatest teachers; and, since his exploration of the 50-mile fjord in 1879, this scenic wilderness on Alaska's southeastern coast has taught the world much about the behavior of glaciers.

Rivers of accumulated snow turned to ice, glaciers within the 4,381-square-mile-monument are remnants of a "little ice age" that began 4,000 years ago; a sheet of ice 4,000 feet deep covered the bay until a warming trend around 1750 made the ice recede. Since then, the glaciation has fluctuated. Some glaciers continue to grind irresistibly down the Fairweather Range into the Pacific Ocean or Glacier Bay. Others retreat. Plateau Glacier (right) recently melted to the point where it is no longer a glacier. Muir Glacier receded five miles in seven years but still presents an impressive 200-foot-high snout of ice.

Here in Muir Inlet, from a cautious half-mile out, the mariner might see the shoreline change before his eyes. Great chunks of ice crack off and crash into the water, sending out huge waves and crowding the inlet with bergs.

From Juneau it's less than 100 miles by boat or plane to park headquarters and a boat dock and lodge at Bartlett Cove, near the mouth of Glacier Bay. Ashore, you can step into virgin forest, haven for bear and marten. Unlimited opportunities for camping and hiking await, but go prepared for temperatures that seldom top 72° even in summer. Afloat, you can share the bay with whales, and fish for king salmon.

And you can marvel at the glaciers, especially the one named for Muir. Here among its cavernous crevasses, he became lost one day. Stumbling back into camp at last, he exclaimed to his partner, "Such purity, such color, such delicate beauty! I was tempted to stay there and feast my soul, and softly freeze, until I would become part of the glacier."

Write Supt., Box 1089, Juneau, Alaska 99802

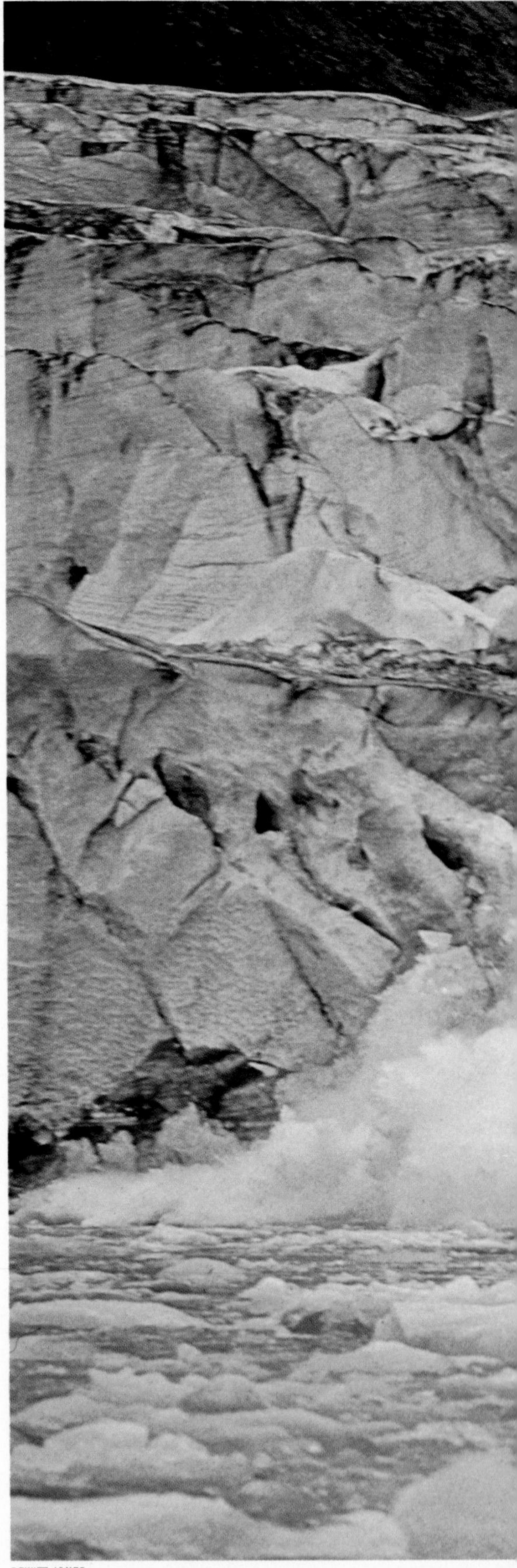

DEWITT JONES

A glacier, crawling an inch or two a day, calves icebergs near Muir Inlet.

Ernest Gruening

Katmai

NATIONAL MONUMENT, ALASKA

I stood in Alaska's Valley of Ten Thousand Smokes, a volcanic wilderness desolate as a shell-torn battlefield. As I gazed at its scarred face, I thought of the momentous events that occurred here. In June of 1912 one of the mightiest eruptions in history rocked this remote corner of the world. Earthquakes shook the northern Alaska Peninsula, and a great cloud of dust darkened the sky. The entire region trembled in the throes of titanic subterranean convulsions.

On June 6, at the southeastern end of the valley, a vent—later appropriately named Novarupta—suddenly opened. Melted rock boiled up from its depths and from a hundred new fissures in the valley floor nearby. Columns of incandescent pumice leaped hundreds of feet. New volcanoes formed, belching flame and rock. Down the valley poured this seething mass, covering an area of 42 square miles—in places to a depth of 300 feet or more. The inferno raged for 60 hours, and then . . . silence.

In 1916 Dr. Robert F. Griggs, leader of a series of National Geographic expeditions to the scene, sighted and named the Valley of Ten Thousand Smokes. "It was as though all the steam engines in the world . . . had popped their safety valves at once and were letting off surplus steam in concert," he reported. By 1918 the tortured geography of this part of Alaska had been set aside by President Woodrow Wilson as a national monument, named for Mount Katmai volcano. The park was later enlarged to protect the moose, bear, red fox, mink, Canada lynx, and other animals outside the valley, and the seals and sea lions along Shelikof Strait.

To reach the monument, visitors fly 289 miles from Anchorage to the village of King Salmon. From there a floatplane takes them to a modern

Mount Katmai cradles a jade lake, tranquil legacy of volcanic cataclysm. Accessible by daily flights, this majestic preserve astride the Aleutian Range encompasses 4,362 square miles; pending legislation would expand it to a national park with 7,280.

WILBUR L. HARTMAN

lodge with cabins at Brooks River; a camp at Lake Grosvenor 15 air miles to the northeast will accommodate a few fishermen. What was once a long hike from Brooks River to the Valley of Ten Thousand Smokes is now a short bus ride.

I first saw the valley from the air, before aircraft landings were prohibited. When bush pilot Ed Seiler's two-seater came in low for a landing and I saw the volcanic wonderland spread out before me, I was startled. Steam from buried rivers and springs in the baking substrata once had risen as far as the eye could see. Now there were perhaps a dozen fumaroles.

Seiler set the tiny plane down, its oversize balloon tires bounding up the slope of Baked Mountain. We squeezed out, and I watched him peg the aircraft to the ground. "Might get a williwaw," he explained—a sudden high wind with rain that funnels through Katmai Pass. Nearby, a lonely fumarole slanted its plumes skyward. I peered down its gaping throat and warmed my hands in its moist heat.

Beyond Baked Mountain lay Novarupta. Hiking in the volcanic debris is strenuous—like trudging through desert sand, only worse. Scramble down the bank of a watercourse and your feet slip out from under you. Coarse sand skins your hands. Struggle up Novarupta's still-steaming side and you step around granite boulders big enough to crush a man.

"The whole valley," rhapsodized Robert F. Griggs in 1922, "...was full of...tens of thousands of smokes curling up from its fissured floor.... Steam rose a thousand feet.... We had...discovered one of the great wonders of the world." His party camped among the vapors and cooked over natural steam; acid fumes ate holes in the pans. Today, most fumaroles in the Valley of Ten Thousand Smokes have vanished.

ROBERT F. GRIGGS

We made our way to Novarupta's edge. From here we saw what had been one of the region's many beautiful valleys. Its lower reaches had been covered with balsam poplar, birch, and white spruce, interspersed with bog. Wildlife had been plentiful: caribou, bear, wolf, wolverine, many kinds of land and water birds.

We could see the beachline left by the flow of white-hot melted rock on the mountainsides 900 feet above the valley floor. At Novarupta itself a plug of viscous rhyolite 1,300 feet in diameter had welled up to seal off that great vent. I marveled at the force required to thrust this mass of lava—weighing millions of tons—up from the depths. In the distance we could see some of the volcanoes that rim the valley. Once in a while they produce a minor eruption, but for the most part the giants lie sleeping.

It was time to leave. We flew to the valley's foot and then, banking right, coursed north nine miles to land on the Ukak River Delta, now also off limits to aircraft. Here we stood well out of the valley but still within its shadow of death. A mile's walk brought us to a stark forest. Pumice carried by the Ukak from the valley had choked these spruce trees to death. They were bleached skeletons in a shimmering desert. A few held hawks' nests. Beside me, etched in the pumice, were a moose's hoofprints.

Back at Brooks River Lodge that night we

Knife Creek carves a pumice plain in the becalmed Valley of Ten Thousand Smokes, where astronauts trained for a moonwalk. Park naturalists lead hikes across the dead land that once spewed fire and rock. Nearby, on the Ukak River Delta, a puff of volcanic fallout makes a fine featherweight beach ball.

FRED W. BELCHER AND (BELOW) NANCY SIMMERMAN, BOTH VAN CLEVE PHOTOGRAPHY

dined on salmon. Some of the world's finest fishing lies but seconds from one's cabin here or at Lake Grosvenor. Anglers come from as far away as Switzerland to try their luck.

Next morning I visited the lake, where grayling, rainbow, and lake trout abound. A man was fishing in the narrows between Lakes Grosvenor and Coville. "I'm a three-cast man," he said. "Three casts, no fish, I quit." On his second cast he hooked a 3½-pound trout.

Not all the fishermen are human. During the salmon migration when sockeyes are jumping Brooks Falls, the huge Alaska brown bear comes looking for a snack. Man and bear often meet, and if wise, give each other wide berth.

Katmai National Monument encompasses a mountain and lake country of unsurpassed beauty. It has a hundred shoreline miles of ocean bays, fjords, and lagoons, and sharp peaks rising sheer from the water. A visitor may rent a boat or, with a permit, shoulder the necessary survival gear and hike anywhere in the backcountry. I mused over a park ranger's observation: "Some of our national parks and monuments are known for one feature or another. In Katmai we have them all—and space to boot. Man doesn't dominate here."

Write Supt., Box 7, King Salmon, Alaska 99613

John M. Kauffmann

Gates of the Arctic

ALASKA

Mountains walled off our campsite from the bite of summer sleet blowing in across the North Slope of the Brooks Range. Though we were miles from humanity, leagues from a road, we felt no loneliness in that splendid valley surrounded by more than nine million acres of solitude called the Gates of the Arctic.

Nor were my canoeing companions and I alone. When I went to the river's edge for coffee water in the morning, I found others had been there not long before. Broad as salad plates, the pads of a grizzly had pressed into the damp sand. Crossing them were wolf tracks big as my fists. Through the forest behind us moose had beaten paths as clear as if made by axmen, and caribou trails crisscrossed a mountainside. Although the dashing white Tinayguk River bade us launch and be off, we lingered a day after the helicopter left, to drink in the magnificent views and scramble up cliffs in hopes of seeing sheep and raptors. As a team of planners studying the area for a national park, we wanted to sample as best we could what traveling this stern landscape afoot or by canoe means to a human being.

I see the Gates as a big, tough adventuring ground for deep immersion in wilderness. Hiking each ravine or slope becomes an intense personal experience, esthetic as well as physical. First comes the misery and fretfulness of unaccustomed toil as one bucks willow thickets. Mosquitoes are myriad. Tussocks of cotton grass turn one's walking into a ceaseless stumble. Storms must be faced and endured. Fears lurk in the mind. There are perils; help is afar. But in time the body toughens and spirits rise. Time stops. Space expands. Humility and confidence mingle and grow. Weather no longer seems to brandish threatening shadows but

Autumn hues blaze in August above the Arctic Circle where the Koyukuk's wild North Fork hurries through the parkland's namesake valley. Overleaf: *Forks in a river of ice grip ramparts of the Arrigetch Peaks.*

BOB WALDROP. OVERLEAF: JOHN P. MILTON

Packhorse of the Far North, a bush plane shuttles campers, airdrops food during extended treks. On April days that may warm to 20° F. frozen breath coats wisps of hair, frozen rivers glaze the way. Beyond gliding skiers bulks Boreal Mountain, one of the gateposts descried by explorer Robert Marshall.

BELOW: BOB WALDROP. LOWER AND OPPOSITE: NANCY SIMMERMAN

works with sun and cloud as with painter's brushes and sculptor's chisels.

Conservationist Paul Brooks once wrote that "early in every wilderness trip there comes a moment of awareness.... It is as if somewhere along the way a door has silently opened and you have been invited to come in." During our nine-day canoe journey back to Bettles Field, departure point for trips into the central range, we gradually lost the feeling of being out of place. Quietly, hoping we were not intrusive, we became part of the environment. In such sovereign country it is difficult for a man to feel arrogant, though elsewhere his race may reign.

Canoeing the Tinayguk and the North Fork of the Koyukuk, we paused often to explore the surroundings. Once we stopped to dry out, after a capsize in 42° water. It was a mild day; in colder weather we might have built a fire of driftwood to avoid the danger of exposure.

We stopped to examine an eerie ice field, walked to quiet lakes, peered into sagging cabins that once were homes to lone prospectors and trappers. Once, a human call, heard

Gold rush relics dot the vicinity of Wiseman, a hamlet at the parkland's east edge. Rhubarb label seems to promise 125 portions, enough to sour a sourdough's winter; bottle goods cheered it. New life stirs here as the Alaska pipeline surges by to siphon black gold from the North Slope.

NANCY SIMMERMAN

startlingly above a roaring rapids, halted us. We thought to find no people in this secluded land. Equally astonished were Mike Malraven and Doug Greenberg, who were making a hundred-mile loop hike from the Eskimo village of Anaktuvuk Pass. "We've wanted to experience this Brooks Range country ever since we heard of it," said Mike, "so we headed up from California right after college graduation."

We wished we could have tramped each valley, but in the short Arctic summer that was impossible. Only by air could we comprehend this vast land in our allotted time. One flight took us down the Koyukuk, plunging from its headwaters into a great gash in the earth. Below the canyon, Mount Doonerak loomed dark and menacing like the Eskimo spirit for which it was named. For a moment we glimpsed the green jewel of Marshall Lake beneath the mountain's shoulder.

The lake is named for Robert Marshall, a founder of The Wilderness Society, who first explored and extolled the region. Below Doonerak the river courses between two massive mountains named by Marshall. To the east stands the mace-head of Boreal Mountain, horned and knobbed. On the west Frigid Crags curls over the valley like a fossil tidal wave. Marshall called this portal Gates of the Arctic, an evocative name applicable to all this area, where canyons and passes offer many gateways. Through them some 240,000 caribou pour each year as the Arctic herd, America's largest, migrates between calving grounds on the North Slope and wintering areas in the Yukon basin.

Heading back up the North Fork, we landed on Summit Lake, surrounded by the elemental beauty of the Arctic. That beauty dwelt even in the lake, living, darting, flashing with color rarely duplicated in temperate fresh waters. The Arctic char that rose to our lures rival brook and rainbow trout as the most beautiful of freshwater fishes. We kept only a supper's

Where outdoorsmen will always "find the freedom of vast uncompromised wilderness": Planners urge a Gates of the Arctic National Park without roads or campgrounds, the icy solitude left as it is. While the vision takes shape in legal process, the Bureau of Land Management (page 436) retains jurisdiction over visitor use and services.

NANCY SIMMERMAN

worth, for in these cold waters fish grow slowly and a lake can be quickly depleted.

Other days, other flights.... Up the majestic John River Valley to Anaktuvuk Pass, where Eskimo children surge merrily about our plane.... Over the western reaches, where granite fingers of the Arrigetch Peaks reach toward us, ice-honed awls and axheads, monoliths such as mountaineers dream of; below, the rocks cup blue-green tarns whose outlets foam through canyon clefts toward the glacier-scoured Alatna Valley.... Igikpak, a swirl of razor-sharp ridges culminating in a double turret of precariously balanced rocks. Incredible!

Memories kaleidoscope when one reviews such a season, hearing the rivers' music in the mind's ear. I remember the Killik and the roar of its Sunday Rapids, where we dodged boulders and guided our heavy-laden craft through white stacks of waves. Lousewort and sandwort, pink and white, brightened the tundra. Gyrfalcon nestlings dozed on a cliff shelf, and on a far hillside five grizzlies grazed.

Beauty and inspiration and challenge. Such is the promise of the Gates of the Arctic.

The Promise of Alaska

New parklands proposed under the terms of the Alaska Native Claims Settlement Act of 1971 would double the National Park System to more than 60 million acres. Proposals include Gates of the Arctic, the eight units on this page, and extensions of Mount McKinley and Katmai. Until authorized by Congress as park areas, these lands will continue to be administered principally by the Department of the Interior's Bureau of Land Management. But for maps, brochures, and general information on the use of these areas, write to Director, National Park Service, Washington, D. C. 20240. Bear in mind that visitor facilities and services are presently almost nonexistent in the proposed new parks.

Wrangell-St. Elias National Park. 8.6 million acres, from Gulf of Alaska through three ice-clad mountain ranges, including 18,000-foot Mount St. Elias and the largest U. S. glacier system. Canyons, tundra uplands, forested lowlands offer fine hiking. Visitors may sight Dall sheep, grizzlies, caribou, wolves. Adjoins Canada's Kluane National Park. Access by highways, air; ferry to Valdez and Cordova from Whittier, near Anchorage.

Lake Clark National Park. 2.8 million acres. Wildly diverse terrain from Cook Inlet to the collision of the Alaska and Aleutian ranges. Rugged high peaks, glaciers, smoldering volcanoes, steep valleys, tundra plains, forested hills, lakes, cascading rivers, waterfalls. Varied wildlife includes moose, caribou, whales, seals. Excellent hiking, camping, white-water canoeing, climbing, fishing, cross-country skiing. Access by air from Anchorage.

Kobuk Valley National Monument. 1.8 million acres. Mountain-flanked Kobuk River Valley north of the Arctic Circle. Forests, tundra, and 25,000 acres of sand dunes. Caribou, wolves, grizzlies, waterfowl. Valuable archeological sites. Good hiking, camping, canoeing, fishing. Access by air from Kotzebue.

Chukchi-Imuruk National Reserve. 2.7 million acres on Seward Peninsula, from low Bendeleben Mountains and 40-square-mile Imuruk Lake north through lava flows and volcanic vents to rolling tundra uplands, coastal wetlands. Prime habitat for nesting and migrating waterfowl, shorebirds. Remnant of Bering land bridge; wealth of plant and animal fossils, archeological sites. Hiking, camping, birdwatching. By air from Nome or Kotzebue.

Cape Krusenstern National Monument. 340,000 acres north of the Arctic Circle. Important archeological sites on beach ridges and coastal hills chronicle more than 6,000 years of Eskimo culture. Grizzlies, caribou, moose; migrating and nesting waterfowl; whales and seals in Chukchi Sea. Access by air from Kotzebue.

Aniakchak Caldera National Monument. 580,000 acres. Aleutian Range uplands, featuring a 19,000-acre volcanic crater with cinder cones, warm springs, ash fields, and Surprise Lake, from which the wild Aniakchak River flows 27 miles to the sea. Grizzlies. Hiking, camping, fishing. By air from King Salmon or Anchorage to Port Heiden.

Harding Icefield-Kenai Fjords National Monument. 300,000 acres. Dramatic scenery highlighted by 720-square-mile ice field rising high in Kenai Mountains. Glaciers flow to rocky shoreline, indenting forested cliffs. Whales, porpoises, sea otters, sea lions, seals, sea birds. By highway, air, water, or rail from Anchorage; by air or water from Seward.

Yukon-Charley National Rivers. 2.2 million acres. Entire watershed of pristine Charley River and a scenic and historic segment of the Yukon River, in a setting of forested valleys, tundra-capped hills. Grizzlies, caribou, Dall sheep, moose, wolves. Ruins of Yukon gold rush camps. Excellent potential for riverboat cruising, white-water canoeing, hiking, camping, fishing. Access by highway or air from Dawson (Canada) or Fairbanks.

Glacier-carved Twin Lakes catch glacial silt and feed the Mulchatna River on the western slope of the Alaska Range in proposed Lake Clark National Park. A score of such lakes provide floatplane access to vast, isolated regions of scenic splendor.

M. WOODBRIDGE WILLIAMS, NATIONAL PARK SERVICE

Paul A. Zahl

Hawaii Volcanoes

NATIONAL PARK, HAWAII

"A spectacle, sublime and even appalling, presented itself before us," wrote a missionary explorer in 1823. He marveled at "pyramids of brilliant flame; several of these... vomited from their ignited mouths streams of lava, which rolled in blazing torrents... into the boiling mass below."

Sightseeing on the island of Hawaii, the clergyman descended the caldera of Kilauea Volcano—legendary home of Pele, goddess of volcanoes. The "boiling mass" was an active lava lake inside the huge crater Halemaumau, known as "Pele's Pit." Geologists from all over the world flocked to see the bubbling caldron that rose and fell at Pele's whim.

Kilauea is one of the world's most active volcanoes. For the last 150 years eruptions have been spaced a few days, months, or even years apart; the goddess once slept for 18 years. In 1959 she staged a spectacular: Fountains of fire from a long-dormant vent soared 1,900 feet, highest ever recorded in Hawaii.

The volcano continued active in the '60's and '70's, and, monitored by scientists at the U. S. Geological Survey's observatory on the crater rim, Pele's whims are predictable. Seismographs record tremors, and tiltmeters measure the mountain's bulge due to rising magma.

Kilauea and its sister volcano Mauna Loa dominate Hawaii Volcanoes National Park, 352 square miles of lava-built scenery on the "big island" of the Hawaiian chain. But the 1¼ million sightseers who visit each year revel in a beautiful and varied landscape. Jungle plants on the island's windward slopes are fed by as much as 180 inches of rain annually; in the rain shadow on leeward slopes the Kau Desert exposes naked lava. Snow at times whitens Mauna Loa's peaks. A black sand beach at Kaimu east of the park came into being when hot lava met cool seas and exploded into fragments of basalt. Waves eventually battered them to sand.

The first day my family and I spent on the island gave us a sampling of its luxuriant rainy side. From the gentle tropics of the east coast at Hilo, we drove up through rolling sugarcane fields into lush green country. Lacy tree ferns, shaded by lofty ohias, overhung the road. In the rain forest's verdant depths we saw flashes of scarlet as tiny apapanes and iiwis—birds native to the Hawaiian Islands—fluttered in the foliage. When we entered the park after a 30-mile drive, we had climbed 4,000 feet.

That evening we joined a group around a blazing fire in the lounge of Volcano House, a hotel perched on the very brink of Kilauea Crater. The inn has welcomed guests since 1866, the year Mark Twain stayed there. "The surprise of finding a good hotel at such an outlandish spot startled me considerably more than the volcano did," he remarked. The hotel fare was superior and featured a "strawberry-fed goose... enveloped in leaves and baked in a hole in the heated earth." This was the *nene,* or Hawaiian goose, still found in the park but reduced to a small flock—an endangered species on its way back from near-extinction.

Tree of fire bursts at Mauna Ulu (Growing Mountain) in 1974. Hawaii's newest landform rises 400 feet on the side of Kilauea Volcano. A geologist in search of lava samples risks temperatures as high as 2,000° F.

ROBERT W. MADDEN, NATIONAL GEOGRAPHIC PHOTOGRAPHER

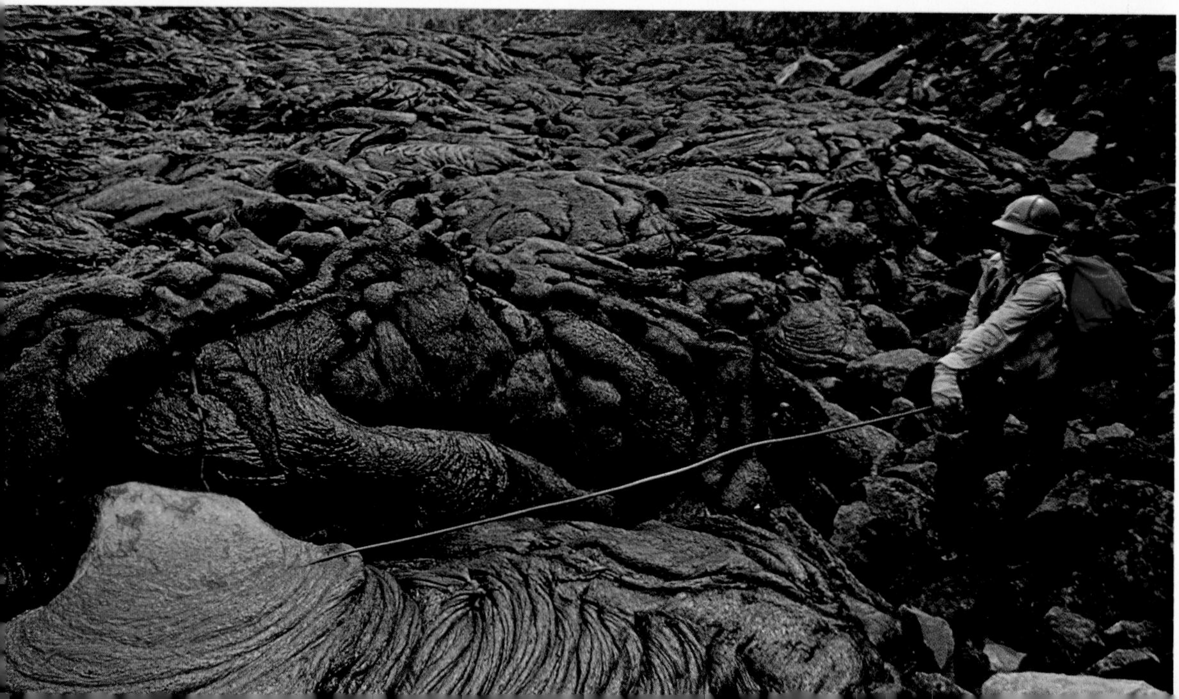

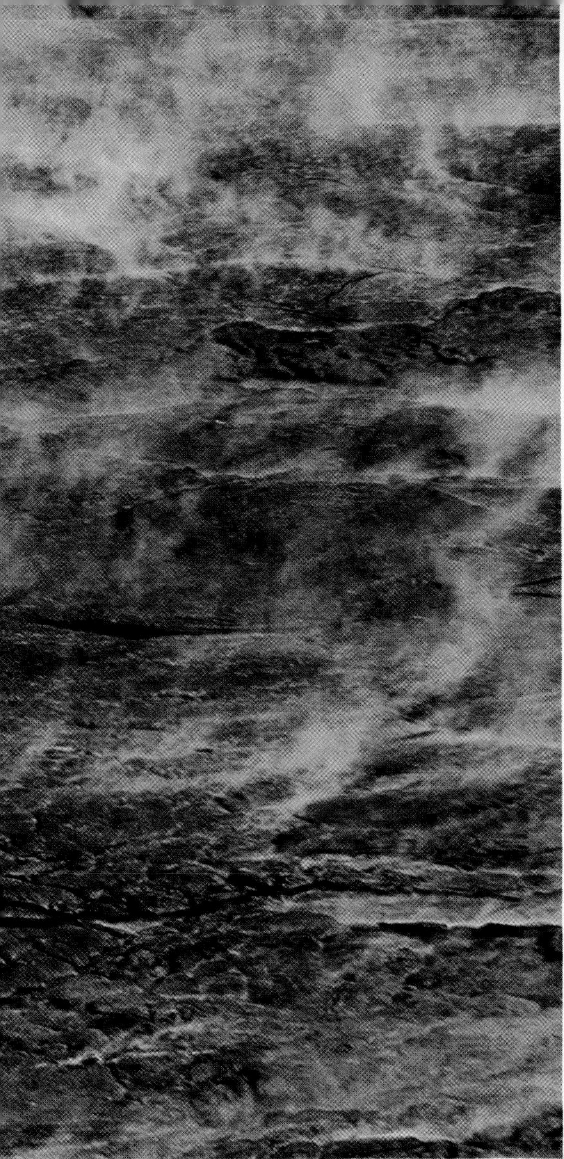

Descent into hell: Steam shrouds a survey team in Pauahi Crater, a lake of crusted lava on the Chain of Craters Road. Scooping samples from the caldron, the scientists inhaled noxious fumes and their boots melted. Visitors could watch from the road. Overleaf: *Mauna Ulu erupts, spilling its incandescent gold.*

ROBERT W. MADDEN, NATIONAL GEOGRAPHIC PHOTOGRAPHER (ALSO OVERLEAF)

The only accommodation except campgrounds and cabins, Volcano House serves as many as 1,500 lunches a day. But it was not always so. The innkeeper told us a story of financial crisis in the 1930's. When Kilauea had slept for nearly three years, the tourist trade slackened and the hotel was in trouble. And so the innkeeper implored Pele to manifest herself, tossing a lei of sacred ohelo berries into the lifeless fire pit and adding a bottle of gin, since the goddess is said to hanker for strong drink. That did the trick. Smoke mushroomed, lava filled the crater, and visitors filled the inn!

At the visitor center across the street we saw a color film on past eruptions and asked for information about trails. From 11-mile Crater Rim Drive, Chain of Craters Road enters the east rift zone, where motorists park and walk on recent lava flows—a series of eruptions that began in 1968. If there are active vents, overlooks provide safe vantage points.

Hikers roam the park on 120 miles of trails. Halemaumau Trail descends Kilauea caldera; the Bird Park Trail threads Kipuka Pualu, a bird sanctuary. We hiked two miles southeast of the visitor center to the Thurston Lava Tube, a conduit in ages past for molten lava. Now the ominous cavern glows with electric lights, and hundreds of tourists stroll through or take pictures of its fern-rimmed entrance.

Lurching and bucking, our jeep made its way upward through a two-color world of blue sky and black lava. With several geologists from the observatory I was headed for Mauna Loa (Long Mountain), 25 miles west of Kilauea. Measured from the floor of the ocean, it rises 30,000 feet, exceeding Mount Everest's stature by a thousand feet. Though the volcano has made news since Captain Cook's day, the last eruption of any consequence had been in 1950.

We parked the jeep and attacked the mountain on foot, camping on top where July's night temperatures drop below freezing. Next day we descended into the grotesque world of the crater floor, passing fantastic crevasses, sulphur vents, and red-lipped spatter cones.

From the same strip of terrain I held in my hand two kinds of lava—rough, clinkery *aa,* and taffy-like *pahoehoe.* One of the geologists explained that aa forms a crust that breaks into pieces while the lava continues to move. "Hawaiian lavas are fluid when they come from the vent," he told me. "Because dissolved gases escape easily, they don't build up pressures that cause a violent explosion."

Back on the brink, I looked down at the crater's cold, harsh, petrified surface. Seeing in my mind's eye the boiling inferno it had been many years before, I wondered when the goddess of volcanoes would speak again....

In the spring of 1974 Mauna Loa began to rumble. By mid-December magma had built up and the volcano was inflating. Earthquakes below the crater increased in intensity....

For information write Supt. *See page 446.*

Kenneth F. Weaver

Haleakala

NATIONAL PARK, HAWAII

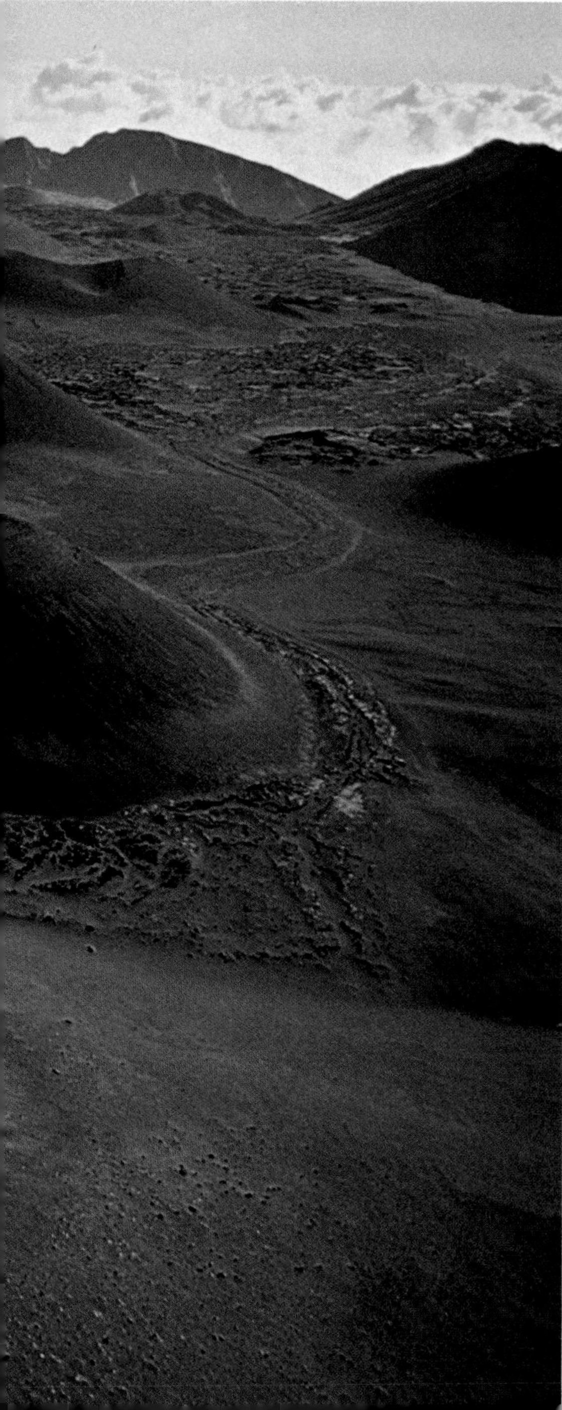

On the island of Maui, in the Hawaiian chain, they tell of a legendary hero who slowed the sun's daily passage through the sky by climbing a great volcano and snaring the rays of the sun as it sped past. From that day to this, according to the story, man has had ample daylight by which to harvest his crops, bring in fish, and dry the tapa fibers that make his cloth. And the great mountain climbed by that long-ago hero has been known ever since as Haleakala—"the House of the Sun."

Today a 42-square-mile national park perches atop the mountain's summit and includes most of Kipahulu Valley, a corridor extending eight miles through lush rain forest to the popular Seven Pools area on the coast.

The huge basin scooped from Haleakala's crown has been called the world's largest extinct volcanic crater, a statement wrong on all counts. Many craters are larger; the volcano is dormant, not extinct; and erosion, not explosion, is chiefly responsible for the "crater."

Early one morning my wife, Modena, and I drove to the top of the mountain to watch the sun come up. From Kalahaku Overlook, north of the visitor center, the basin wall dropped frighteningly into a black abyss. With the coming of daylight—as pinks turned to yellow and gold and overwhelmed the purple shadows—Haleakala's full dimensions spread before us.

On the floor half a mile below, a black river of lava and a dozen or so huge cinder cones—red and brown and black—gave evidence of volcanic eruptions since the present crater was carved by water. On the rim's southwest corner and just under its 10,023-foot summit, we saw several white domes, observatories of "Science City" that take advantage of the rarefied atmosphere to explore the heavens and monitor the passage of satellites.

Cinder cones parade past hardened lava flows within Haleakala's mountaintop crater on Maui, second largest of Hawaii's islands. This remote park shelters rare bird and plant species, some seen only in Hawaii.

GORDON W. GAHAN, NATIONAL GEOGRAPHIC PHOTOGRAPHER

Jewel of the wasteland, a silversword gleams on the cindery floor of Haleakala Crater. The plant, related to the sunflower, grows 100 or more down-covered leaves. At the end of its lifespan—from 7 to 20 years—it erupts into glorious bloom but once, then dies.

No road enters the crater. But two well-marked trails totaling 30 miles do: Halemauu Trail, a series of steep switchbacks best descended on horseback, and the Sliding Sands Trail, a longer but gentler route. We opted for Sliding Sands and, in the company of a ranger, began a two-day trek through the crater.

Sliding Sands is well named. For several miles it loops across a smooth slope of cinder and ash, where shoes grip with difficulty. An unearthly silence settled over us shortly after we began our descent. The only sound was the scuff and crunch of our boots on the path. We had entered the House of the Sun, but the sterile wasteland of broken lava dotted with rock and boulder seemed more lunar than solar.

On the bottom we found bracken fern, bunch grass, a shrub called pilo, and a heather-like evergreen known as pukiawe. But most exciting was an occasional glimpse of the silversword, found nowhere else except on the arid volcanic heights of Maui and Hawaii.

After a brief lunch at Kapalaoa Cabin, one of three shelters maintained by the Park Service, we moved on eastward through a sea of cinders, clinkers, and increasing vegetation. Waist-high ferns almost blocked the trail at times. We passed a rare sandalwood tree heavily festooned with moss.

Throughout the day we had seen clouds flowing through two huge gaps in the rim. Now, as we rounded Oili Puu, last of the cinder cones, mist dampened our faces. Rain threatened.

Paliku Cabin, standing in a meadow of heavy grass at the base of a steep, 700-foot cliff, was a welcome sight after our ten-mile hike under lowering skies. No sooner were we indoors than the rains came down. The ranger explained that this end of the crater gets a great deal of spillover from torrential downpours that give Haleakala's windward slopes as much as 400 inches of rain a year.

Early next morning we headed out by way of Kaupo Gap. Misty veils drifted across the precipitous cliffs and gulches. Our trail led through sopping-wet grass, sometimes waist high, and our shoes squished with every step. Against the thunder of waterfalls, aftermath of the rains, we heard the song of the crimson apapane and the squeaky call of the iiwi, whose vermilion feathers were eagerly sought for cloaks by Hawaiian chiefs of old. Ferns, mosses, trees, and flowering plants created a lushness here that had been starkly absent where we entered the crater's western slopes the day before.

The rank growth reminded me of Kipahulu Valley. Along a water-logged ridge, I had climbed through tangled ferns and vines and fallen trees to a promontory called Palikea. Behind me the green land ended in a froth of white surf against black lava and the endless wash of blue Pacific. Ahead, all the way to the crater's eastern rim, swept a magnificent valley choked with green, thousands of barely explored acres set aside as primitive wilderness. Surely, I reflected, Haleakala is a very special place.

HAWAII VOLCANOES and HALEAKALA NATIONAL PARKS

Areas 358 and 42 square miles

Features: *Volcanic wonderlands on islands of Hawaii and Maui. Craters, lava tubes, colorful cinder cones, fern jungles, bird park; Kau Desert (Hawaii).*

Activities: *Visitor centers at Kilauea (Hawaii) and Haleakala summit (Maui). Scenic roads; rim, crater, and self-guiding nature trails; horses at Haleakala. Talks, exhibits at both parks.*

Weather: *Pleasant days, frequent showers; cool nights. Parks open all year.*

How to get there: *By air (several flights daily) or unscheduled ship from Honolulu. Taxis, tour cars to parks; car rentals at Hilo and Kailua-Kona (Hawaii), Kahului Airport (Maui). Write Hawaii Visitors Bureau at Honolulu, Hilo, Wailuku, or 3440 Wilshire Blvd., Los Angeles, Calif. 90005.*

Accommodations: *Volcano House, Kilauea (c/o park); for Haleakala, write visitors bureau. Hikers' cabins, campgrounds at both parks.*

For further information write Supt., c/o Hawaii Group, NPS. Pacific International Bldg., 677 Ala Moana Blvd., Honolulu, Hawaii 96813

GORDON W. GAHAN, NATIONAL GEOGRAPHIC PHOTOGRAPHER

Nathaniel T. Kenney

Virgin Islands

NATIONAL PARK, VIRGIN ISLANDS

In only one national park was I ever followed by a barracuda. It happened, of course, in Virgin Islands, where the most popular trail is blazed in ten feet of water.

The sight of the four-foot silver torpedo sent me racing for the beach. I doffed flippers, mask, and snorkel, and reported my experience to the ranger on duty at Trunk Bay.

"Nothing to worry about," said he. " 'Cudas seldom bother people. But they're curious, and sometimes follow my weekly snorkeling tours over the underwater trail."

Reassured, I went back into the water. The barracuda had left and the bay's other denizens had come out of hiding—tiny damselfish, brilliant blue wrasses, and big-eyed squirrelfish; schools of jacks and yellowtail snappers; and fat blue-green parrotfish which, by chewing coral into fine white sand, add their bit to Trunk Bay's crescent of sun-kissed beach.

Face down on the surface of Caribbean Sea water so warm you can laze in its embrace until you pucker like a dried apricot, I feasted my eyes on one of nature's most exquisite sights, a coral reef in a tropic sea.

Plaques set on the bottom marked the trail and identified its inhabitants. Sea whips and sea fans waved in submarine currents. An octopus ducked into a forest of elkhorn coral as I passed above. Diving for a close look at a massive brain coral, I flushed a big spotted eagle ray out of the shadows.

A family of children, parents, and grandparents joined me. First-time snorkelers, they had learned the art from the ranger in an hour. Few dangers faced them on the trail, only stinging fire coral, the sharp spines of sea urchins, and—sunburn!

More than a score of sparkling hideaway bays like Trunk form the main attraction of this

Trunk Bay's turquoise waters and dazzling beach lure yachtsmen to a storybook anchorage. Sea mist shrouds Britain's Great Thatch Island (left) across The Narrows, once a pirates' passage.

JAMES L. STANFIELD, NATIONAL GEOGRAPHIC PHOTOGRAPHER

JAMES L. STANFIELD, NATIONAL GEOGRAPHIC PHOTOGRAPHER

southernmost of our national parks. Each has coral reefs, dozens of them in the 5,650 acres of waters closed by park rules to spearfishing and collecting of coral and shells.

I have visited most of these bays in a jeep rented in the village of Cruz Bay just outside the park's 9,500 land acres, all of them on the island of St. John. But you can see them on bus tours that travel the 15-mile loop road through the island's mountainous, forested center and along its north shore. They make swim stops beside at least one bay.

Myself, I am partial to the park's marinescapes. But there are other pleasant things. Tropical flowers—hibiscus, bougainvillea, flamboyants—thrive in temperatures that average 79 degrees and vary only six degrees from winter to summer. Colorful or not, other plants bear intriguing local names like clashie melashie, bellyache balsam, better man better, and jumbie cutlash.

Vines and strangler figs everywhere crawl over crumbling stone walls—ruins of the sugar plantations that once dotted St. John. The Park Service preserves one of the larger estates, Annaberg, now roofless, on a hill above the azure sea. Here I heard a ranger smilingly claim, for a tour group, Christopher Columbus as the first park visitor.

Columbus was, probably, the first European to see the lush Virgins. He came in 1493 on his second voyage to the New World. After him, adventurers of many nationalities sailed in from the Spanish Main. Tradition says they included such swashbucklers as Drake, Morgan, Blackbeard, and Laffite. Only Denmark, however, established a lasting claim to ownership.

Beginning in the 1670's, Danish planters grew rich making sugar, rum, and molasses. The end of slavery in 1848 made estates unprofitable, and proprietors began to abandon

Ruins of Annaberg sugar factory brood on a hilltop, reminding park visitors of Danish colonial times. Hop, skip, and a jump will land the campers at right in Cinnamon Bay's warm, translucent water.

Grunts school under an elkhorn coral as snorkelers invade their domain: Buck Island Reef, just north of St. Croix. Swimmers tour the national monument's underwater trail, following markers and arrows easy to read beneath the crystal water. Buck Island itself offers a nature trail through tropical vegetation.

JAMES L. STANFIELD, NATIONAL GEOGRAPHIC PHOTOGRAPHER

them. The United States bought the Virgin Islands from Denmark in 1917.

Congress established the park in 1956. Laurance S. Rockefeller and his Jackson Hole Preserve, Inc., donated the initial 5,000 acres of land. Today 150,000 visitors a year can be grateful for the gift. Most of them come by plane to St. Thomas, a half-hour's ferry ride from the park. St. Thomas, a duty-free port, has lodgings, bargain-filled shops, sailing yachts for charter, and captains who know where to find tuna, marlin, dolphin, and bonefish on some of the world's finest fishing grounds.

I usually stay on St. John, either in plush Caneel Bay Plantation or the park's Cinnamon Bay Campground, a beachside complex of tent sites, cottages, general store, and cafeteria beneath tall palms and huge kapok trees.

Always I catch a flying boat to St. Croix, 40 miles away, and snorkel the underwater trail at nearby Buck Island Reef National Monument. Guided-tour boats run regularly out of Christiansted harbor. You can swim the trail over this magnificent coral garden in half an hour.

The superintendent of Virgin Islands National Park also has charge of Buck Island. A letter to him at Box 806, St. Thomas, Virgin Islands 00801, will get you full information about both vacation paradises.

He may or may not mention mongooses. The Danes imported these Asian animals to control sugarcane-destroying rats. You'll see mongooses by the score. They look like out-sized weasels. Leave them strictly alone. They bite.

Additional Areas of the Park Service

The National Park Service (NPS) also administers the following natural and recreational areas, listed in its booklet, *National Parks and Landmarks* (for sale by Superintendent of Documents, U. S. Government Printing Office, Washington, D. C. 20402). The areas include national parks (NP), monuments (NM), recreation areas (NRA), seashores (NS), lakeshores (NL), and scenic riverways (NSR). Acreage figures are authorized acreage; at some parks, land acquisition is still in progress. Addresses provided are sources of further information. Or write to the National Park Service, Department of the Interior, Washington, D. C. 20240

ALABAMA

Natchez Trace Parkway. See Mississippi.

ARIZONA

Lake Mead NRA. See Nevada.

ARKANSAS

Hot Springs NP. 3,535 acres. Mid-city woodland spa, rocky hills, 47 mineral springs. Camping, hiking. Box 1219, Hot Springs, Ark. 71901

CALIFORNIA

Golden Gate NRA. 34,200 acres. San Francisco area urban park. Includes ocean beaches, redwood forests, Alcatraz and Angel islands, historic sites. Hiking, picnicking, fishing. Fort Mason, San Francisco, Calif. 94123

Whiskeytown-Shasta-Trinity NRA. Three units total 255,970 acres. Whiskeytown (42,570) administered by NPS, others by Forest Service. Scenic mountains, lakes. Water sports, hiking, camping. Box 188, Whiskeytown, Calif. 96095

COLORADO

Curecanti NRA. 41,103 acres. Eroded volcanic terrain. Rugged mountains, streams, 20-mile-long Blue Mesa Lake. Water sports, camping, hiking. 334 S. 10th St., Montrose, Colo. 81401

Florissant Fossil Beds NM. 5,992 acres. Insect and leaf fossils. Petrified sequoia stumps. Box 164, Florissant, Colo. 80816

Shadow Mountain NRA. 18,240 acres. Three lakes in Colorado River Valley. Water sports, camping, hiking. Administered by Rocky Mountain NP, Estes Park, Colo. 80517

DISTRICT OF COLUMBIA

Chesapeake and Ohio Canal National Historical Park. 20,239 acres. Scenic 184-mile Potomac River canal from Washington, D. C. to Cumberland, Md., begun in 1828. Towpath hiking, bicycling, canoeing, camping. Unit of National Capital Parks.

National Capital Parks. Over 700 units, including the White House, Washington Monument, John F. Kennedy Center for the Performing Arts in Washington, D. C.; Oxon Hill Children's Farm, Md.; Great Falls Park, Va.; Harpers Ferry National Historical Park, West Va. 1100 Ohio Drive, S.W., Washington, D. C. 20242

FLORIDA

Big Cypress National Preserve. 522,000 acres. Lowland and swamp, vital wildlife habitat and water source for adjacent Everglades NP. c/o Southeast Regional Office, NPS, 3401 Whipple Ave., Atlanta, Ga. 30344

Canaveral NS. 67,500 acres. Lagoons, marshes, barrier dunes; south of Daytona Beach. c/o Southeast Regional Office, NPS. See Big Cypress.

Biscayne NM. 95,064 acres. Mostly water and coral reef. Primitive campground, small boat marina on Elliott Key. Snorkeling, scuba diving, swimming. Box 1369, Homestead, Fla. 33030

Gulf Islands NS. (Also in Mississippi.) 125,000 acres. 150-mile stretch of islands in Gulf of Mexico. Historic ruins. Camping, fishing, swimming. Box 100, Gulf Breeze, Fla. 32561 or Drawer T, Ocean Springs, Miss. 39564

GEORGIA

Cumberland Island NS. 36,876 acres. Pristine sandy beaches, dunes, freshwater lakes, forest. Not yet open to the public. Box 960, Kingsland, Ga. 31548

INDIANA

Indiana Dunes NL. 8,721 acres. Beaches, marshes, 200-foot-high dunes on south shore of Lake Michigan. Swimming, picnicking, hiking, biking. Rt. 2, Box 139-A, Chesterton, Ind. 46304

MARYLAND

Assateague Island NS. (Also in Virginia.) 39,630 acres. 37-mile Atlantic barrier island. Includes

Chincoteague National Wildlife Refuge. Camping, swimming, fishing, hiking, bird-watching. Rt. 2, Box 294, Berlin, Md. 21811

MICHIGAN

Sleeping Bear Dunes NL. 71,105 acres. 31 miles of Lake Michigan shoreline, two islands. Sandy cliffs, forests, luxuriant bogs. 400 Main St., Frankfort, Mich. 49635

MINNESOTA

St. Croix NSR. See Wisconsin.

MISSISSIPPI

Gulf Islands NS. See Florida.

Natchez Trace Parkway. (Also in Alabama, Tennessee.) Follows 450-mile Indian and pioneer trail. Historic sites, nature trails, recreation areas. Rt. 1, NT-143, Tupelo, Miss. 38801

MISSOURI

Ozark NSR. 72,101 acres. Camping, caving, boating on 150 miles of Current and Jacks Fork rivers. Box 448, Van Buren, Mo. 63965

MONTANA

Bighorn Canyon NRA. (Also in Wyoming.) 122,623 acres. Reservoir 71 miles long in deep rugged canyon. Water sports, camping, hunting. Box 458 YRS, Hardin, Mont. 59035

NEBRASKA

Agate Fossil Beds NM. 2,269 acres. World-renowned deposit of Miocene mammal fossils. Box 427, Gering, Neb. 69341

NEVADA

Lake Mead NRA. (Also in Arizona.) 1,936,978 acres. Vast reservoirs amid desert canyons, plateaus. Water sports, hiking, camping, tours of Hoover Dam. Boulder City, Nev. 89005

NEW JERSEY

Delaware Water Gap NRA. (Also in Pennsylvania.) 70,000 acres. Scenic Delaware River pass. Water and winter sports. Historic sites. Interstate 80, Columbia, N.J. 07832

Gateway NRA. See New York.

NEW YORK

Fire Island NS. 19,311 acres. 30 miles of barrier beach, thickets, salt marshes, and grassy wetlands. Box 229, Patchogue, L.I., N.Y. 11772

Gateway NRA. (Also in New Jersey.) 26,172 acres. New York Harbor beaches, marshlands, islands. Swimming, camping, fishing. Floyd Bennett Field, Bldg. 69, Brooklyn, N.Y. 11234

NORTH CAROLINA

Cape Lookout NS. 24,500 acres. Lower Outer Banks barrier islands. Adjoins Cape Hatteras NS. Box 690, Beaufort, N.C. 28516

OHIO

Cuyahoga Valley NRA. 29,000 acres. Scenic stretch of Cuyahoga River between Cleveland and Akron. c/o Midwest Regional Office, NPS, 1709 Jackson St., Omaha, Neb. 68102

OKLAHOMA

Arbuckle NRA. 8,851 acres. Man-made lake in wooded hills. Water sports, camping, nature trails. Box 201, Sulphur, Okla. 73086

Platt NP. 911 acres. Eastern hardwood forest and midwest prairie. Rolling hills, streams, mineral springs. Box 201, Sulphur, Okla. 73086

OREGON

John Day Fossil Beds NM. 14,400 acres. Animal and plant fossils. c/o Pacific Northwest Regional Office, NPS, 1424 Fourth Ave., Seattle, Wash. 98101

PENNSYLVANIA

Delaware Water Gap NRA. See New Jersey.

TENNESSEE

Natchez Trace Parkway. See Mississippi.

TEXAS

Amistad NRA. 65,000 acres. Immense reservoir on Rio Grande. Water sports; camping, hiking in desert plains, rugged mountains. (Joint project of the United States and Mexico.) Box 1463, Del Rio, Tex. 78840

Big Thicket National Preserve. 84,550 acres. Bayou, forest, and uplands of unique "biological crossroads." c/o Southwest Regional Office, NPS, Box 728, Santa Fe, New Mex. 87501

Lake Meredith NRA. 41,097 acres. Scenic lake in high-plains setting. Water sports, camping, picnicking. Box 325, Sanford, Tex. 79078

Padre Island NS. 133,918 acres. 67-mile stretch of broad, windswept barrier island. Box 8560, Corpus Christi, Tex. 78412

VIRGINIA

Assateague Island NS. See Maryland.

WASHINGTON

Coulee Dam NRA. 100,059 acres. Columbia River reservoir, 151 miles long. Water sports, camping, hunting. Summer tours of Grand Coulee Dam and historic Fort Spokane. Box 37, Coulee Dam, Wash. 99116

WISCONSIN

Ice Age National Scientific Reserve. 32,500 acres to be included in nine widely separated units containing significant features of continental glaciation. Cooperative state and federal project. c/o Midwest Regional Office, NPS, 1709 Jackson St., Omaha, Neb. 68102

Upper St. Croix NSR. (Also in Minnesota.) 62,622 acres. Waterfalls, rapids, and wide placid stretches in deep gorges along 200 miles of the St. Croix and Namekagon rivers. Also **Lower St. Croix NSR,** 9,223 acres: A 52-mile segment flowing into the Mississippi. Box 579, St. Croix Falls, Wisc. 54024

WYOMING

Bighorn Canyon NRA. See Montana.

Fossil Butte NM. 8,178 acres. Abundant deposits of Paleocene-Eocene fossil fish, 40 to 65 million years old. c/o Grand Teton NP, Moose, Wyo. 83012

John D. Rockefeller, Jr., Memorial Parkway. 23,700 acres. Scenic 82-mile drive. Includes corridor linking Yellowstone and Grand Teton NPs. Tent and trailer camping, lodge, horseback riding, swimming, float trips, snowcoach tours. c/o Grand Teton NP, Moose, Wyo. 83012

Appalachian National Scenic Trail. 2,000-mile footpath through the Appalachian Mountains from Mt. Katahdin, Maine, to Springer Mtn., Georgia. Northern Unit: 143 South 3rd St., Philadelphia, Pa. 19106. Southern Unit: 3401 Whipple Ave., Atlanta, Ga. 30344

Migrating ducks rise with the sun at Assateague Island National Seashore. Travel-worn birds and city-worn people alike find rest and refuge here along 37 miles of Virginia and Maryland coastline.

JOSEPH R. SPIES

How to Enjoy Your National Parks Vacation

What do you want to see? Geysers? Caverns? Cliff dwellings? Wildlife? Do you want to boat, fish, climb, hike, or just absorb the view? This book will help you choose.

Major parks such as Yellowstone and Acadia are often seriously overcrowded. Consider an off-season visit, climate permitting. (In northern mountain parks, roads may be closed in winter; in many desert areas, summer months are uncomfortably hot.) Also consider visiting one of the lesser-known parks.

The National Park Service has a pamphlet on each area it administers: Write to the superintendent of the park, or order from Superintendent of Documents (SOD), U. S. Government Printing Office, Washington, D. C. 20402.

Planning Is Vital

BUDGET YOUR TIME. How many days in the park, how many to and from? Remember that mountain driving can be much slower than map-measured mileage may indicate.

Consider an extended stay in one or two areas rather than hurrying from park to park. You will save gas and gain a deeper appreciation for the park by learning to know it well.

BUDGET YOUR MONEY. How much for transportation, how much for lodging, food, incidentals, tours, emergencies? Will it be a luxury hotel or lodge, a modest cabin, a campground? A useful listing, *Visitor Facilities and Services Furnished by Concessioners* in park areas, is available from SOD (#726-549/150). For out-of-park accommodations, write local chambers of commerce. If you have never traveled by camper, trailer, or motor home, consider renting one. You may spend more on gas and take longer reaching your destination, but you will save money on lodging and food.

How to Travel

The energy crisis of the 1970's added a new dimension to travel planning—the need to conserve gas. Keep in mind that your driving time may be increased by lower speed limits and by stopping to fill your gas tank before it drops below half-full. Plan to take advantage of in-park mass-transit systems.

Before loading the car, consider other means of transportation. Fly-and-drive plans save time; buses, trains save driving. Amtrak serves many parks (see insert map). Group tours take care of planning details.

CAR TOURING. Get road maps, travel data from auto club or oil company. Don't plan more than 350 miles a day; fatigue invites accidents.

Think twice about taking pets. In most parks, pets must be kept on leash and are not permitted inside buildings or caverns.

Purchase of the annual Golden Eagle Passport lets driver and passengers enter free any park where entrance fees are charged, as often as they wish. But "special recreation use fees" (campgrounds, boat launching facilities, etc.) must still be paid. Passports are available at park entrances.

OF SPECIAL INTEREST. Persons over 62 can obtain free a lifetime Golden Age Passport, which covers admissions and allows a 50 percent discount on some recreation use fees.

Facilities and obstacles in each park area are described in *National Park Guide for the Handicapped.* Order #2405-0286 from SOD.

What to Take

In most parks, informal sportswear is all you need. Include denims, khakis, rugged boots, if you plan to rough it.

Wear glasses? Take an extra pair, also your prescription. See a dentist before you leave; a toothache far from help can spoil your trip. And don't forget nature guidebooks.

Car Camping

Camping in the parks can be a rewarding, inexpensive family vacation. Check out any NPS campsite reservation system that may be in effect. If you are heading for a first-come, first-served campground, get there early in the day and have an alternate plan in mind. Many park campgrounds are free, or nominal in fee. Most parks offer trailer sites; check length limits and access road conditions in backcountry areas.

BASIC CAMPING SUPPLIES. Tent, travel trailer, or compact camper (over-large camper vehicles require more gas, are prohibited on some park roads); air mattresses (don't over-inflate); sleeping bags and/or warm blankets; camp stove. Veteran campers also suggest:

tarpaulin	plastic plates, cups, utensils
lantern	dishpan
sheath knife	can opener
water jug	spatula
aluminum pots	potholders
skillet	soap
coffee pot	scouring pads
plastic bags	paper towels
toilet tissue	matches, candles
whisk broom	flashlight
small hatchet	extra batteries
folding table	

Forget bulky cots (chill air freezes you from below) and gadgets (keep things simple).

Optional: ice chest. Canned, instant, and freeze-dried foods allow variety, need no refrigeration. Camping stores offer specially packaged foods, but many items—powdered milk, soups, fruit drink mixes, dried fruits—are available, and cheaper, at local groceries.

Caution: Bears will rip tents open to get food. Hang it from a line high between trees or put in closed car. Put scraps in garbage cans. Never feed wild animals.

WHERE TO CAMP. Most national parks have campgrounds. En route you can camp in hundreds of state parks and national forests, and on public lands. For listings, order these guides from SOD:

Camping in the National Park System #1972-483-79

National Forest Vacations #0101-0072

Room to Roam: A Recreation Guide to the Public Lands #1971-0438-167

Write to the Director of State Parks at the state capitals for listing of campgrounds.

Wilderness Camping

A night—or a month—in the backcountry, away from cars, crowds, and amenities, is for many people the most meaningful way to enjoy a park visit. Backpacking requires careful preparation and special equipment. The sleeping bag you carry in your car may be too heavy to carry on your back! Information is available from hiking clubs, outfitters, conservation groups, and a wealth of literature, including the Society's book *Wilderness U.S.A.*

Park Safety

Nature rules in the national parks. Visitors must respect it or suffer the consequences. Don't risk accidents by climbing or swimming alone or by disturbing wildlife. Don't let children stray, especially near thermal pools, cliffs, waterfalls. Ask about particular local hazards. Obey regulations and warning signs.

Photo Tips

Good photographs will help you relive your park vacation for years afterwards. Follow these hints for better pictures:

Always frame your picture; don't just point and shoot. Take a broad general view, then move in on details. Don't overlook signs; they can take the place of copious notes.

Avoid self-conscious posing. Catch subjects in natural activities. Close-ups are more dramatic than full-figure shots.

Obey your light meter, but vary the exposures to be sure. Mountain, desert, and seashore light can be deceptive. See page 171 for special hints on cave photography.

Store your film and camera away from direct sunlight and such warm spots as car windows and glove compartments. Remember that airport X rays may ruin film.

Index

Text references in roman type; illustrations in **boldface;** picture captions in *italic*.

Key to abbreviations for National Park units:
NP – Park
NM – Monument
NS – Seashore
NL – Lakeshore
NRA – Recreation Area
NSR – Scenic Riverway

The editors thank the National Park Service for its cooperation in the preparation of this book. Specialists at Washington, D. C., headquarters and in regional offices helped keep us abreast of emerging parks and policies. Superintendents, naturalists, historians, and archeologists in the field assisted our staff and checked every story for accuracy.

Composition by National Geographic's Phototypographic Division, Lawrence F. Ludwig, Manager. Color separations by Chanticleer Company, Inc., New York; Progressive Color Corporation, Rockville, Md.; The J. Wm. Reed Company, Alexandria, Va. Printed by Fawcett Printing Corporation, Rockville, Md. Binding by R. R. Donnelley & Sons Company, Chicago, Ill. Paper by Oxford Paper Company, New York.

Library of Congress CIP Data

National Geographic Society, Washington, D. C., Book Service
The New America's Wonderlands

(World in Color Library)
Published in 1959 and 1966 under title: America's Wonderlands.
1. National Parks and reserves—United States. 2. United States—Description and travel—1960-
I. Title
E160.N24 1975 917.3'04'92
74-32377 ISBN 0-87044-004-7

NATIONAL GEOGRAPHIC SOCIETY

WASHINGTON, D. C.

Organized "for the increase and diffusion of geographic knowledge"

GILBERT HOVEY GROSVENOR
Editor, 1899-1954; President, 1920-1954
Chairman of the Board, 1954-1966

THE NATIONAL GEOGRAPHIC SOCIETY is chartered in Washington, D. C., in accordance with the laws of the United States, as a nonprofit scientific and educational organization for increasing and diffusing geographic knowledge and promoting research and exploration. Since 1890 the Society has supported 1,095 explorations and research projects, adding immeasurably to man's knowledge of earth, sea, and sky. It diffuses this knowledge through its monthly journal, NATIONAL GEOGRAPHIC; more than 50 million maps distributed each year; its books, globes, atlases, and filmstrips; 30 School Bulletins a year in color; information services to press, radio, and television; technical reports; exhibits from around the world in Explorers Hall; and a nationwide series of programs on television.

NATIONAL GEOGRAPHIC MAGAZINE